VERSIONS OF MEDIEVAL COMEDY

VERSIONS OF
MEDIEVAL COMEDY

Edited and with an Introduction by

PAUL G. RUGGIERS

UNIVERSITY OF OKLAHOMA PRESS : Norman

By Paul G. Ruggiers

The Art of the Canterbury Tales (Madison, 1965)

Florence in the Age of Dante (Norman, 1964)

Library of Congress Cataloging in Publication Data
Main entry under title:

Versions of medieval comedy.
   Includes index.

   1. Literature, Medieval—History and criticism—Addresses, essays, lectures.   2. Comic, The—Addresses, essays, lectures.   I. Ruggiers, Paul G.   II. Genre.
PN682.C55V47   809'.9'17   77–6384
ISBN 0–8061–1425–8

Copyright 1977 by the University of Oklahoma Press, Publishing Division of the University. Reprinted from *Genre* magazine, Ronald Schleifer, General Editor. Composed and printed at Norman, Oklahoma, U.S.A., by the University of Oklahoma Press. First edition.

809.917
Ver

CONTENTS

VERSIONS OF MEDIEVAL COMEDY

Introduction: Some Theoretical Considerations of Comedy in the Middle Ages

Paul G. Ruggiers
University of Oklahoma

This small volume of essays attempts to increase our knowledge of the comic impulse in the Middle Ages, mainly in the Latin and thereafter in the vernacular traditions of Europe and England. The period covered—from Plautus to Ariosto—is so vast as to daunt in advance any systematic investigation of a coherent theory. Nonetheless, I have felt it better to make a start on so extensive a field with the expectations that other collections may ensue, and that other studies may be stimulated on topics suggested by this group.

For a variety of reasons, an overview of medieval comedy has failed to materialize in the welter of materials dealing with comedy generally. This, in spite of the fact that data does exist in the Latin Grammarians, in the philosophical and theological writers of a millenium who manifest a high tolerance for a comic view of the world, and in the poetry of the late Middle Ages, in which the poets express concern about the language and the subject matter they are using, and who feel called upon to justify themselves to their audiences. These matters are the subject of this introduction, to which I will add a set of fundamental questions to be confronted before laying out a theory of comedy in any age, our own as well as the Middle Ages.

Because the traditions of comedy, like those of tragedy, have been handed down in a greatly distorted and fragmentary way, largely through the grammarians of the late classical period, I have thought it of some value to give a brief account of Aristotle's views on comedy (found not only in the *Poetics*, but also in the *Nicomachean Ethics*, and the *Rhetoric*). I have no intention of demonstrating a point-by-point correspondence between his views and those of later times—I doubt if that is possible—but only of laying out the complex of ideas which have filtered down through Theophrastus and Menander into Hellenistic writers and thereafter into the mainstreams of medieval thought.

I

Aristotle attributes the origins of both tragedy and comedy to primitive improvisations: the tragic from the improvised dithyrambs, the comic probably from the phallic processions. The nature of the subject matter attracted the appropriate kind of poet: that is, the "base" kind of poet was attracted to the non-serious, the "noble" kind was attracted to the serious. The "base" kinds first produced invectives, but eventually Homer, in the *Margites*, found the ridiculous to be a good content for fictional presentation. Thereafter, in the evolution of forms tragedy emerged from epic and comedy from epic satire to their full stature as forms of imitation.

The actual history of early comedy is somewhat hazy, Aristotle offering the view that there are rival claims to inventing the form by the Dorians (Megarians) of Greece, by the Megarians of Sicily (on the ground that the first true comic poet, Epicharmus came from Sicily), and by the Athenians. And according to the Dorians, comedians acquired their name not from the verb to revel (*komazein*) but from their habit of strolling from village to village (*komai*) when a lack of appreciation forced them out of the city. Whatever the origins, the Sicilians Epicharmus and Phormis actually invented plots for comedy; and the Athenian Crates was the first to abandon invective and to construct plots of a more universal nature. Furthermore, while both tragedy and comedy deal with their materials in a manner essentially different from history, comedy gives up any reliance upon history, i.e., upon specific persons. In particular, the writers of Middle and New Comedy invented their plots and added the names of the characters, while tragedy continued to cling to the heroes of the past for its plots.

Aristotle's definition of comedy is memorable: "Comedy is an imitation of baser men. These are characterized not by every kind of vice but specifically by the ridiculous, which is a subdivision of the category of deformity. What we mean by 'the ridiculous' is some error or ugliness that is painless and has no harmful effects. The example that comes immediately to mind is the comic mask, which is ugly and distorted, but causes no pain."[1]

As to the form of the plot, Aristotle makes a distinction which, though implied rather than explicitly stated, is clear enough to have influenced

[1] The translation is that of Leon Golden, *Aristotle's Poetics, A Translation and Commentary for Students of Literature* (Englewood Cliffs, N.J.: Prentice-Hall, Inc., 1968) p. 9.

all definitions of comedy from his time on. In discussing the kinds of plots to be avoided, he points out that plots in which the deadliest of enemies become friends and quit the stage without anyone slaying or being slain give the distinctive pleasure not of tragedy, but of comedy. Thus, while he may not mean exactly that a comedy ends happily (*Iphigenia in Tauris* he deems a tragedy), he suggests that the reversals in comedy dissolve earlier rancor by reconciliations of various sorts.[2]

As for the agents depicted in the drama, they must be either of a lower or a higher type. Comedy tends to represent the agents as worse, and tragedy as better, than the norm. And the characters of comedy, as opposed to those of tragedy who are "noble" and mainly historical or legendary, are of a "lower sort" and are invented, that is, with names given them by the poet. Aristotle has in mind here, not Aristophanic comedy, but rather the Middle and New Comedy coming more fully into existence in his time, in which the agents have proclivities or evince humours such as were defined in the *Nicomachean Ethics* as to their ages, social status, and "psychology." Such analyses were to be seen in the definitions provided later by Theophrastus and in various other treatises of Aristotle's time.

The function of character, it must be remembered, is not to particularize, but rather to generalize, to create an easily recognizable type.[3] And just as the tragic hero was to have a defect of character (something between a moral and a purely intellectual flaw or perhaps an error in calculation), so also the comic hero would demonstrate a defect crucial to the plot. And the flaw in character, perhaps even indicated by the name of the character, like the flaw which is the mainspring of tragic suffering, should produce in comedy the equivalent of the tragic catastrophe: beatings, punishments, even the threat of death from which the audience derives its own peculiar measure of gratification. In his discussion of the kind of character defects to be employed in comedy, Lane Cooper offers this note:

[2] See the conjecture of O. B. Hardison, Jr., in *Aristotle's Poetics*, p. 188.

[3] Gerald Else, *Aristotle's Poetics: The Argument* (Cambridge, Mass.: Harvard University Press, 1957) pp. 311–12, puts it this way: ". . . Greek comedy had two principal resources, the humorous representation of ordinary life, and parody of myth. . . . In dealing with a heroic figure, say Heracles, the tragic poet begins with the deeds or adventures traditional to the individual Heracles. The comic poet, in the other hand, begins with the concept 'glutton' or 'enormously powerful individual' and develops an action or scene which fits the concept; the action or scene will then almost certainly be new, i.e., fictitious, and may develop in any direction the poet pleases."

3

The faults which it would appear were suitable for comic characters might, therefore, be almost, if not quite, all the vices listed in *Nicomachean Ethics* 2.7, so long as these vices produced neither pain nor harm; but, particularly, certain of the vices that were nearer to the main state, or state of virtue . . . such as foolhardiness, prodigality, vulgarity, vanity, impassivity, self-depreciation (= 'irony'), buffoonery, obsequiousness or flattery, and bashfulness. Yet the opposite and more extreme vices might be so represented as not to be painful or injurious—as cowardice, illiberality, or avarice, boastfulness, boorishness; perhaps also quarrelsomeness, licentiousness, and envy; possibly shamelessness and malice. It has been thought by some that Aristotle deemed the buffoon or low, jesting parasite, the ironical man or type of dissembled ignorance, and the boastful man or type of imposters and braggarts, as *par excellence* the characters (*or ethe*) of comedy.[4]

The advantage to a writer in creating a character whose name suggests his character lies in the tendency towards the stereotype that underlies grotesque or exaggerated types; the disadvantage may be the inner tendency of such characterization to diminish seriously the moral significance of character. But the fact remains that subsequent literature has made capital of the stock characters that have become the staple of comedy.

Setting aside the truly vexing questions of catharsis in comedy (whether it operates homeopathically, allopathically, or even whether it exists at all), we revert here to views about imitations that are fundamental in Aristotle's conception of art. He is firm in his views that imitative art generally has as its chief characteristic the pleasure that results from learning for all men, even when the objects depicted are in real life ugly or fearful, like corpses and hateful animals. Somehow, in art, they become a source of pleasure. And this pleasure is not merely that of learning; it is intimately welded to another pleasure, that of feeling the cessation or alleviation of painful emotions aroused in the course of a presentation.

The question of catharsis is defined with regard to music in the *Politics*,[5] in which we read that pleasure and pain as mere representa-

---

[4] Lane Cooper, *An Aristotelian Theory of Comedy, with an Adaptation of the Poetics and a Translation of the 'Tractatus Coislinianus,'* (New York: Harcourt, Brace and Co., 1922), pp. 176–77.

[5] 1340a 17–1342a 16. Catharsis continued to surface among later Greek writers: Iamblichus (A.D. 330?): "When we witness the emotions of others, both in comedy and tragedy, we halt our own emotions, work them off more moderately and are purged of them"; Proclus (A.D. 410–85); and John Tzetzes (A.D. 1110–80) "Comedy

tions are close to our feelings about realities, and that music has the capacity to lighten and delight the soul through purgation of adverse emotions aroused by the presentation. These statements have suggested to me that a certain kind of pleasure, along with a certain kind of laughter, are alleviated in the manner suggested by the *Tractatus Coislinianus*. And elsewhere I have summarized the matter at length.[6] Whatever is meant, Aristotle seems to be saying that in the process of enlightenment and learning, we enjoy the proper function of art, namely to yield a special pleasure in the process of apprehending the universal in the particular.

ii

In one way or another, this complex of ancient views filtered into the Hellenistic and Imperial periods and, subsequently, into the Middle Ages and the Renaissance. For the grammarians, it is useful to employ a scheme like that offered by Spingarn and by McMahon[7] in their list of the comic topics found in Diomedes, Evanthius, and Donatus.[8] I have presented these topics synoptically in order to make, though artificially, a more coherent statement of their principles to be viewed against the backdrop of antiquity. And I should state here that the terms for comedy and tragedy among the grammarians are still reserved for the drama and have not yet come to be applied to the versified tales in later Latin and in the vernacular languages.

    1. *The Origins and History of Comedy*: Comedy originated in religious festivals to give thanks for harvest. The name is derived either from villages (*komai*) plus song (*oide*) or from revel singing. Homer provided the models for both comedy and tragedy. Early comedy named

---

is an imitation of an action . . . purgative of emotions . . ." (texts are given in Cooper, pp. 82–87).

  [6] In "A Vocabulary for Chaucerian Comedy: A Preliminary Sketch," *Medieval Studies in Honor of Lillian Herlands Hornstein*, ed. Jess B. Bessinger, Jr., and Robert R. Raymo (New York: New York University Press, 1976), 193–225.

  [7] Joel Spingarn, *A History of Literary Criticism in the Renaissance* (New York: Columbia University Press, 1920) pp. 66–67; and A. Philip McMahon, "Seven Questions on Aristotelian Definitions of Tragedy and Comedy," *Harvard Studies in Classical Philology*, XL (Cambridge, Mass.: Harvard University Press, 1929), 104.

  [8] The texts of Evanthius and Donatus are to be found in Alex Preminger, O. B. Hardison, Jr., and Kevin Kerrane, *Classical and Medieval Literary Criticism* (New York: Frederick Ungar Publishing Co., 1974), pp. 301–309. The text of Diomedes (?) is to be found in Cooper, p. 85.

real persons and thus served as a corrector of morals. A new form, the satyr play, evolved, which attacked vice, but without naming specific persons; and this form gave way, because of abuses, to New Comedy in which the situations are typical and describe middle-class life. It had a close-knit plot, good characterization, was apt in prosody, afforded useful sentiments, yielded delight and pleasure.

2. *The Structure of the Plot*: The opening of comedy is turbulent, yet the outcome is happy, as opposed to tragedy in which the actions undergo a reversal towards the worse, heroic fortunes being seen there in adversity. Comedy, thus, fulfills an inner law of its subject matter, dealing with "taking hold of" life rather than, as in tragedy, giving it up. Thus, the petty onsets of danger are resolved in comedy into a cheerful outcome.

Comedy is divided into four parts: 1) a prologue in which the poet vindicates himself; 2) a protasis, the first action of the drama, where part of the story is explained, and part held back to arouse suspense; 3) the epitasis, the complication, the development and enlargement of the conflict, the "knot"; 4) the catastrophe in which the unravelling of the story produces a happy ending made possible by the recognition of past events.

3. *The Subjects of Comedy*: While tragedy offers accounts of lamentations, exiles, and murders, comedy offers stories of love and the kidnapping of virgins. These stories are in a happy vein, providing in one way or another, by means of a middle or ordinary view of things, an imitation of ordinary life. (This view is attributed to Cicero, who is supposed to have said that comedy is a mirror of human actions, the image of truth.) The actions are invented by the writer rather than taken from historical personages and events; they are typical actions of the middle class of persons.

4. *The Characters of Comedy*: The characters of comedy are humble, private persons, usually in humble villages. Since comedy originated in village song and festivals as a kind of entertainment for the local audiences, the villagers themselves, the persons depicted are those of the "middle state." On stage these characters may be distinguished by their garments: short garments for slaves (so as to leave them free for action and also to mark their poverty), a purple garment for the rich man, varicolored garments for the young, yellow for the prostitute, etc.

5. *Style and Delivery*: Comedies are distinguishable into various types: lively, quiet, or a mixture of the two. Lively comedies contain turbulence and movement; quiet comedies are characterized by tranquility and seriousness. A musical prelude played on either right- or left-hand flutes

provides the clue to the audience that the play to be presented is either quiet or spritely.

6. *Function*: From comedy one learns what is useful in life and what is to be avoided. The emotional effect of tragedy is to arouse the audience to tears, while the aim of comedy is to move the hearer to laughter. Comedy's function is to afford pleasure by its plot and by its truthfulness to life, its sentiments, its wit, its language. The level of comedy, here, is to be distinguished from older forms of lampoon or satyr plays in which the vices of the upper classes were attacked and actual names were used. Further, while tragedy deals with the dissolution of life, comedy consolidates it.

Such a complex of Hellenistic ideas, reaching back into a classical antiquity long past and often little or totally unknown at first hand, survived in one form or another as formulae in various writers of the Middle Ages, to surface once again with renewed vigor and enlarged commentary in the comic theory of the Italian Renaissance.[9] Yet, the complex of ideas has its own kind of sophistication, a grasp of the essentials of the comic impulse seen critically and there is nothing quite like it again in any language of the Middle Ages.

It is now fairly well-accepted that the forms of comedy and tragedy inherited from classical antiquity had no real impact upon the like modes of experience manifesting themselves principally as irony and romance in the Middle Ages. Only with the recovery in Italy and elsewhere of a more self-conscious use of the Roman dramatists in the fifteenth century may we speak of drama revitalized along the lines of the ancient tradition. Between the time of the dying Empire when the theater was degraded and the early Renaissance, there was a separate survival and development of the narrative prose forms along with the survival of epic, lyric, and philosophical and didactic discourse. To these narrative forms were attached the considerations of their serious and non-serious biases and of the subject matter and vocabulary once reserved for the dramatic forms, but now applied inadvertently to the narrative fictions. Thus, the tales of Chaucer's Monk were deemed tragedies like those of Boccaccio's "illustrious" men and women, and Dante could call his splendid pilgrimage a comedy to which later writers added the term "divine" indicating a sensitivity to the wide range of comic possibilities.

[9] Marvin Herrick, *Comic Theory in the Sixteenth Century* (Urbana: University of Illinois Press, 1971), pp. 57ff.

The other late development, the direct presentation of action before an audience in the liturgical drama, seems to have been made possible by the persistence of popular entertainments and the techniques of various kinds of entertainers. It is still possible to talk in terms of a separate evolution of the dramatic forms of miracles, mysteries, and moralities, even though they show similarities to the inner forms and devices of actions of a pagan sort. The matter remains open for scholarly investigation, though even here the documents are few both for the origins and for the transitions from liturgical practices to secular ones, and for what it is worth, it should be obvious that the cycle dramas are narratives which have been converted into drama.

It seems fairly obvious, too, that neither the forms of drama, nor those of narration, whether in Latin or in the vernacular, could have come fully into existence without radical changes in the social structures: the ingredient of an audience of listeners or readers of a certain kind and status. The refinement of a literary form seems, somehow, to be concomitant with caste systems, perhaps, or with sophisticated economic practices of an age expressing itself in the material pleasures of the merchant classes; with an increasing liveliness of the city and a widening of the attitudes towards entertainments on the part of the Church. And at the same time, the stability of faith seems to have freed medieval writers from excessive concern for the appearance of things. Blasphemy, parody, burlesque, the juxtaposition of sacred and profane, all become possible ingredients of comedy.[10]

[10] The "lower" comic elements would have been part of the larger "divine" comedy evolving in the overall structure of the cycles. See O. B. Hardison, Jr., *Christian Rite and Christian Drama in the Middle Ages: Essays on the Origin and Early History of Modern Drama* (Baltimore: Johns Hopkins Press, 1965), p. 83, who offers the view that the entire cycle of plays would have been a comedy in the Dantean definition going back to Evanthius; that just as the Church year and the plot of the liturgy follow the line of a ritual birth, death and resurrection, so the cycle plays would have a comic, yet serious form. And Arnold Williams, "The Comic in the Cycles," *Medieval Drama*, ed. Neville Denny (London: Stratford on Avon Studies XVI), p. 123, writes: ". . . the comic . . . bulks large in its total effect. With a few exceptions . . . the comic is always intrinsic to the dramatic structure. . . . the comic always flows directly from the method of the cycles, which the attempt to make the scriptural story human and contemporary. We see everything through the eyes of the common citizen, and the disparity from that point of view and the one we are accustomed to in 'religious' literature produces a comic irony that is never absent for long in any of the cycles . . . the constant undertone of comic irony preserves them from the sanctimoniousness which mars most postmedieval dramatic treatments of scriptural themes."

By its inner law of trivializing experience and making capital of the defects of human nature, comedy lends itself, though in a largely non-serious way, to depictions of the ugly and even the painful. Readers of Boccaccio's *Decameron*, for example, frequently find themselves repelled by a spirit of something close to hard-heartedness, by its derision of human defects, and by what may be called an all-pervasive naturalism. But such sentiments are proper to comedy, as several of the papers in this collection demonstrate.

The demonic and the ugly, always recognized as a possible subject of painting and fine arts, had produced as early as St. Augustine's *Soliloquies* the view that the depiction of the ugly, the image of a demon, for example, must be regarded as beautiful if the depiction is a good one. This notion was already an ancient one, going back at least to Aristotle, *Poetics* IV, when St. Augustine adopted it. Much later, Hugh of St. Victor, in describing the beauty of God in terms of the beauty of His creatures, tells us that some forms please us because they are beautiful, but others please because they are suitably absurd (*convenienter ineptae*) and incongruous. The underlying notion is that of aesthetic optimism,[11] a view of the universe as a reflection of the divine, best expressed by Plotinus whose influence is discernible upon a number of later writers in the Latin tradition. He writes,

> Do you criticize the Divine Intellect because It has created monsters? It resembles a painter who endows his animals with other things besides eyes. And, we, in our astonishment, resemble ignorant critics who reproach a painter because he has not laid on beautiful colors everywhere, when actually he has placed in each area the colors best suited to it. . . . We do not find fault with a tragedy because its characters are not all heroes; abolish the lesser roles of servants and common people, and the drama will lose its beauty, because it needs them in order to be a complete whole.[12]

And Alexander of Hales saw the necessary relationship of the monstrous

---

[11] See Edgar De Bruyne, *Études D'Esthétique Médiévale*, 3 vols., (Brugge: De Tempel, 1946). Recent studies in Germany find the source of the grotesque in native, un-Christianized forms of drama surviving concomitantly with liturgical types. In any case, the subject matter of fifteenth-century German and Austrian forces contained familiar subject matter: attacks on professions, gluttony, avarice, lack of self-control. And among the characters, tricksters and the fool, dupes and dupers.

[12] *Enneads* III, 2. 11.

to the beautiful, of moral error to virtue, remarking, "just as the beauty of a picture may be enhanced by a dark color in the proper place, so the beauty of the universe is enhanced by moral errors."[13] In this view, moral error always reminds us of the beauty of the physical world.

But the boldest defense of the ugly comes from Hugh of St. Victor, who reminds us that God may be discovered more easily in ugly forms than an outwardly beautiful ones, the ugly forcing us away from contemplation of itself, urging us to transcend it. He writes: "When we praise God for His beautiful forms, we praise Him in terms of the beauty of this world. But when we praise Him for His ugly forms, we praise Him transcendentally—in terms far superior to any others we normally use to praise Him. . . . The ugliness of base objects does not allow us to linger quietly over them, but drives us away to seek other objects which are true and beautiful."[14]

Among poets, Dante makes capital of the demonic, the horrid, the ugly with no faltering of his intention to write a poem calculated to arouse the proper emotions in us; and as readers we come to understand how imperfection taints the human condition as an inevitable consequence of its material nature. It is a view that afflicts the medieval mind occasionally with melancholy over the perishable quality of beauty in the world.

There was, too, the medieval recognition that poetry, music, and painting as forms of play, all produce pleasure, and that that pleasure may derive from the expression as much as from content; that is to say, that works of art must appeal both to the senses and to the heart. Various writers were eager to make the distinction between a pleasure that leads to the contemplation of the Divine and a pleasure that leads in the opposite direction, towards carnal desire. Poetry, in particular, carried the ancient paradox derived from painting in that the more it deceived, the better it was as art. And this tenet had the support of the best thinkers of the Middle Ages. St. Thomas, who recognized the play element in poetry, in discussing the despised art of comedians and actors in general, writes:

Their art in all its forms is oriented towards pleasure and even amusement. But we need not condemn it, provided it does not definitely endanger morals, and does not upset the equilibrium of life as a whole by being excessive. In truth, play (that is, the enjoyment of an activity which is its own end) is necessary in the total rhythm of human life; consequently, if we

[13] De Bruyne, III, 112.
[14] De Bruyne, II, 215.

define the arts in terms of basic needs or essential satisfactions, we need not exclude the arts of pure play.[15]

The statement does, indeed, constitute an ancient topic justifying the value of leisure as essential to the good life, leisure involving the simple and pleasant entertainments, such as are provided by the various verbal arts.

From the early Church Fathers, through the various Church Councils, fear of the theaters' power and contempt for the actor's art characterized the early Christian attitude towards the art. Chief of these is, of course, Tertullian's attack on the immorality of the theater in his *De Spectaculis* (A.D. 198), and, thereafter, the various injunctions to priests that they must not, under pain of excommunication, attend the various *ludi* at feasts and marriage ceremonies. But the theater, in the loose sense of the word, persisted; and there are references to *histriones*, a broad term that includes various kinds of wandering entertainers, throughout the theological writings of at least a thousand years.

The Church was also steadily opposed to the participation of priests in the acting and presentation of plays. The reasons are familiar: diversion from duty, the inherent hypocrisy of the actors' art, and the abhorrence that attaches to impersonation generally, particularly when men play women's parts. But with the shift to secular control by the guilds, particularly in England and Germany, and with the availability of money, time, and, perhaps, unique talents, the arts of theater could once again emerge as a separate and autonomous art.

Though couched in negative terms, the fourteenth-century Lollard *Treatise against Miracle Plays* echoes and reinterprets some of these aesthetic considerations. From the earliest times, going back at least to Strabo, it was assumed that a picture was a means of teaching the ignorant. Gregory the Great writes in a letter to Sirenus of Marseilles, "A picture is as a book to the common people; it is one thing to adore a picture, another to learn by means of the content of the picture, which is rather to be adored."[16] This sentiment reverberates throughout the centuries, both in eastern and western church writers, to be picked up by St. Thomas Aquinas in the *Summa Theologica* and in his *Commentary on the Sentences*.[17] The notion became a staple of defense for the use of

[15] De Bruyne, III, 341.
[16] Rosemary Woolf, *The English Mystery Plays* (Berkeley: University of California Press, 1972), pp. 86–87.
[17] *Summa Theologica*, III, xxv, 3; and *Commentary on the Sentences*, III, ix, 2.

images at least through the sixteenth century. The arguments in favor of images works equally well with plays. If we take our example from the *Treatise Against Miracle Plays*, we may see that the argument boldly presents its case on this point, namely, that plays are presented to the honor of God, and the viewer learns from them about human folly and the snaring devices of the devil; furthermore, the audience is moved by compassion and tears to devotion. Even conversion of the recalcitrant may result from the powerful effects of a play. Besides, as the *Treatise* points out, a religious play is a better form of entertainment than secular pastimes. Anyway, if it is permissible to portray religious matters in painting, why not in the drama, since drama is more memorable by virtue of being "alive," while painting is "dead."

Some of these attitudes are anticipated in the thirteenth-century glosses on a decree of Innocent III condemning the comic aspects of the Feast of Fools, but tolerating serious representations as inducements to devotion and as curbs to lewdness. And these sentiments are echoed in one form or another in Robert Manning's *Handling Synne*, which is itself based on an Anglo-Norman *Manuel des Péchés* by William of Waddington. Wherever these sentiments occur, there is a clear recognition of the pleasure inherent in the arousal of emotion by the dramatic presentations, though the clerical mind is reluctant to see that pleasure as a good in the ancient Aristotelian sense.

iv

By the late Middle Ages, the technics of comedy had reached a level of great sophistication. In the *Roman de la Rose*, held together by its various strains of irony and by its extravagant humor, Jean de Meun exploits a wide range of comic devices and a number of comic contents. A satiric bent impels him to deal in strongly anti-feminist travesties as well as anti-masculine ones: he knows the value of stereotypes and makes them the vehicle for comment on a wide range of manners. His resolutions on the side of human dignity, personal liberty, equality and toleration are the eminently sane conclusions of an urbane and witty mind. The style of presentation, its somewhat eclectic demonstrations of alternating values and conventions (a pattern Chaucer was to emulate), is in fact the soul of satiric comedy. And what later writers like Chaucer may have derived from the *Roman* is that nice balance between a hard surface and an inner allegorical tendency, in an exemplar of the subordination of literality, akin to realism, to the service of allegory.

Later, writers would recognize that the characters depicted in the *Roman* are stock characters deriving from a long tradition of types: the bawd, the drunkard, the angry man, the dissolute clergyman, the jealous man, the lover, the old lady, the flatterer, and so on. They would have seen in their conventional nature an accordance with the inherited theory of the day that the poet assigns to each of his conventional persons or his stereotypes the proper ethos. This, of course, was a dim reflection of Aristotle's strictures about making characters true to life and true to type, a notion that was filtered through Horace into the later Middle Ages, at least from the eleventh century on.[18]

But more important for our purposes here, I wish to cite three defenses of plain language which, in essence, are defenses of the poet who writes comedy. Noteworthy in the *Roman de la Rose*, the first of our examples, is the speech of Raison, shocking the young Amant into considerations of the relation of language of thought. I quote only a small section:

> "... you commit a great fault against me ... when you rebel and call me a foolish ribald. ... God my father ... taught me his behavior. With his permission it is my custom to speak properly of things when I please, without using any gloss. ... You oppose to me that, although God made things, at least he did not make their names. Here I reply to you: perhaps not, at least the names that things have now; however, he could indeed name them then when he first created the whole world and whatever exists in it, but he wanted me to find names at my pleasure and to name things, individually and collectively, in order to increase our understanding before God who hears me: if, when I put names to things that you dare to criticize thus, and blame, I had called testicles relics and had declared relics to be testicles, then you, who here criticize me and goad me on account of them would reply that 'relics' was a base ugly word. 'Testicles' is a good name and I like it, and so in faith are 'testes' and 'penis'. ... I made the words and I am certain that I never made anything base. ... how would I dare not to name the works of my father properly? ... If women in France do not name these things, it is only that they are not accustomed to, for the right names would have been pleasing to those who are accustomed to them; and if they named them correctly, they would commit no sin in doing so."[19]

Misunderstanding De Meun's comic practices, Christine de Pisan and

[18] See Edmund Faral, *Les Arts Poétiques du XII*^e *et du XIII*^e *Siècle* (Paris: E. Champion, 1924), pp. 78–79; and Lionel J. Friedman, "Jean de Meun, Anti-feminism, and Bourgeois Realism," *MP*, 55 (1959), 13–23.

[19] Guillaume de Lorris and Jean de Meun, *The Romance of the Rose*, trans. Charles Dahlberg (Princeton, N.J.: Princeton University Press, 1971), pp. 135–36.

Gerson were to decry his anti-feminism more than a century later, along with charges of carnality, unnecessary frankness, and general contempt for women (familiar topics of comic satire). Gerson, while specifying the poet's lewdness, his spreading of false doctrine, and his capacity for corrupting the young, offers the argument that certain parts of the body, being sinful in themselves, should not be mentioned. These views are those either of gentility or of biased clericalism, or in Rosemund Tuve's sense, an allegorism imposed upon the text by the preoccupations of a later age.[20] When Pierre Col answers their excessively genteel piety, he restores our confidence in the ability of a good mind to honor both common sense and a hallowed tradition in literature: we need words for things, we need to be able to describe even what is sinful; and we should not identify the poet with the characters he creates or impute their utterances to him.

The charges against Jean de Meun are equally applicable to other writers, notably Boccaccio and Chaucer whose self-exonerations and defenses of comic vocabulary I wish to cite as answers to an increasingly narrower humanism. Both writers had a rich poetic past reaching back through Dante and Jean de Meun's part of the *Roman de la Rose* to the Latin poets. And both had inherited the fertile technics and contents of comedy, including irony and allegory.

Whether Chaucer knew the *Decameron* of Boccaccio we cannot be sure; but, the *Decameron* contains a defense of frankness and a special sensitivity to the level of language and subject matter in a tradition repeated by writers before and after him. The defense is spread out in three places: in the Introduction to the collection, in the Introduction to the fourth day, and in the Epilogue. Boccaccio's defense would seem to us now to be conventional: at times a writer should offer useful counsel as well as pleasure, and yet he should remain faithful to the original of his tales; for faithfulness to one's material dictates the level of diction and is of greater concern to the artists than opinion of prudes who boggle at the word rather than at the deed, at appearances rather than at realities. Moreover, a writer should be free to tell the truth just as a painter is free to depict the nude body. Anyway, the tales are not for the churches or the schools, but for mature societies; they entertain at time when the necessity of sheer survival has somewhat overwhelmed moral considerations. Consequently, a writer cannot worry about his readers' responses;

[20] Rosemond Tuve, *Allegorical Imagery* (Princeton, N.J.: Princeton University Press, 1966), pp. 219–333.

in fact, some of the readers may be adversely affected by the tales, for literature, like wine, like fire, like scripture, may be badly used. Furthermore, the character of the reader will determine the value of the tale for him. Since each tale is preceded by a summary of its argument, the reader must make up his own mind, assuming responsibility for himself according to the various subjects offered. Thus, where some of the tales are long, they were meant for leisure use; and where some are light or comedic (imitating the sermons of the Friars!), they were meant for pleasure. Anyway, who in Florence at this time could possibly be corrupted?

These sentiments are the conventions of a long tradition and though colored strongly by irony were later to be recanted on the grounds that the tales were less than decent and were, in fact, calculated to arouse the passions. This rejection of his comic strain in the short, narrative form was to become one of the elements of the last two books of the *Genealogy of the Gentile Gods* in which Plautus and Terence are exonerated on the ground that though they are not allegorical—the ideal function of poetry is to be the handmaid of theology—they describe the universal manners of mankind. Others, like Ovid, weaken the moral order and prompt men to crime and thus should be, not merely expelled, but exterminated.

Both of these attitudes, that is, the defense of the comic and the desirability of the higher *sentence*, appear in Chaucer. But in the structure of the *Canterbury Tales*, the defenses of the comedic come properly at the beginning of the action, that is to say, at the end of the *General Prologue* and in the Prologue to the *Miller's Tale*; while the emphasis upon the higher meanings comes later, in the Prologue to the *Tale of Melibee*, in the Prologue to the *Parson's Tale*, and in the *Retraction*. They are uttered, furthermore, by the persona-reporter, a device that increases the irony of the statements and deceives us into accepting the utterances as presented at face value. Thus, Chaucer's two defenses of the comic, whatever our views about the tone in which they are offered, summarize the earlier sentiments of Boccaccio: a) Do not attribute the words or views of the created characters to me, I am merely being faithful to the tales I have heard and now offer to you. Everyone will admit that a writer should not falsify his materials, even if the materials are offered in a manner "rudeliche and large." b) I defend myself by the examples of Christ in Scripture and Plato, who tells us that words must truly represent the thing described. Anyway, there are lots of tales to pick from, some of them on holy and serious subjects. But do not blame me if you choose badly. Furthermore, you cannot expect very much from rascals like the Miller and the Reeve. In any event, do not take the game so seriously.

V

We turn, now, to more pragmatic considerations. In the gathering of these essays, my assumptions have been that a theory of comedy for the Middle Ages ought to emanate, principally, from an examination of texts and that we do well to resist imposing theories arising in the Renaissance or later upon the materials of the Middle Ages. Not that there is not some insight to be gleaned from imposing later theory upon the forms of the Middle Ages, but only that one ought to start from the texts themselves. I have felt it more profitable in a field of observations so vast historically, and so varied in forms, to start from a series of questions aimed at empirical considerations rather than from a series of philosophical or theoretical constructs—questions in which I have deliberately blurred the distinctions between dramatic and narrative forms. These questions were earlier submitted to several of the authors whose essays are collected here; taken together they describe the overarching concern of this volume:

Plot: Is the plot one of character or situation? Does it have an amorous conclusion? How do the actions begin and end? Is the plot a parody of a classical theme? Is the plot propositional, that is, does it set forth an absurd law at the outset? What happens to the proposition in the course of the action? Is the plot episodic? Does the plot contain "suffering?" What kinds of reversal are there? recognitions?

Character: Is there a single character that dominates the action? Is the character a "humour," a stereotype? Does the hero undergo a transformation for the better?[21] Is the character outwitted or unmasked? Does the character dupe all the others in the action? Are characters given ethical dimension?

Content: Is there a serious content? How is the serious content transmitted? What is the role of maxims and proverbs?

Function: Are the works frankly aimed at entertainment? Is pleasure a

---

[21] See Frances McNeely Leonard, "The School for Transformation: A Theory of Middle English Comedy," *Genre*, 9 (1976), 179-91.

stated goal of the work? Is there a definable audience or reader? Is the audience directly addressed? Are the values of the audience obvious from the context? Are such values corroborated, challenged, vindicated? Does the author impose his presence upon the content by direct comment? What is purely medieval about the content?

Style and Diction: What devices are used to elicit laughter? What technics are employed to maintain audience distance or to reduce audience concern? What is the role of various kinds of irony? What uses does literary theory have for the materials? Are there elements of the ugly and the grotesque in the content?

In this brief essay I have attempted only two things: 1) To make a presentation of an Aristotelian theory of comedy with its ramifications and result in the late classical Grammarians. To this presentation I have added some justification for the comic mode generally in the writers, theological and secular, of the Middle Ages. 2) To append a series of questions to these initial remarks aimed at opening up an entirely pragmatic examination[22] of the literary forms of the period. Beyond these I think it would be unnecessary in an introduction to go, in so broad a range of topics as are contained in the essays that follow. In brief, it has seemed to me that both the theoretical and the practical considerations offered here constitute an *a priori* set of assumptions about the sense and value of comedy in general, and it is against the background of these assumptions that the essays presented here should be read.

[22] A splendid example is the work of Philippe Ménard, *Le rire et le sourire dans le Roman Courtois en France au Moyen age* (Geneva: Droz, 1969).

Adaptation and Survival: A Genre Study of Roman Comedy in Relation to its Greek Sources

Elaine Fantham
University of Toronto

"I want to tell you the name of our play. In Greek it's called Klerou-menoi, in Latin, Sortientes. Diphilus wrote it originally in Greek, and Plautus, the fellow with the name that barks, translated it later into Latin."

> Plautus, *Casina*, Prologue 30–34, trans. Casson

"Today I am presenting the Self-Tormentor, a fresh comedy from a fresh Greek source."

> Terence, *Heautontimoroumenos*, Prologue 4–5, trans. Radice

Within its genre, the sub-species of Roman Comedy occupies an anomalous position, since its historical importance is quite out of keeping with its derivative form. First a brief sketch of the afterlife of Plautus and Terence, the surviving master of Roman comedy.[1] Twenty-one of the one hundred and thirty plays attributed to Plautus were acknowledged as authentic by the encyclopedic scholar Varro in the last century before Christ. Gradually with changing literary tastes and the new moral standards of Christianity, the plays lost their appeal, and were almost forgotten when Petrarch quoted from and adapted the eight plays which were known in his generation. But in 1429 Cardinal Orsini's manuscript containing the last twelve plays was eagerly reproduced by humanists, and before 1500, Plautus' plays were performed in the original and in translation at various courts of Italy. More "theatrical" than Terence's comedies, they were repeatedly adapted from the time of Ariosto and Machiavelli, and it is notable that in German and in English as well as

---

[1] See G. E. Duckworth, *The Nature of Roman Comedy* (Princeton, 1952), pp. 397–423; T. A. Dorey and R. Dudley, eds., *Roman Drama* (London, 1965), pp. 51–86 and pp. 87–122; and R. R. Bolger, *The Classical Heritage* (Cambridge, 1954), pp. 532–33, 536–37.

Italian, *Menaechmi*, the original of Shakespeare's *Comedy of Errors*, was one of the first plays to be translated.

Terence, as a model of propriety in Latin speech, quickly became a school text, so that the continued study of his plays was ensured, and aided by a cumulative commentary based on the work of the fourth-century grammarian Aelius Donatus: this was a pedagogic work, in which language and formal rhetorical features received more comment than dramatic technique, but it preserved some useful information about Terence's Greek source-plays. The plays survived in the schools; they were even used as models for the edifying Christian comedies of the nun Hroswitha of Gandersheim; in the fifteenth century they were studied and memorised at Erasmus' school in Deventer, and shaped his Latinity. In England they were not only read but performed annually at Westminster school after its refounding in 1560, but it is noticeable that translation of Terence largely came a generation later than translations from Plautus, because Terence's work was studied for its Latin, and adaptations seem to have been proportionately fewer than those based on Plautine comedies.

Any reader of Roman comedy knew from Plautus' and Terence's own statements that these plays were converted from the theatre of another language, society, and century, but even after the coming of Greek to Western Europe in the fifteenth century, the texts of these Greek comedies, the Athenian "New Comedy" of the late fourth and early third century B.C., were known only from fragmentary quotations preserved without dramatic context by anthologising moralists. It is from Plautus' "The Bacchis Sisters,"[2] for example, that scholars discovered the context of the famous "he whom the Gods love dies young"; Menander was not lamenting the early death of heroic youth, but his character, a cynical slave, inverted the adage to abuse his master as a repulsive old man who would be better dead. Only with the twentieth century have students of Roman comedy been able to sample the Greek plays of Menander, as papyri from Egypt have been pieced together and deciphered to produce the first substantial Greek texts; in 1907 excerpts were published from four of Menander's plays: "The Arbitration," "She who was shorn," "The Samian Girl," and a smaller section of "The Cult-Hero," enough to give an accurate picture of Menander's technique in language, metre, dialogue, characterisation, and even dramatic economy.

[2] *Bacchides*, ll. 816–17; noted by F. H. Sandbach in A. W. Gomme, F. H. Sandbach, *Menander: A Commentary* (Oxford, 1973), fr. 4.

In the last generation we have been able to read the first complete play. "The Bad-Tempered Man" from the Bodmer papyrus and large sections of at least five others—more of "The Samian Girl," "the Shield," "The Sicyonians," "The Man whom she Hated," and "The Double-Deceiver."[3] Only with the last-mentioned comedy have scholars recovered the original text—for rather less than an act—of one of our Roman plays, Plautus' "The Bacchis Sisters," offering us scope for direct comparison of technique between original and adaptation.

So students of Roman comedy are working with a secondary literature: for there is no good reason to doubt that all the surviving Roman comedies are versions of Greek plays. So long as the Greek originals were unknown no-one could challenge the literary importance of the Roman dramatists. But now much of Menander is available, his text superbly edited, and his techniques analysed by a generation of scholars. If the complete Menandrian model of Plautus' "Casket-play" or Terence's "Brothers" were recovered, could we justify the continued interest of students of drama in Plautus and Terence? True, no texts survive of any plays by Menander's contemporaries and rivals, Diphilus and Philemon, or his pupil Apollodorus, from whom Terence adapted two plays. But if they were resurrected from the sand, would Roman Comedy dwindle into mere source-material, a body of work without intrinsic value on the margins of literary history?

Obviously I intend to champion Roman comedy, and on literary grounds. It would be quite possible to argue, like the teachers of the Middle Ages or contemporary linguists, that we should study the Comic dramatists for their value as Latin, or as evidence for the evolution of the language; again a historian can argue for their importance as documents of social history, class structure and family law. But their claim to our interest is as literature, and the individual qualities of the Roman plays can be best appreciated by understanding the transformations which their authors imposed on the Greek models from the same genre. In this paper I hope to show, by applying to our plays the schema of Aristotle's *Poetics* for the components of drama, how Roman comedy evolved as a new species, differing in almost every aspect of its art from the primary Greek comedies.

One fundamental cause of this change was the difference in society

[3] These Menander titles are in Greek respectively Epitrepones, Perikeiromene, Samia, Heros, then Dyskolos; then Aspis, Sikyonioi, Misoumenos and Dis Exapaton.

and education between the primary and secondary dramatists. It is not possible to do justice to this change without describing the inspiration and distinctive features of Greek New Comedy. As its name implies this was itself a modified form, deriving its nature from the contrasted genres of Euripidean tragedy and Aristophanic "Old" Comedy. During the cruel decades of the Peloponnesian war which brought Athens to near-starvation and defeat, tragedy and comedy had been converging towards a greater realism. It was not only the war which led Euripides to strip the heroic dignity from his mythological roles, to depict them in poverty, madness or sordid adulterous passion (I am using the cliches of his accusers, quoted in Aristophanes' "Frogs"), but it was certainly defeat which deprived Aristophanes and his audience of their joy in fantasy, and glee at the triumph of the trickster and his or her Utopian schemes. In Aristophanes' last extant comedy "Wealth" the world of the play is reduced to that of domestic comedy, preoccupied with private morals and economics. For two generations comedy (often known as "Middle comedy") seems to have survived on semi-satirical plots, deception intrigues of the city-streets, exploiting the humour of easily mocked professions—doctors, soothsayers, philosophers, fishmongers and cooks. The surviving fragments are limited by the interests of their sources, but suggest a clubman's world of gossip and amusement: personally I do not regret their loss. But at the same time the two strongest forms of prose literature, court oratory and Aristotelian philosophy, helped to change the consciousness of the audience. The Athenians had always relished the rhetoric of making a case, for in their society all citizens could serve on the jury panels in criminal and political trials which tended to base their verdicts on moral rather than legal considerations. Now Aristotelian philosophy studied the psychology of morals; virtue was seen as having many forms manifested in different circumstances, but based always upon a mean between the extremes of contrasted vices, as economy is a balance between extravagance and miserliness. Aristotle studied human relationships, the different bonds of affection (*philia*) between friends, lovers and members of the family; he analysed the prejudices and passions to which different groups, young and old, rich and poor, educated and ignorant, were prone, and he considered moral problems from recognisable social contexts. Here was a rich stimulus for drama. His successor, Theophrastus, has left us a marvellous collection of "Characters" —some thirty social types, characterised by their foibles (it would be too much to call them humours or ruling passions)—The Ironical Man, The

Boor, The Superstitious Man, The Boaster.[4] His sketches portray men by their words, gestures and public behaviour. Menander was his pupil, and applied this psychological expertise in moods and mannerisms, and problem situations to create a new kind of play.

A predecessor, Antiphanes, in a comedy called "The Creative Art" (*Poiesis*), had complained that tragedians did not have to find a plot, nor even name their characters:

> Now tragedy's a lucky sort of art.
> First the house knows the plot before you start.
> You've only to remind it, "Oedipus"
> You say, and all's out—father Laius,
> Mother Jocasta, daughters these, sons those
> His sin, his coming punishment. Or suppose
> You say "Alcmaeon," in saying that you've said
> All his sons too, how he's gone off his head
> And killed his mother . . .
>   We comic writers have more clamant needs
> There's all to invent, new names, new words, new deeds,
> Prologue, presuppositions, action, ending. . . .
>
>   (fr. 91, trans. Edmonds)

One source of themes for New Comedy was to scale down the plots of tragedy—not the dreadful agony of Oedipus or Alcmaeon, but the all's-well-that-ends-well tragedies of later Euripides. The rescue of Helen from the lusts of her Egyptian captor by Menelaus becomes the rescue of an Athenian courtesan from the custody of a Mercenary Captain in Ephesus by her lover and his loyal slave (the original for Plautus' "Braggart Soldier," and ultimately *Die Entführung aus dem Serail*), or the recognition of the bastard child of a god and a princess after its de-

---

[4] These are numbers 1, 4, 16 and 23 in Menander, *Plays and Fragments*, with *Theophrastus' Characters*, trans. Vellacott, 2nd edition (London, 1973). Aristotle recognised the ironical man and boaster, and the boor together with his opposite the buffoon (bomolochos) as types whose deviations from the mean of truthfulness and wit belonged to the world of entertainment: in *Nicomachean Ethics* 4, 7–8, he contrasts the abusive buffoonery of the Old Comedy with the innuendo of the New, which he sees as an improvement in good taste. But we should not follow Northrop Frye, when in his influential *Anatomy of Criticism* (Princeton, 1957) he tries to fit all the standard roles of New Comedy into framework based on these four types. To represent the heavy father as an *alazon* (p. 172) or the hero as an *eiron* is to falsify these terms by extending their application beyond anything which Aristotle or Menander would have recognised. Theophrastus has no buffoon, but offers about thirty other deviant types, many identifiable in Menander.

liberate exposure to die (Euripides' lost plays *Alope* and *Auge*), becomes the recognition by a husband that his wife's baby, which he thought the result of rape or infidelity, is his own child (Menander's "Arbitration"). In Euripides' *Ion*, a parent is deceived into mistaking her own child for an enemy, and saved in the nick of time from procuring his murder; a wartime situation makes possible a similar theme in the original of Plautus' "Prisoners." When in Menander's "The Shield" the returning heir, thought dead, drives off the false suitor and restores the threatened woman to the right husband, Menander can be seen to go back even to Homer, and the ending of the *Odyssey*.[5]

Menander's plots were above all domestic: his chief roles the respectable male citizens, middle-aged fathers of adolescent sons whose love affairs often provide a starting point for the action, along with slaves and such members of the family or families as the plot required. Although the plots were usually motivated by a love-intrigue, the female roles were unimportant. Since the stage represented the street or other public space, and bourgeois women were discouraged from appearing in public, wives and young girls of good family remain offstage, or keep modest silence; women servants or entertainers, on the other hand, offer small parts for old nurses, or lively soubrettes. In plays where the young man had fallen for a girl "entertainer" the audience would be content with a temporary liaison as the romantic solution. In others the happy ending would be an approved marriage if the girl was found to be stolen or kidnapped from respectable parents, and was restored to them by a Recognition scene: but this type of solution required that she should have preserved her virginity. Menander is as versatile as any mystery writer in ringing the changes on his plots, introducing elements of misunderstanding and unexpected but well-motivated turns of the intrigue. His craftsmanship controls the action from the prologue, often offered in Euripidean fashion by an omniscient deity, through the economy of each scene; characters are brought on stage when they are most needed, after the audience's interest has been whetted by anticipation. Menander wrote in the five-act form which Horace later canonised as the ideal framework,[6] separat-

---

[5] On the Euripidean sources of plot and motif see T. B. L. Webster, *Introduction to Menander* (Manchester, 1974), pp. 56–67, and W. Geoffrey Arnott, "Menander, Plautus and Terence," *Greece and Rome, New Surveys in the Classics*, 9 (1975), 12; on the Odyssey and *Aspis*, see H. Lloyd-Jones, "Menander's *Aspis*," GRBS 12 (1971), 192, n. 40.

[6] Horace, *Ars Poetica*, 189–91.

ing each act from its successor by an interlude of song and dance un-
related to the play; but he knew how to maintain audience commitment
from act to act by the introduction of a new role or phase in the plot
shortly before the interlude. His alternation of monologue and dialogue,
the unobtrusive entrances and exits are all calculated, consistent and
swift-moving. An anecdote reports that a month before the dramatic
festival Menander was asked about his forthcoming play. It was, he said,
as good as written; he had worked out the plot, and now had only to
compose the text.[7]

Plot, then, was important to Menander, but if it had been his only
excellence he would never have earned such praise from poets, moralists
and literary critics after the Greek theatre had faded away. We might
add that on the evidence of his two known plays adapted into Latin,
Diphilus at least seems to have had more diversity of action and a
stronger element of spectacle and stage business than Menander. "The
Lottery" (Plautus' *Casina*) takes its name from the lively scene where a
lecherous husband and his nagging wife hold a lottery, ostensibly to decide whether his slave or hers shall obtain a pretty slave girl in "marriage." In fact the husband wants her for himself, and his wife is schem-
ing to frustrate him; the finale of this play employs the folk-motif of the
"bride" who is a disguised man, armed and threatening homosexual as-
sault upon the would-be lover.[8] Diphilus' model for Plautus' *Rope* involves the shipwreck of two beautiful girls, their rescue by a priestess, an
attempt by the villain to drive them from sanctuary by fire, a tug of war
for the chest "fished up" from the sea, and two arbitration scenes, in one
of which the arbiter recognises his long-lost daughter.

Since Menander seems to have reduced the element of professional
humour in his plays, concentrating on the family circle, we might fear a
certain monotony in dramas repeatedly focussed on respectable fathers,
foolish but honourable sons, and helpful slaves. But "stock characters"
can stimulate subtlety and refinement of detail. We know that New
Comedy used many varied masks for each age, sex and class of person.
Thus masks of old men might be fair and curly haired or dark and
straight, or bearded in different styles, some suggesting a severe, some a
mild disposition. A famous relief depicts Menander sitting to compose a
play, with three masks before him; he has picked one up and is gazing

[7] Plutarch, *Moralia*, 347f.
[8] See MacCary, "The Comic Tradition and Comic Structure in Diphilus'
Kleroumenoi," *Hermes*, 101 (1973), on the transvestite motif in ancient drama.

at it for inspiration.[9] However much plot should, according to Aristotle, predominate over character, it is clear that character decided the shape of each encounter that composed the plot, just as it inevitably determined the denouement.[10] Yet we have fixed ideas about character which were alien to the Greeks, and the authors of New Comedy were far more alert to the details of behaviour from one moment to the next, than concerned with long-term character as a determinant in fictional biography. The Aristotelian term ethos was also applied to the language and attitudes that an orator would build into the speech he composed for a client—say an old countryman—using his sophistication to portray a convincing simplicity. Commentators praise Menander for his ethos when he gives a role the right turn of phrase or gesture for his immediate argument.[11] At the same time the audience had their stereotyped expectations of old men, or courtesans, and the playwright will allow his own personae to voice these stereotypes in their judgements of each other, particularly when he intends to take his characters one stage further and reveal the discrepancy between prejudice and reality. Such subtlety is only possible at the end of a dramatic tradition.

But ethos had another application to the moral tone of a composition. Here, too, Menander advanced beyond his predecessors. In criticizing comedy it is useful to distinguish the "ethical" play, in which the audience is encouraged to measure the characters by their moral intentions, and the solution must satisfy the audience's conception of justice—what Aristotle called "human feeling."[12] Menander wrote many such plays, often using the omniscience of a divine prologue to reassure the audience that under supervision by the deity all obstacles would be surpassed to reach a just and happy outcome. The other, "amoral" type of comedy is much nearer to farce. In this the audience takes sides with youth, or the lovers of physical pleasure (greedy parasite and cheating slaves) and support an intrigue of deception to override justice (and indeed all es-

[9] See Webster, "The Poet and The Mask," *Classical Drama and Its Influence* (London, 1965), 5ff., and MacCary TAPA, 101 (1970), 277f.

[10] *Poetics*, trans. Grube (Library of Liberal Arts: New York, 1958), VI, 1450a. "The purpose of an action on the stage is not to imitate character, but character is a by-product of the action. . . . the plot is the first essential of a tragedy, character comes second." For the conformity of the *peripeteia* with characterisation see XIII 1452b–53a.

[11] For illustration of this craftsmanship see Arnott, *Phoenix*, 18 (1964), 110f., and Sandbach, "Menandre," *Entretiens de la Fondation Hardt*, XVI (1970), 111f.

[12] This concept first appears in the discussion of *peripeteia* at XIII, 1452b, and is related to our idea of poetic justice.

tablished authority) and victimise members of outsider groups—repressive older men, tradesmen, or foreigners—in order to obtain their goal of pleasure.[13] When Menander's plays used traditional comic motifs and roles, they neutralised them: the lowlife characters, the element of deceit, are subordinated to a legitimate purpose, and both in roles and scenes the serious and respectable element predominates. This is what the Greeks called *spoudaion*, a quality that Aristotle expected of gentlemen in life, and of the main figures in tragedy.[14]

Two plays will illustrate Menander's control of comic elements and admixture of serious, sometimes tragic forms. First "The Badtempered Man." The presupposition is that a rich but honourable young man, Sostratus, has fallen in love at sight with the daughter of a misanthrope living in rural isolation. His and the audience's common goal is an approved marriage, and the misanthrope Knemon's unmanageable nature is the chief obstacle. After a prologue by the god Pan, promising this outcome, the young man appears; he tells his companion, an expert in handling difficult people, that he has sent a slave to request an interview with the girl's father. At this moment the terrified entry of the slave ("the old fellow's crazy!") leads the expert to advise withdrawal, but Sostratos, made brave by love, waits to greet the returning Knemon, and is rudely rebuffed. A brief chaste encounter with the girl puts him under suspicion with her half-brother who lives nearby, but his misunderstanding and intervention (in a scene whose appeal is moral and psychological) leads to their alliance, and the only element of deception in the play, as the hero takes up the hoe and sets to work in the fields in order to seem an honest farmer and please the misanthrope. At the end of this second act the only non-serious characters appear, as the hero's slave and a boastful cook come to prepare a sacrifice to Pan for his superstitious mother. Their attempts to borrow pots and pans from Knemon (a traditional comic motif) relate both backwards in their pattern (for

[13] Compare Frye, pp. 163–65 and the introduction to E. Segal, *Roman Laughter, The Comedy of Plautus* (Cambridge, Mass., 1968), although he mistakenly relates these features only to the Roman context of Plautine comedy. These stereotyped plot requirements are ironically reflected by the young man in an excerpt from a Roman comedy, "The Fellow-Cadets," probably adapted from Menander. He complains that he is deprived of the plots against a mean father which are the chief delight of lovers, by his father's generosity, which makes deceit impossible. Another character is quoted expressing amazement that a courtesan is refusing to take money from her lover. In its mockery of the tradition this shows itself to be a play late in the evolution of comedy.

[14] XV, 1454a, where, however, he uses the synonym *Chrestos*.

the expert who reproves the amateur and boasts he can handle the difficult old man returns defeated, like Sostratos and his other slave) and
forwards to the finale. There is traditional comedy when the hero enters
from the fields bemoaning his aching back, but it is kept brief: the crisis
of the play approaches. In Act I we heard that the old man's bucket had
fallen into the well: now the old maid comes lamenting that she tried to
recover it and lost the spade, all because her master was too mean to
replace the rotting rope. Now it is his turn to go down after it, and he
falls. This is the pathos[15] (in tragic terms) which will bring him understanding. The amoral slave and cook see his fall as dramatic justice, but
rescue comes in the next act, when the old maid seeks help from the half-
brother Gorgias. News is brought of this peripeteia by the hero, in a
speech derived from the tragic messenger tradition, but comic in its explicit address to the audience.[16] Again in tragic fashion the messenger
speech is followed by the bringing on of the wounded victim like Euripides' Hippolytus. But this is comedy, so Knemon will live: his great
speech cast in an expressive trochaic metre, raising the tone above the
level of a dialogue, is a recognition[17] of his previous error: he was foolish
to think that he could live without dependence on others; now he ac-
knowledges the generosity of his stepson and gives him control over the
family affairs, and with it the right to choose the daughter's husband—
naturally this will be our hero. But in Greek society a rich boy's father
might well object to his marriage to a "poor" girl. This figure and his
influence over the outcome is no sooner mentioned than he appears, but
the hazard of his consent is postponed to the final act. This has two
scenes, both of which surprise the modern reader. In the first, the interview between father and son, the consent, easily obtained, is followed by
a fresh demand for another union, that of the hero's sister with a large

[15] *Poetics*, XI, 1452b specifies *peripeteia* (reversal) ,*anagnorisis* (recognition) and
pathos (suffering) as features of the tragic action. For a speculative but illuminating
appraisal of "The Bad-tempered man" as the reflection of Aristotelian ethical and
poetical theories in Comedy see Michael Anderson, "Knemon's Hamartia," *Greece
and Rome*, 17 (1970), 199f.

[16] "Athenians, by holy Demeter and Asclepius / by all the gods, I never yet in
my whole life / saw any man drowned at a more opportune moment." Both the
address to the audience and the formula "I never saw / heard a worse / bigger
etc., than just now" are found in Aristophanes and Middle comedy.

[17] *Poetics*, XI: "a change from ignorance to knowledge." Aristotle limits
hamartia and by implication *anagnorisis* to mistakes about personal identity, but
Anderson (pp. 213–15) makes a good case for a special kind of anagnorisis of moral
error in comedy which would have been an Aristotelian counterpart for tragic
hamatia.

28

dowry, to the helpful friend, the poor Gorgias; not only the father must be won over, by a moralising argument about the proper use of wealth, but Gorgias, who fears a change in his way of life and the loss of independence. This gratuitous second marriage, while in the comic tradition of multiple unions (we may compare the four marriages in the finale of *Measure for Measure* or *As You Like It*)[18] also depends on the social habits of the Greek bourgeoisie, which favoured marriage within the clan, or cross-marriages to reinforce the bonds of allied clans. Despite the criticism of foolish extravagance which Menander gives to Knemon, despite his sympathetic delineation of the poverty and hard work of Gorgias, Menander in this play and others accepts the discrepancies of Athenian society and rewards the deserving with social promotion; there is no intention of criticism, or pressure for social change, in the New Comedy.

The second phase of the finale revives the conflict of Knemon with the cook and slave from Act III. Despite his concession from the sickbed, the old man has not changed, and the misanthropy that keeps him back from the wedding party exposes him to the mockery of the pair, who bombard him with requests for impossible kitchen equipment, in a scene set to musical verse to match the offstage wedding music. The tone of the finale offends the reader who has given Knemon some respect: his discomfiture (like that of Shylock) is to some extent Menander's concession to the "other" morality, the partisanship of the farcical tradition, but there is again a moral purpose. Knemon must not be allowed to dilute the happiness of his daughter's wedding by his absence. His voluntary surrender of power in the fourth act is now echoed by reluctant physical surrender as cook and slave carry him to the party and ask the audience's approval for their victory in the *Agon* (a formal feature of both tragedy and Old Comedy) "over the troublesome old man": the obstacle is removed, and the blocking figure, for the time being, included. There are many ways in which this play satisfied the familiar comic pattern,[19] but

[18] See Frye, p. 163, and Walter Kerr, *Tragedy and Comedy* (New York, 1967) on the comic ending. Hymen himself intervenes ex machina to bring *As You Like It* to an end, and the withdrawal of Jaques offers a rough parallel to the behaviour of Knemon below.

[19] It can be seen as Frye's comic solution by the expulsion or inclusion of the blocking figure (163f.) provided we recognise that the most significant aspects of Menandrian finales are the exceptions and variations which do not fit the formula. It is a pity that students of comparative literature so often misapply Frye's analysis, using it, not to understand the underlying myths of comic fiction, but as a framework to impose on half-studied plays. In the context of ancient comedy Frye's own

rises above it to offer lifelike and serious characters and provoke thoughtful criticism of the audience's own habitual attitudes and assumptions.

In contrast "The Shield" is a deception play, nearer to ethos in traditional farce, and similar in plot to several Plautine comedies. A complex family structure determines the situation. Of three brothers, one is dead, leaving a son absent on military service, and a marriageable daughter: she is about to marry the stepson of the second brother, the sympathetic Chairestratos, who has generously provided the dowry for his niece's forthcoming wedding. But the eldest brother, Smikrines, is an unmitigated villain, avaricious and hypocritical. The crisis with which the play opens is the return of the soldier's loyal slave Daos bearing the news of his death in battle: the body could not be recognised, but was identified by his shield lying nearby. Smikrines, learning of the rich booty left by his nephew, decides to overthrow the family plans by claiming his legal right as senior kinsman to marry the girl, who is now heiress to this wealth. In a postponed prologue, a favourite Menandrian device, the goddess Fortune reassures the audience; the recognition of the body was false, and the soldier will return to put things to right. There is a farcical scene over the dismissal of the wedding cook, who catalogues his professional frustrations, and then the sudden collapse of Chairestratos at the news of Smikrines' evil plans inspires Daos to mastermind the deception. Chairestratos will be reported sick, and a sham doctor fetched in to report his "death"; then Smikrines will drop his designs on the niece so as to claim instead the daughter of Chairestratos, since her father's death will leave her a far greater heiress: thus the niece will be free to marry her suitor and the deception will be revealed before Smikrines can do any more harm. Act III is particularly close in technique to Plautine versions of Greek comedy.[20] Daos, pretending to be unaware of the listening Smikrines, rushes from the house noisily lamenting in tragic quotations an unspecified doom: Smikrines, his curiosity provoked, only gradually extracts the "news" from the slave, when the mock doctor appears, and is ushered inside. The return of the doctor after twenty lines, with his

---

deliberate *reductio ad absurdum* should make his reader cautious: "At this point we realise that the crudest of Plautine comedy formulas has much the same *structure* as the central Christian myth itself, with its divine son appeasing the wrath of a father and redeeming what is at once a society and a bride" (p. 185). This is too universal to foster understanding of the individual playwright or phase of dramatic creation.

[20] See below and W. S. Anderson, "A New Menandrian Prototype for the *servus Currens* of Roman Comedy," *Phoenix* 24 (1970), 229–36.

comic Doric accent and medical mumbo-jumbo, is a perfect scene in the tradition of Middle Comedy and a foreshadowing of many doctors in Moliere (not to mention Despina in *Cosi Fan Tutte*). Although the last part of the play is lost, there is enough to indicate the soldier's timely return, with a scene in which the slave initially refuses to "recognise" him, and a finale based on the villain's discomfiture and a double wedding of the paired cousins. It is natural to speak of this play in theatrical cliches, because of its extravagant operatic devices of conspiracy, impersonation[21] and tragic parody; yet it also contains a uniquely realistic report of battle, to be taken seriously by an audience who has not yet been told that the soldier's death is a misunderstanding. It would seem, too, that in Daos we have a portrayal drawn from the tragic tradition, and without known comic precedent, of the completely unselfish slave, whose concern for the family contrasts both with the villainy of Smikrines, its theoretical head, and the stereotype of his slave role. There are no scenes preserved in musical metre, but this would be most likely to occur in the finale, which has been lost. "The Shield" is probably an early play; certainly it represents those aspects of comedy which Menander later eliminated, but which appealed most to the Roman comic tradition, and for students of the Roman playwrights, this most recent discovery offers the best connection between the Greek and Roman forms.

Whatever informal stage performances the Romans enjoyed before they encountered Greek drama have left no indisputable evidence.[22] Romans first saw Greek tragedies and comedies during their campaigns in South Italy against Tarentum (when Diphilos and Philemon were still alive and composing new plays), and in Sicily against Carthage, from 264 to 241. In 240 the first officially sponsored Latin adaptations, made by a bilingual Tarentine Greek, Livius Andronicus, were pre-

[21] Outsiders are imported for such impersonations in Epidicus (the flute-girl as long-lost daughter); "The Braggart Soldier" (the two soubrettes as matron and maid); "The Persian Girl" (the parasite's daughter); "The Carthaginian" (the bailiff as a tourist hitting the town); *Pseudolus* (the trickster Monkey impersonates the messenger); and "The Three-bit Trickster" (the title-role as messenger). Members of the plot themselves assume disguise in *Curculio* (the parasite as messenger) and "The Braggart Soldier" (the lover as ship's captain).

[22] See W. Beare, *The Roman Stage*, 3rd Ed. (London, 1963), Ch. 2. The most important influences on Roman comedy outside Greek New Comedy were Sicilian and South Italian Greek-language Phlyax farces (often travesties of Myths, like Amphitryo) and the Oscan Atellane farces, improvised and later composed around the stock roles of trickster, glutton and old fool. Plautus' second name Maccius derives from the trickster hero of these farces, perhaps a relic of his earlier career on the stage.

sented at the games celebrating the Roman victory over Carthage. From that time versions of Greek tragedy and comedy became a regular component, *the Ludi Scaenici*, offered on two or three days of the public festivals each year. Plautus, our first great comic playwright, is also the earliest Latin author to survive in complete works rather than fragmentary quotation. Roman tradition claimed he was an Italian who worked as a stage artist, and his plays show so many techniques in common with the fragmentary excerpts of his predecessor Naevius that it is natural to believe he learnt the craft of playwrighting from experience, and inherited a developed tradition of presentation. Menander had been dead eighty years or more before Plautus' earliest play (probably "the Braggart Soldier") and a generation had passed since the deaths of Philemon and Diphilus, but although the Greek tradition had continued in Athens and spread to Sicily, Plautus seems to have ignored contemporary Greek comedy and preferred the "classics." Among his extant plays four can be attributed with confidence to Menander, three to Philemon and two to Diphilus,[23] while dramatic features of others have suggested attribution to one or other of these authors, but scholarly disagreement is likely to continue unless more Greek model plays are recovered. If Plautus, then, inherited the material of his plays from Greek dramatists, what did he contribute to their form? And if he was offered such material ready-made, can we assume he adopted it whole and unabridged?

Aristotle analysed dramatic mimesis in the *Poetics* into six components: plot (*muthos*) and the media of language (*logos*) and metre or song (*mousike*), with the modes of characterisation (*ethos*) and argument (*dianoia*, explained later as the dramatist's ability to say what the situation admits and requires) and finally the mode of spectacle (*opsis*). Formally the essential is plot, since though different plays may handle the same plot or story, any significant change in the plot by an adapter would make it a different play.[24] Naturally this element in Greek comedy is the one least altered in adaptation. There was at one time a scholarly conviction, based partly on faith in the harmonious unity of

[23] From Menander, "The Pot of Gold" (probably) and "The Bacchis Sisters," "The Casket-play" and *Stichus*, with certainty; from Philemon, "The Merchant" and the "Three-Bit Trickster" and probably the "Little-Ghost Play"; from Diphilus, *Casina*, and "The Rope."

[24] *Poetics* VI, 1450a. For the fuller explanation of "argument," or "thought," see 1450b. On plot as the differential, compare XVIII 1456a, "It is with regard to plot more than anything else that one is justified in calling one tragedy the same as another, that is two tragedies that have the same involvement and unravelling."

composition of Greek drama, that plays of Plautus which employed two successive intrigues, such as "The Braggart Soldier" or "The Carthaginian," must have amalgamated the plot of a second Greek play into that of the chief model. This belief was reinforced by the actual practice of Terence, who in three of his six plays borrowed one or more scenes from a second Greek comedy to enrich the action of his main original. His enemies called this *contaminatio*, "spoiling" the Greek plays:[25] he, in rejecting the abusive term, confirmed his practice, referring his critics to Naevius and Plautus, with the implication that they had amalgamated plays, but in language which permits us to doubt it.[26] There are scenes in Plautus whose action seems not to be required by the original play; we may instance the tableau scene of the brothel inmates from the *Pseudolus*, manifestly added by Plautus since it converts the girl-entertainer of the plot into a low-status brothel slave. This is also, incidentally, the only clear instance of innovation for the sake of spectacle, in the form of the parade of female extras. In general we have little chance of discovering this element of ancient production, although there must have been plenty of stage business; two samples are the mime implied by the elaborate description of the poses of the plotting slave in "The Braggart Soldier" (200–16), and a later scene in the same play which combines on opposite sides of the stage symmetrical dialogues between the soldier and his deceitful slave, and the two women conspirators; in the grouping and regrouping which orchestrates such scenes Plautus obviously exploited visual production-patterns, but they may also have featured in the script he was adapting.

Other scenes may be suspected as insertions because they damage the dramatic economy: in "The Braggart Soldier" the long monologue of the elderly bachelor describing the woes of marriage is a *tour de force* for a leading actor, but an unnecessary postponement of the action; again a scholar has recently suggested that the scene of the doctor in *Menaechmi* is a Plautine insertion, because it is seen as spoiling the symmetrical structure of the original.[27] But the only incontrovertible evidence we have of Plautus' technique is the sixty surviving lines of Menander's "Double-Deceiver," set against the corresponding scenes in Plautus' "The Bacchis Sisters." In Menander the young man has repented and determined to pay back to his father the money he cheated from him. When his father

---

[25] Compare Duckworth, pp. 202–08.
[26] Terence, "The Andrian Girl," Prologue 15–21.
[27] Steidle, in *Rheinisches Museum*, 114 (1971), 247f.

comes home from the marketplace the son explains and they enter the house, leaving an empty stage for the act interval; both return in the next act and the father leaves before the young man meets his friend (whom he believes to be false to him). Plautus did not want the father on stage, so his young man assumes that the father is already at home (although the audience last saw him going in the other direction) and declares he is going in to pay back the money. But Plautus had a further problem to overcome, that of form, for his plays were presented without act interludes, offering continuous action. To fill the empty stage Plautus brings the "false" friend out prematurely, and the confrontation between the young men follows almost immediately upon the hero's exit monologue. Plautus' interest in exploiting the young man's emotional confusion and the cross-purposes of the encounter leads him to give the scene a fuller scale than he found in Menander.[28] It is typical of his handling of dramas scene by scene that he should compress (or even suppress completely) scenes with little emotional or comic appeal, even when they are essential to the flow and understanding of the action. Nevertheless this alteration of balance between scenes, while it inevitably changes the emphasis of a play, does not entail substantial changes in the plot itself.

I spoke of the elimination of act divisions; this adoption of continuous action can be shown in the texts of both Plautus and Terence, although act divisions were imposed, in rough correspondence to those of the original Greek plays, by later editors.[29] Menander and his colleagues had dropped the participating chorus of Aristophanic Comedy, in favour of disconnected interludes of song and dance. The texts of Menander simply indicate the word *Chorus*, but at the first appearance of the dancers there is usually some allusion in the actual dialogue: "We had better get out of the way. I hear some revellers approaching."[30] Some chorus-like groups of people appear in Roman comedies: the hired witnesses who describe their trade and enter into conspiracy with the hero of "The Carthaginian" and the poor fishermen in "The Rope" who similarly describe their way of life and exchange information with the young lover. These plays are

[28] The definitive reconstruction and analysis is in Handley, *Menander and Plautus: A Study in Comparison* (London, 1968).

[29] Duckworth, pp. 98–101.

[30] Compare "The Bad-Tempered Man," at the end of Act I; "There are people coming / with offerings for Pan. They've had a drop to drink; / this is no time to get involved with them. I'm off." Plautus leaves one of these formulae at 106 in "The Bacchis Sisters": Is he referring it to the stage character who approaches, or is this a sign that he too had some kind of interlude?

not Menandrian, and we may surmise that other writers of New Comedy retained a participatory chorus in some plays. Plautus has his own solutions to the act division that cannot be written over. In *Curculio* the wardrobe master emerges between acts III and IV explicitly to give the audience a tour of the Roman forum while he and they await the parasite's return; in *Pseudolus*, the protagonist tells the audience that a flute player will amuse them while he goes inside to think (a necessary rest for an almost continuous role). We might expect the elimination of act divisions to increase the hazard of audience fatigue: would they not miss the musical interludes? The Roman audience had never known such choruses in comedy and if Plautus lost an element of spectacle in omitting the dancing chorus, he enriched the plays musically. The predominant metre in Menandrian drama is the iambic trimeter: Aristotle tells us that as tragedy evolved "the iambic trimeter replaced the trochaic tetrameter, which had been used at first because the poetry was then ... more closely related to the dance. When spoken parts came in, nature herself found the appropriate metre, as the iambic is of all metres most like ordinary speech."[31]

The trochaic tetrameter found in some scenes and choruses of Aristophanes is also used in Menander for Knemon's great scene of realisation and the dialogue which follows it to the end of Act IV of "The Bad-Tempered Man" (708–84) as it is for lively dialogue scenes in "The Samian Girl" (421–615) and "The Sicyonians" (110–49); but there is no evidence that this metre had musical accompaniment. The only certain instance of music seems to be the finale of "The Bad-Tempered Man," where the iambic tetrameters are enhanced by the festive flute music of the offstage wedding. Although there is now firm evidence for these longer verses with their heightened tone of anger or excitement in Menander and the fragments of his contemporaries, there is still no sign of any lyric forms. The contrast is great when we turn to Plautus. In his plays the longer metres predominate over iambic dialogue, and his most favoured metre is the Latin version of the trochaic tetrameter, the septenarius, a curtailed eight-foot line; this coincided with a traditional Italian accentual verse form which survives in some old songs and chants. In taking over Greek quantitative metre the Roman dramatists had to cater to the greater proportion of heavy syllables in Latin, by ignoring the Greek rythmic refinements which distinguished the purer, more formal, tragic iambic from the freer comic form. One consequence was

---

[31] IV, 1449a.

that loss in the Latin of a subtle element of Menandrian versification—
the ability to heighten the tone of a scene by adopting not only tragic
diction but tragic verse-rhythm.[32]

Plautus' plays contain whole scenes in the trochaic septenarius and
other longer metres (trochaic octonarius, iambic septenarius and octonarius), and scholars generally believe that these rhythms were sung
or intoned to the accompaniment of the double-flute; but in addition all
his plays except "The Braggart Soldier" and "The Merchant" contain
lyric, often as many as five songs for one or more performers. Thus, in
Menaechmi, fairly representative in its musical distribution, the iambic
prologue and exposition monologue lead into a lyric of two approximately corresponding stanzas in mixed metres for the husband, then a
scene in trochaic septenarii. The pattern is repeated with the new persons of the second "act"; iambic dialogue leads into a lyric of welcome
sung by the courtesan, followed by a scene in trochaic septenarii. After
another moment of empty stage, and an assumed lapse of time, a trochaic
monologue is followed by several short iambic scenes; then another song
—the play's longest, in several sections and metres—for the returning
husband, leads into a confrontation scene in septenarii. In the next unit
of action (called Act V in our manuscripts) dialogue leads up to a song
by the old father-in-law, characterising his feebleness, followed by an
excited "Mad" scene in trochaic septenarii. The last phase of action
similarly proceeds from spoken dialogue to trochaic septenarii; then a
song by the loyal slave is followed by a high-pitched kidnapping scene in
which trochaics are briefly replaced by a long iambic octonarius for the
crisis of physical action, and the finale of the play exploits the symmetry
of the trochaic septenarius for the echoes and antiphonies of the slave's
interrogation of his master and the twin brother.[33] Out of 1162 lines,
over 600 are in trochaic septenarii, and 122 lines are in lyrics shared by
four characters, making use of iambic, anapaestic, and trochaic lines and
the uniquely Plautine five-beat rhythms of the double-stressed cretic
($\angle \cup \angle$) and Bacchiac ($\cup \angle \angle$).[34]

[32] See Webster, pp. 60–65.
[33] The pattern can be expressed schematically:—
    Act I. Iambic dialogue (110v)—Song (25v)—Trochaics (90)
    Acts II and III. Dial. (125v)—Song (18v)—trochaics (96)
    Act. IV. Dial. (105)—Song (35v)—trochaics (96)
    Act V (really IV) Dial. (52)—Song (22v)—trochaics (97)
    Act Vb from 881 Dial. (17)—Trochaics (67)—Song (22v)—Trochaics,
    with song-inserts of Iambic Octonarii (160v)
[34] I offer as accentual equivalents of the regular cretic four-foot line "témperánce

It is not unfair to suggest that Plautus has effectively turned a straight play into an Opera Buffa, with spoken dialogue, recitative and arias. But it is in language (or expression, as Aristotle's term *logos* can be interpreted here) that Plautus was most original. Latin as a literary language was unformed, and what he chose to make of it; it is a reflection of the unsophisticated quality of Latin that early writers both of tragedy and comedy parade alliteration and conspicuous sound patterns, based on anaphora, repetition, homoeoteleuton (a kind of rudimentary rhyme), and other word play. For Plautus, words, whether they were in usage or he had to invent them, were a medium of play, to be juggled, punned upon, misunderstood, distorted and elaborated into fantastical formations, as imaginative in conception as in form and second.[35] Plautus excels in the humorous epithet: an old nurse is accused of reconnoitring eyes, and a turtlish tread; another, very fond of drink, is offered a statue of solid wine. Cause and effect are inverted, as shackled slaves are accused of wearing down their shackles, or shattering the rods that rain upon their backs;[36] resemblances limited to one aspect are transformed into riddling identifications: "My father's a housefly." "How's that?" "Because you can't keep anything from him." Fleecing was a standard image for the confidence trick in the ancient world, so the old man who is cheated becomes a sheep; the metaphor once started is kept moving for a whole duet of lyrical fantasy by the two temptresses in the finale of "The Bacchis Sisters"; neither the lyrical form nor the verbal pyrotechnics are likely to have occurred in Menander's original finale. Echoes of religious, legal and military formulae vary the tone and contribute to grandiose effects, whether mock-tragic, or triumphant; units of metre and speech coincide with comic precision, and over much of the dialogue, especially the metres for long lines, like the septenarius, with their scope for fuller expression, ideas are embroidered with variation and exaggera-

---

/ cáuses mén / língeríng / síghs of páin"; The Bacchioc has a slow effect, suited to old men and drunken singers: "a lóng sóng / is tóo lóng, / that mákes síngers bréathléss."

[35] The classic study of Plautus' verbal creativity, Eduard Fraenkel's *Plautinisches in Plautus*, (Berlin, 1922 as *Elementi Plautini*; Rome, 1960) has unfortunately not been translated into English.

[36] *Aulularia* 41, 49; *Curculio* 139; *Most.* 356, *Trin.* 1021, *Per.* 795. On Plautine imagery compare Fantham, *Comparative Studies in Republican Latin Imagery*, (Toronto, 1972), pp. 95–114.

tion from sheer joy in verbal display; it is the verbal equivalent of dance, but certainly did not exclude gesture and visual flourish.

American writers have succeeded better than the British in conveying the uninhibited vitality, the puns and slang, the oaths and abuse and pomp and sheer unflagging inventiveness of Plautus. But his *logos* is untranslatable, and the best incentive I know for Mahomet to come to the Mountain; it is up to lovers of comedy to learn Latin.

Meanwhile the dramatic critic is entitled to ask how such flights of language effect the two most intellectual components of drama, which Aristotle identified as characterisation and argument. How do they survive the pyrotechnics? Does not this kind of language play belong to farce and is it not incompatible with the subtle characterisation and relationships of High Comedy? If we divide the roles of New Comedy roughly into the serious—respectable figures, though they may not be wise—and the carriers of humour[37]—men who without being ridiculous are sufficiently free of dignity to create comic scenes—we will find that Plautus shows respect for the respectable. He may favour plays that feature irresponsible and lecherous old men ("The Comedy of Asses," "The Bacchis Sisters," "The Merchant") but he will leave virtuous elders their dignity of language and behavior. In "The Three-Bit Trickster" there are long scenes of undiluted earnest between old men (there are four of them in the cast, all sober-sides) and serious young men. A long opening scene provoked by one good old man's misunderstanding of the other's behaviour provides a moral discussion of gossip and its evils;[38] later a young man explains in a lyrical *tour de force* why he has rejected romance from his life. There is a serious argument with his father about a man's duty to his friends in trouble, and an even more earnest dispute with his impoverished friend, who refuses to let his honour be impaired by accepting the honourable generosity of the other. This conflict of principle lets argumentation dominate over action, and the scene's length is dramatically undesirable, but Plautus finds the rhetorical element in such

[37] These correspond approximately to Frye's "buffoon or entertainer" (p. 175) but should not be thought of as clowns.

[38] It looks as though Plautus has tried to ease this scene with extraneous wise-cracks; the Roman allusions of 83–85 are certainly his, but we should be more cautious about holding him responsible for the time-honoured jokes against wives (42, and 51–56; compare the jokes of the good man in "The Rope," 904–05, 1045–47, 1203–04): though they may offend modern readers, they are not too crude for the misogyny of Attic comedy. Menander would have known better, but the models of these two plays are not Menandrian.

scenes attractive, another aspect of his preoccupation with verbal texture at the expense of structural values. His audience enjoyed emotional conflict and moral dispute. The supreme example of this tendency is "The Prisoners," a play in which a slave impersonates his master when taken prisoner of war, in order to aid his escape. The whole play is carried by social irony based on the inversion of slave and gentleman (we might compare the sexual irony of *Fidelio*, also comic, in terms of genre) and the almost tragic irony that the slave is in fact the kidnapped child of his new master, the old man who condemns him to the murderous work of the stonequarries.[39] All three leading figures are *spoudaioi*—honourable men. Only the element of misunderstanding based on two changes of identity, one partly known, and one unknown to any of the three, creates the drama finally resolved by the return of the escaped master with evidence leading to a happy recognition. Almost every ingredient of tragedy recommended by Aristotle is to be found in this play, but to the audience Plautus affirms its status as comedy: "It'll pay you to give this play your attention. It's not a hackneyed theme like the others; it has no dirty lines unfit to quote, no lying pander or naughty courtesan, nor any braggart soldier. Don't be anxious because I said there was a war going on. . . . the battles will all be offstage, for it would be unfair if we used our comic production to present you with a tragedy."[40] Serious the play was, and something new and special, but no tragedy.

From this play and "The Three-Bit Trickster" we may infer that Plautus and his audience valued explicit moralising more than would be acceptable in modern comedy. His characters can be earnest enough, or actively comic: what is missing is the relish for the absurdity of human inconsistency which distinguishes Menander. Plautine comedy comes nearest to this sense of absurdity in its treatment of lovers, for sentiment clearly embarrassed the Roman spectator, and Plautus prefers to offset lovers' exchanges with the cynical comments of a bystander, most often

---

[39] Compare *Poetics* XIV, 1453b: "There is still a third way; when someone who intends to do the deed is ignorant of the relationship, but recognises it before the deed is done. . . ." and 1454a, "best of all is the last alternative, the way of Merope in *The Cresphontes* when she intends to kill her son, but does not do so when she recognises him."

[40] "The Prisoners," Prologue 52–62 (my translation). We can compare the assurances given in the prologue to *Amphitryo*, 60–64 that the play is not a tragedy. "I can't rightly make it a continuous comedy, since kings and gods appear in it, but as there's a slave role too, I'll make it a tragicomedy, like I said." The audience defines genre by the social circumstances of the cast and the action.

the young man's slave.[41] Plautus' slaves are his glory, and his most successful plays are intrigues conducted with little moral scruple by a loyal and ingenious slave to help his young master outwit his father or some less reputable obstacle to happiness; "The Bacchis Sisters," "Epidicus," "The Little-Ghost play," "The Carthaginian," "The Braggart-Soldier," "Pseudolus," and to some extent "The Rope" are variations on this form. Not even Daos in Menander's "Shield" reaches the inventive scale of Tranio in "The Little-Ghost Play" or Pseudolus in his own play. It was the personality and actions of these slaves which started a European tradition leading to characters as diverse as Mosca, Scapin, Figaro, Leporello, The Admirable Crighton, and Jeeves.

The glorification of the slave figure came more easily to the Romans since the plays represented another society; if the Lord of Misrule took over, and responsible citizens were fooled, these were Athenians, not the Roman paterfamilias. Plautus never tried to naturalise the Greek milieu. Instead he exploits in both ways the alienation effect of deliberate Roman allusion. 'Pseudolus," says the pimp fantastically, "has brought me to trial before the Centuriate assembly." On another occasion Plautus will make a Greek-style reference to Roman or Italian practices as "barbarian."[42] Since the scene is not Rome, Plautus can employ every dramatic means to exalt his slave-protagonist and let him dominate the free members of society. The play *Pseudolus* opens with the suppliant appeal of his helpless young master for Pseudolus' intervention, which he generously guarantees. From then on he is the young man's patron, spokesman and negotiator; it is his master's claim to glory that he commands Pseudolus

> T'is thee I seek, your majesty, yea thee
> whom thy servant Pseudolus serves. T'is thee I seek
> to give thee thrice in triple-wise, in form
> three-fold, three thrice-deserved delights derived
> from dumbbells three and by devices three,
> deceit, deception and double-cross. (697, cf. 703ff., trans. Casson)

[41] Compare *Menaechmi* I.iii., "The Carthaginian" I.iii. and the reading of the love-letter in *Pseudolus* I.i. The only unchaperoned love-scene seems to be the last ten lines (295–305) of "The Little-Ghost Play," I.iii. Even when the girl appears on stage, the plays may contain no love-scenes, as in "The Braggart Soldier" and "The Rope"; the extreme case is *Casina*, where the prologue assures the spectators that Plautus has kept both lovers offstage.

[42] Pseudolus 1233: for barbarian = Roman compare "The Braggart Soldier," 211, *Stichus*, 193 and "The Three-Bit Trickster," Prol. 19–21; "Philemon wrote this play: Plautus made the barbarian version, and called it *Trinummus*."

In a direct proclamation to the audience Pseudolus braves the world, and challenges it to beware of his tricks (124–28). As he later warns Simo, his master's father (511, 517), so Simo in turn warns Pseudolus' other enemy, the pimp Ballio (1096, 1228). The four lines of proclamation that end the first scene of the play are only the first of Pseudolus' many scenes alone with the audience; he is their window on the play, imparting his doubts and fears directly to them at 404ff., 561 ff., 573ff., 617ff., 756ff., and 1016ff.; even in dialogue he keeps other characters only half-informed; his responsibility is to the audience. (385 and 720, "Look, this play's being given for the benefit of these people, and they were here, they know all about it. I'll tell you later.") Pseudolus has to take on two adversaries, father Simo, who is determined not to pay for his son's mistress, and the pimp, Ballio, who must be paid for her, and has partly sold her to a soldier rival. The play becomes a triangular contest elaborately bound by a series of waters, as Pseudolus, acting like a free economic agent, wagers the cost of the girl against a stiff beating that he can get her away from the pimp; then the pimp bets father Simo the same amount that he can foil Pseudolus. The fact is that every character in his own way treats Pseudolus with respect; the pimp declares that if he died, Pseudolus would be the worst villain in Athens (336); father Simo calls him a veritable Socrates (465); neighbour Callipho, asked by Pseudolus to cancel his business for the day so that he can watch Pseudolus' trickery, sums it all up for us: "I've decided to stay for your sake, Pseudolus: I'm dying to watch your act" (551–52). Pseudolus is putting on an expert performance of which the actors are spectators as well as the audience. Plautus gives him all the glamour of imagery: he is the poet and deviser of plots (in both senses, 404f.) the professional inventor (700); the philosopher (678f.); the military commander going through siege (385, 571, 576f.), battle (525f., 760f.), and triumph (1051). As Simo reluctantly declares, his Pseudolus has outstripped Ulysses, and the trickery of the Trojan Horse (1244).[43]

Pseudolus' opportunity comes with the coincidental arrival of the messenger sent to complete the purchase of the girl from Ballio. In swift succession he impersonates Ballio's steward and awes the messenger into handing over the seal, then takes the intrigue into his hands, persuading his young master's friend to provide a loan (which will cover the last installment of the purchase price) and a trickster to be disguised as the

[43] These mythical comparisons are combined with Roman military imagery in Plautus' most splendid lyric aria, The Triumph-song of Chrysalus, "Bacchis Sisters," 925–79.

purchaser's agent; in this scene there are details of dialogue and construction closely parallel to "the Shield." Curiously Plautus outdoes himself at this point, by representing the new trickster as even sharper than
Pseudolus, who temporarily becomes a mere witness to the prowess of
his emissary; the latter is given a display scene with Ballio (960–1016)
like the mock-doctor's fooling of Smikrines, and the girl is successfully
led off to rejoin her young lover, who does not reappear. In the fourth act
Pseudolus is not on stage, but dominates the consultation of his enemies,
Simo and Ballio, in temporary alliance. Ballio is now confident that
Pseudolus is foiled, and it is this confidence which makes him enter the
wager with Simo, just before the real messenger returns. In the peripeteia
of the play, Ballio first cruelly mocks the man, thinking this is Pseudolus'
contrivance; it is only when this innocent describes the preposterous
physique of Ballio's "steward" to whom he gave the seal that Ballio experiences the recognition; "the moment you mentioned those feet you
did for me. It was Pseudolus all right. Simo, it's all over with me. I'm a
dead man" (1220–21). This marks his downfall, the outcome of his fatal
error. The victory is Pseudolus', and the last act is his song of triumph.
He opens with a forty line aria describing his drunken dance of celebration, then approaches his master's threshhold and calls him out. Simo
too must yield, because he owes Pseudolus money, and comic justice requires that he keep his bargain;[44] but Pseudolus is generous in victory;
he will remit half the debt, if Simo will drink with him. So in the final
indignity not only the young master, but the authority figure carouses
with the slave triumphant.

Other Plautine comedies take the slave within an inch of disaster; he is
besieged with fire as he seeks sanctuary on the street altar (a motif known
from Menander's *Perinthia*, and Plautus' "Little-Ghost Play") or bound
fast ready for thrashing. But even this can be used to exalt his ultimate
victory. Chrysalus in "The Bacchis Sisters" (747, cf. 855) and Epidicus
(684) have their masters tie them up so that their triumph will be more
absolute when their masters are compelled by circumstances to release
them (cf. Ba. 861). Such comedies use every physical and verbal device
to reinforce the message of escape from authority.

Characterisation, then, in Plautus represents stereotypes, sober or

[44] Where Menander's gentlemen are concerned with their propertied interests,
Plautus' characters, slave and free, are preoccupied with ready money, and the
comic justice of a Plautine finale several times involves a financial settlement,
(*Curculio, Pseudolus*, "Rope"). See Segal, Ch. 1

comically distorted; he excels in representing the consummate rascal, or villain, but he does not try to reproduce either the delicate instantaneous words and gestures that make a personality vivid, or the paradoxical counter-types which are Menander's chief innovation—the sensitive and honourable soldier, or the generous courtesan. In the third sense of ethos, however, he does not limit himself to amoral farce, but in plays such as "The Prisoner," "The Three-Bit Trickster," or "The Rope," seeks out the serious element as a desirable ingredient in his comic world.

Where Plautus had advertised the Greek authorship of his plays in his own interest, Terence was proud that his plays derived from originals by distinguished authors, and prouder of his own ability to convey their qualities to his audience; but then Roman society had evolved rapidly since Plautus' heyday. Although Terence's first play is dated to 166 B.C., only sixteen years after Plautus' death, he was not one, but two generations younger, a captive from Carthaginian territory, so well educated in the household of his Roman master that his Greek was fluent, and his Latin partook of Greek simplicity and elegance. Rumour accused young Philhellene noblemen of writing Terence's plays: he tactfully made no outright denial, but it was for these men, the new intelligentsia, travelled in Greece and versed in Greek rhetoric and philosophy, that he made his versions. Greek comedy was no longer something that could be adapted to amuse an audience: it was a model of sophistication, whose standards must be reproduced; let the audience adapt themselves to the requirements of art. But his ideal was not slavish adherence to the plots of his models; with the first play to be performed, "The Andrian Girl," Terence boasted that he had adapted the opening exposition scene not from Menander's "Andrian Girl" but from another play with a similar plot; no doubt he preferred a dialogue to a monologue exposition, but even then he changed the interlocutor of the elderly father from his wife (for whom Terence had no further use in the play) to a freedman cook, who disappears as soon as the exposition is ended. The play was based on the recognition of a beloved girl as freeborn, so that her union could be regularised in marriage. In New Comedy such secrets of identity had always been made known to the audience in a prologue. Plautus had largely respected this practice, preserving the dramatic assets of irony and the audience's confidence of a good outcome. Terence's first prologue takes the form of a literary vindication, and uses his critical concerns as an excuse to omit the usual advance information; but none of his prologues ever serves to inform about the plot. We might say that he preferred suspense to irony,[45] but since he takes great pains to write in hints that would lead experienced spectators of comedy to foresee the outcome, it might be fairer to assume that he disliked not irony, but the alienation inherent in an expository prologue.

Yet the biggest innovation in his "Andrian girl" is not acknowledged in his prefatory speech; we only know from the commentary of Donatus[46] that Terence inserted two new roles, a second young man and his servant, into the Menandrian action. Following the scenes in which they appear we can easily see how Terence wrote them into the play, even resorting in one scene to the inartistic device of an eavesdropper who arrives and departs unnoticed (II.v.); with these roles he is also able to bridge over the formal act-divisions of the Menandrian framework, so that there are only two moments in the play when the stage is left empty. But continuity of action was not his motive for the new personnel. He is said to have introduced the second young man so as to provide a husband for the girl left unmarried by the hero, but his practice in other plays suggests a more structural explanation. Of Terence's six plays, five construct their plot around contrasted pairs; indeed three ("The Self-tormentor," "Phormio" and "The Brothers") offer contrasted pairs of both fathers and sons. Terence translated only Menander, and his pupil Apollodorus, but since the model of "the Phormio" is not by Menander, it is fair to see this kind of doubling as the product of Terence's preference, rather than a mannerism of Menander.[47] In "The Andrian girl" he had to impose this duality; all our evidence suggests that he then looked for it and found it ready-made in his other plays. Such double plots multiplied the action, and Terence's other innovations in incorporating borrowed material into "The Eunuch" and "The Brothers," like his conversion of monologues into dialogue, suggest that he was seeking a fuller action. But contrast is intrinsically attractive and the opposition of severe and indulgent fathers in "The Self-tormentor" and "The Brothers" provides symmetrical scenes of confrontation and a dramatic reversal based on the changed balance and success between the contrasted but parallel roles.

[45] Duckworth has a good discussion of this over-simplification, pp. 231–35.

[46] Donatus, on *Andria*, 301. They may be free invention or possibly roles imported from Menander's "Perinthian Girl," the second play used. See W. Ludwig, "The Originality of Terence and his Greek Models," GRBS, 9 (1968), 169f.

[47] Four plays of Plautus have contrasted pairs of young men ("Bacchis Sisters," *Epidicus*, "The Merchant," and the "Three-Bit Trickster") but significant contrast of fathers only arises in "Bacchis Sisters" and "The Merchant" (based on Philemon).

In his use of metre and musical form Terence drew back from the variety of Plautus: he ventured lyric metres only for two songs in his first play, and again, surprisingly, in his last play, "The Brothers." But these are not new conceptions; the song of the lovesick young man describing his emotional torment appears in similar form in Plautus' "Casket-Play" (Cist. 202ff.), and the brief midwife's song in "The Andrian girl" echoes the rhythms of the old woman in Plautus' *Curculio*.[48] Terence did not feel at ease in song, but preferred to convey moments of emotions by frequent syncopating changes from the lost iambic octonarius to the trochaic septenarius, or by other interchanges of iambic and trochaic rhythm. Where Plautus tended to use a change of metre to mark a change of scene, as the exit or entry of a character raises or slackens tension, Terence constantly and less obtrusively registers each shift of mood within a scene by altering the metre: tone and tempo change to express *ethos*, not to create musical variety.

His language, too, aims at naturalism. While neither Plautus nor Terence used dialectal differentiation or lapses of grammar to convey social distinctions, Terence plays down the form of language to concentrate his audience on its implications. Slaves or parasites are allowed their pithy sayings and colourful metaphors,[49] but in general his dialogue is neat, swift without haste, elliptic and allusive. Terence handles asides, interruptions and aposiopesis with a special dexterity, to convince the audience that they are not watching a conscious performance but overhearing excerpts from natural talk. There are no extraneous wisecracks, no anachronistic Roman allusions, and amazingly few references to the physical world about them. Without reaching the rarified conversational level of characters in the novels of Ivy Compton Burnett, Terence's people largely avoid naming food, drink, clothing, furniture or aspects of crafts and trades. When the midwife in a small fragment of Menander's "Andrian girl" leaves the new mother, she calls back into the house "wash her, and give the baby the yolks of four eggs, please"; Terence's midwife suppresses the egg yolks: "Now first see that she's washed, then give her what I ordered for her to drink, in the quantity I specified."[50]

[48] *Andria*, 625–38 (dactylo-cretic); *Adelphoe*, 610–17 (choriambic-dactylic, then long iambic and trochaic lines); compare *Andria*, 234–53 for iambic-trochaic alternation. For the midwife, compare *Andria*, 481–85 in bacchiacs.

[49] See Arnott, "Phormio Parasitus," *Greece and Rome*, 17 (1970), 32 f. and Fantham, pp. 72–81.

[50] Terence, *Andria*, 483–85; the Menander fragments are quoted by Donatus here.

In keeping with his ideal of naturalism Terence offers virtually no scope for spectacle, except in "The Eunuch," his most successful play. (As Horace tells us, Roman audiences always loved spectacle.)[51] Act II opens with a competitive display of slaves presented to the courtesan Thais; her lover's slave leads across the stage a eunuch in distinctive costume and an attractive "Ethiopian" girl—quite irrelevant to the plot, but presumably a curiosity available for the production. His rival's agent outshines him with the beautiful Greek girl whose rape, recognition and marriage will shape the intrigue of the play; this is integral, then, but her presentation on stage goes beyond the requirements of the action, or the known practice of Menander, from whom Terence was adapting. Later in the same play there is scope for spectacular business when the warrior Thraso advances to besiege the house of Thais with two slave lieutenants and three extras. The small scale of ancient theatrical troupes did not allow crowd scenes: Menander's plays, like all Greek comedy, had to be performed with a troupe of three players, although this often entailed the splitting of roles between two actors. For Plautus five players are usually needed to handle the action. Oddly it is Terence who seems to have required the biggest cast; "Phormio" and "The Brothers" require six players, and it is probable that in "The Andrian girl" and "The Eunuch" seven were needed. It seems that his desire for fullness of action led him to increase the number of participants by retaining characters on stage or bringing them out before they were required by the action of his model play.[52]

I have spoken of his handling of plot, music, language and spectacle. In ethos and in argumentation Terence shows his individuality more in the choice of plays to adapt than in deviation from what he adapted. His plays are predominantly ethical in type, assuming a need to justify his characters and stimulating the audience to assess and reassess their be-

[51] Letter to Augustus (2.1), 187–207 quotes stage armies, horses, chariots and works of art (in fact a full Roman triumphal procession) and the applause of the audience at an actor's purple costume. It was no better in Cicero's day; he quotes 600 mules crossing the stage for Accius' tragedy *Clytemnestra* at the grand opening of Pompey's new theatre in 55 B.C.

[52] cf. Ludwig 176–77, 181. The larger number of players available to Roman comedy was also exploited by Plautus to increase the busy-ness of the stage by retaining or introducing characters where they did not appear in the Greek models. The scéne à quatre of the "Braggart Soldier" quoted above would not have been possible in the Greek model-play; when Plautus detains the two girls on stage for the arbitration scene of "The Rope" (1045 f.) it must be for their contribution to visual interest, that is, spectacle.

haviour as understanding of the circumstances is gradually increased. He takes from Menander the use of misjudgment as a dramatic element. In the first three plays, he aimed at a serious tone, playing down the "comic" roles to focus attention on relations between citizen equals, and in particular the moral impact of father on son, and the crisis of growing up to responsibility. In his later plays, "The Eunuch," "Phormio," and "The Brothers" there is much more opportunistic comedy. Thus the cast of "The Eunuch" contains only one older man, limited to a scene in the last act; three young male citizens, absurd either through love or vanity; a comic soldier Alazon and his parasite; three or four slaves, one of whom is cynical, witty and inventive; and a virtuous courtesan, Thais, who must have been an even greater novelty in Rome than she was in Menander's original play. The plot contains an impersonation, and a titillating report of a rape which is only regularised by the arrival of a stranger *ex machina* bringing recognition and marriage for the victim. This could have been an undiluted farce; instead the moments of sentiment, the serious comments on humane or civilised values, help decency to prevail; the rapist is in love, ashamed of his act, and glad to marry, while the courtesan earns the patronage of her lover's father, the only recognition possible for her status. There is however an apparent breach of ethos when in the spirit of comic reconciliation (to recall Aristotle again)[53] the soldier-rival is offered a share in Thais' sexual favours in return for expenses. Scholars offended by this have blamed Terence for the scene, arguing that he imported this bargain, like the roles of the soldier and parasite, from Menander's "The Flatterer," where the tone was immoral and the courtesan a coarser, more stereotyped figure than Thais. Similarly students have found an offence against ethos in "The Brothers," where the indulgent father, who has kept the audience's sympathy from the opening exposition to the main peripeteia in Act IV, is in the last phase of the play fooled by the feigned generosity of his stricter brother, and weakly consents to an absurd marriage. A mere hint in Donatus' commentary that "in Menander the old man does not object to the wedding" has led to long controversy. Did Terence in this play and "The Eunuch" change the finale and harm the fastidious ethos of his Greek model? It is a measure of his skill that the controversy continues unsettled.[54]

[53] *Poetics* XIII, 1453a. "It is in comedy that those who in the story are the greatest enemies . . . are reconciled in the end."

[54] On the endings of "The Eunuch" and "The Brothers," see Lloyd-Jones, CQ 23 (1973), Arnott, pp. 53–55; and most recently Grant, AJP 97 (1976), 42–60.

When I offered analyses of plays by Menander and Plautus, I chose an extreme to illustrate Plautus' farcical powers. May I be forgiven if for Terence I chose the opposite extreme? His best play is probably "The Brothers," his last composition and a blend of his own interest in problems of upbringing with a double love intrigue, farcical elements of boys-in-hiding and old men sent on wild goose chases, a series of false tales from a wily slave, and a lively crescendo of action. But I suspect that he was proudest of "The Mother-in-Law." He tried to put it on twice, and the audience deserted. It may have been seen through at its third showing after his death. For the plot he went to Apollodorus, an imitator of Menander, who himself derived the story line from Menander's "The Arbitration." The "hero" has married, five months before the play begins, a girl whom he has raped at a night festival, without, however, either party recognising the other. She was in fact pregnant from the rape by the time of the marriage but concealed it; he, loving her submissive nature, has been forced to leave on a four-month business voyage. In his absence the girl, who has been living with his mother (the Mother-in-Law of the title), has made a pretext of illness so as to return home and conceal her condition, which is known only to her mother. When the play opens, the older generation is baffled by her departure and the mother-in-law is blamed; embarrassment mounts as the young husband is expected back, and he arrives at the moment when his wife produces a boy child. He, stumbling upon the crisis, knows the baby cannot be the product of their marriage but promises her mother secrecy. Although he has the social right to refuse to take back his wife, and repudiate the child, the new grandfathers see the baby as an heir, a joyous reason for reuniting the couple: they blame the husband's desperate prevarications first on the mother-in-law and then on his supposed love for his former mistress Bacchis, from whom he had separated on his marriage. Bacchis, who was described as cast off at the beginning of the play, is now brought in to heal the crisis: she is able to prove by means of a signet ring which the girl snatched from her ravisher that the husband was the unknown father of the child, so that the wife he loves has truly given him an heir. Apollodorus almost certainly spared his audience some of the tension by reporting the identity of husband and rapist in an expository prologue: for Terence's audience the husband's horror at his wife's shame is fresh and justified. The mistrust between the three married couples and the false suspicion of the old fathers (interestingly the misjudgments of this play are all inflicted by men upon women, who are revealed as superior

48

to their stereotypes) make this play a sequence of anxious soliloquy and unhappy prevarication. The exposition is provided by outsiders from the demi-monde, and there is a small part for the slave Parmeno, but essentially the audience is made to live through the claustrophobia (Huis-Clos?) of this family torment until Bacchis releases them in the final act.

The writing is subtle, expressive, economical, the characterisation vivid and empathetic, from the warmth of the maligned mother-in-law to the worldly materialism of the wife's father; the action is well-organised, and the logic of the plot flawless, but where is the wit, the variety, the freedom of comedy? High comedy as Menander and Terence represent it was an overbred species in danger of extinction; if the Greek comic tradition was approaching its end when Menander gave it his delicacy, its remodelling in Roman hands led it on two divergent ways, from all-but-farce, to all-but-tragedy. The ancients were too genre-conscious to write bourgeois tragedy, so Terence's "Mother-in-Law," like Plautus' "Prisoners" could lead nowhere: the comedies of Plautus and Terence might be performed and read for more than a century, but they had no legitimate heirs; other forms, bastard or improvised from popular vaudeville, took over the Roman stage. But the rebirth of comedy is beyond the confines of my theme.[55]

[55] I would like to express my considerable debt to Professor John N. Grant of Scarborough College, for his valuable suggestions and comments which I have exploited in this paper.

Latin "Elegiac Comedy" of the Twelfth Century

Ian Thomson
Indiana University

About the middle of the twelfth century a French cleric named Vital de Blois wrote a comic tale in Latin elegiac couplets, entitled *Geta*. It is a third person narrative—Vital calls it a *fabula* in his prologue—with an abundance of direct speech. The story begins with the return of Amphitryon from Greece, where he has been studying philosophy, attended by his slave Geta. But before Amphitryon gets home to his wife Alcmena, the god Jupiter avails himself of her sexual favors in the guise of her husband. He puts Archas (Mercury), disguised as Geta, on guard at the door, with instructions to keep everyone out. Before Jupiter's arrival, Alcmena had sent her slave, Birria, to meet the real Amphitryon and Geta. Seeing Geta from a distance, he hides in a cave to avoid having to carry the packs. But Geta has seen him, and pretending to hear a hare in the cave, he pelts him with stones. A debate follows in which Geta "proves" by "logic" that something can never become nothing. Birria goes on to meet Amphitryon, while Geta goes to the house, where Archas, (as Geta) "proves" by the same specious "logic" that he is the real Geta. Thoroughly confused, Geta reports to Amphitryon that neither he (Geta) nor Amphitryon exists. Dismissing such stupidity, Amphitryon suspects the presence of an adulterer in the house. With Geta and Birria, he bursts in, but the gods have departed. Everything now moves very fast. Alcmena is terrified by what she thinks is a sudden change of mood in the "husband" who has just made love to her. She senses that something very odd has happened, but showing the wiles of her sex as *hominis confusio*, she claims to have had a very vivid dream. Birria chirps in, "Yes, dreams it is!" and everyone, content not to probe too deeply, accepts this as the best solution. All is well again.

This tale is the earliest of about twenty other extant so-called "Latin elegiac comedies" of the twelfth century. They were widely circulated in their own time and for several centuries afterwards.[1] The most popular was the anonymous *Pamphilus*, edited and printed about 1470 by the French humanist, Jean Prot. Traces of the influence of some of them can be seen in works by later dramatists such as Molière's *Les Fourberies de Scapin* and Ben Jonson's *Volpone*, but no serious scholarship was devoted to them before Edmond Faral's long article, "Le fabliau latin au Moyen Age," published in 1924.[2] Then in 1931 Gustave Cohen published a two-volume collection of fifteen of them,[3] ranging in length from 22 to 792 lines.[4] He assigned one "comedy" (two in the case of Paul Maury and Alphonse Dain) to each of thirteen new editors, who reconstituted the Latin text and provided a French translation with notes and a brief critical introduction. Cohen himself wrote the general introduction.[5] The result was a model of cooperative scholarship, which remains the major study and the fullest sampling of these "comedies" in print.

Partly because these "comedies" are written in difficult Latin and partly because very little has been written about them in English, they are still too little known in the English-speaking community of scholars.[6] My purpose therefore is first to discuss briefly what generic name suits them best; second, to describe them as a whole; and third, to provide some notes on comic force as it relates to these works.

Cohen favored the name "elegiac comedies" as a generic description. Faral had earlier proposed "Latin fabliaux." Both terms are somewhat unsatisfactory. "Comedy" normally implies a play with dialogue and no narrative, and no ancient drama would ever have been written in elegiacs.

[1] Manuscript tradition, printed editions, and literary *Nachleben* are all discussed in the editors' introductions in Cohen's edition (see n. 3 below), and will not be treated in this article.

[2] *Romania*, 50 (1924), 321–85.

[3] *La "Comédie" Latine en France au XIIᵉ Siècle*, 2 vols., ed. G. Cohen (Paris, 1931); hereafter referred to as Cohen I or Cohen II.

[4] The 15 works with the number of lines in each are: *Geta* 530; *Aulularia* 792; *Alda* 566; *Milo* 256; *Miles Gloriosus* 366; *Lidia* 556; *Babio* 484; *Baucis et Traso* 324; *Pamphilus, Gliscerium et Birria* 208; *Ovidius puellarum* (= *De nuncio sagaci*) 376; *Pamphilus* 780; *De tribus puellis* 300; *De clericis et rustico* 62; *De tribus sociis* 22; *De mercatore* 100. The end of *Ovidius puellarum* is missing.

[5] Cohen I, pp. v–xlv.

[6] Notices, where they occur, are invariably brief. The most recent is in *Medieval Comic Tales*, ed. Derek Brewer (Towata, New Jersey, 1973) p. 148. For general bibliography see Cohen I, pp. 31–32; also the chapter "Elegische Komödie und Tragödie," in M. Manitius and P. Lehmann, *Geschichte der lateinischen Literatur des Mittelalters* (Munich, 1931), pp. 1015–40, which mentions some "comedies" not in Cohen.

Moreover, none of them, except for *Babio*, is even remotely like a play in form.[7] To the theoreticians of the Middle Ages, however, a *comoedia* meant simply a narrative with a light or humorous theme written in the "simple" style appropriate to it.[8] Only with that specialized definition of "comedy" in mind can we accept Cohen's nomenclature.

Faral's proposal is equally misleading. The French vernacular fabliaux,[9] of which the earliest, *Richeut*, was written about the same time as Vital's *Geta*, were drawn from that vast body of humorous anecdotes, jokes, and salty stories about cuckolds and fools of all kinds, lecherous priests, vigorous gallants and the women who accommodated their desires, either as partners in the sex act or as female pimps. They often contain much obscenity and knockabout comedy. It is now agreed that they were first written by court poets as a kind of foil to the romance, but their origins were definitely popular. They are simple and direct, with almost no rhetorical elaboration, whereas most of the works in Cohen's collection are crammed, almost choked with rhetoric. This in itself would deny them the name "fabliaux," but as Maurice Hélin has pointed out, only *Milo, Miles Gloriosus*, and *Lidia* are at all like the fabliaux.[10] What generic name, then suits them best? The adjective "elegiac" would best be dropped, if only because two of them, *De tribus sociis* and the much more famous *Ovidius puellarum*, are actually in hexameters. I would propose "Latin comic tales." Though not fully informative, it is at least not inaccurate.

What common characteristics do the works in Cohen's collection possess to justify grouping them together? Hélin in 1943 made the comment: "Ce recueil, en permettant de comparer aisément des textes jusqu'alors très dispersés, a précisément montré que leur seul caractère commun est d'être en distiques élégiaques."[11] This is inaccurate about the metres, and as a judgement too harsh. There are features which bind these works together, as I hope to show in the general description that follows.

[7] It is the only one that contains no narrative. F. Ermini printed it as a play in his 1928 edition.

[8] See note 46 below.

[9] About 160 of these are extant, most of them from the thirteenth century, when they flourished in Northern France. The major studies are J. Bedier, *Les Fabliaux*, 5th ed. (Paris, 1925); P. Nykrog, *Les Fabliaux* (Copenhagen, 1957); J. Rychner, *Contribution à l'étude des fabliaux*, 2 vols. (Geneva, 1960).

[10] M. Hélin, *Littérature d'Occident: Histoire des Lettres Latines du Moyen Age* (Brussels, 1943), p. 69.

[11] *Histoire des Lettres Latines*, p. 68.

All of them are anonymous, except for *Geta* and *Aulularia* by Vital de Blois, *Alda* by Guillaume de Blois, and *Milo* by Matthew of Vendôme. The short *De tribus sociis* is quoted in Geoffrey of Vinsauf's *Poetria nova* (c. 1216) as an example of how to write in the comic style, but it is almost certainly not by him.[12] Except for *Babio* and *De mercatore* (a version of the well-known Snow-child story), which may date from the early thirteenth century, all of them belong to the second half of the twelfth.

Another link is that their authors seem all to have been clerics, most of them French (to judge from the occurrence of certain place names such as Évreux in *Pamphilus, Gliscerium et Birria* and certain French usages in the Latin), although the authors of *Babio* and *Baucis et Traso* may have been English. In any event, they were all products of Anglo-Norman culture, educated in the cloister and shade, yet not untouched by knowledge of the world. Except for the author of *Pamphilus, Gliscerium et Birria*, a curious work which might, I suspect, repay study as an extended blasphemy, their allusions are to pagan myths rather than to Christianity. This is no argument against their ecclesiastical status. Apart from the fact that only clerics at that time had the training in language and rhetoric necessary to write anything at all in Latin, it is easy to imagine ecclesiastics, surrounded daily by the symbols and services of the Church, turning in their poetry to lighter, even earthy themes. As members of what was probably a largely idle clergy,[13] they knew the value of a good tale, especially if it could be spiced with their hard-won learning, satire against other clerics, and, of course, women, or even, as I think conspicuously in the case of *De tribus puellis*, made a vehicle for sexual fantasy.[14]

[12] Maury in Cohen II, pp. 255–56, argues that Geoffrey had produced in hexameters an "improved" version of the same story that already existed in elegiacs.

[13] Those who doubt their idleness should read *Records of Civilization, Sources and Studies* LXXII: *The Register of Eudes of Rouen*, trans. Sydney M. Brown (Columbia U.P.; New York and London, 1964). The clergy depicted are of the thirteenth century, but there is no reason to believe the situation was any better in the twelfth.

[14] In this first-person narrative the poet meets three girls, judges a singing contest between them and declares the most beautiful one the winner. She promises him a reward. Hesitatingly, he requests sexual intercourse. She takes him to a castle and proves to be the aggressor sexually. It contains much lascivious and explicit detail. Elsewhere, I hope to show that this work is a parody of the form known as the *pastourelle*, for which see F. Brittain, *The Medieval Latin and Romance Lyric to A.D. 1300* (Cambridge 1951; rpt. New York, 1969), p. 31. In the *pastourelle* the male is the aggressor. The author of *De tribus puellis* turns this and other conventions around. These reversals are found elsewhere, so far as I know, only in *El libro di buen amor*.

All of them seem to have been educated in one or other of the schools of the Loire, at Tours, Chartres, Vendôme, Blois, Fleury, or Orléans, which emphasized the study of poetry and rhetoric. Cohen and his editors see in various passages an antipathy towards the schools of Paris, where philosophy was beginning to receive marked attention. If this is correct, it never operates as a direct violent attack, such as John of Salisbury's on the "Cornificians,"[15] but by gentle, implied mockery. I am inclined, however, to believe with Hélin that the twelfth century is too early a time in which to postulate any systematic attack on scholasticism, which did not reach its heyday until the thirteenth century.[16] The ignorance of the learned, however, is timeless. It is satirized in fools like Querolus (*Aulularia* 61–67) who wishes he had a better-omened name like Plato, Socrates, or Pythagoras, then immediately rejects "Pythagoras" because that philosopher forbade meat-eating and thought he was related to a pig; or others like Babio, who claims to be a rhetorician and "by making the correct premises" to be able to "prove that Socrates is Socrates and a man is a man."[17] The best examples of this kind of "in-joking" are in the exchanges of Geta and Archas. Geta first proves to Birria that "something can never become nothing," then Archas (as Geta) proves to Geta that he does not exist.[18] Geta's mood is near panic. If he is not Geta, who is he? Plato perhaps? Impossible, because Plato is dead. Finally, he sees that something really can become nothing and with the despairing cry, "Logic has turned me from a fool into a madman!"[19] he swears off philosophizing. Whether or not such passages were directed specifically against the schools of Paris, their general message is plain: a little learning is dangerous.

The other targets of satire are women, whether as fickle wives, outright whores, venal go-betweens, or young maidens who act coyly but are ready vessels for the lusts of men. A good example of the fickle wife is Lidia, who in the "comedy" of that name deceives her husband under a pear tree (*pirus*) with a gallant appropriately called Pirrus.[20] Another is

[15] For John's attack on "Cornificius" (probably Adam du Petit-Pont) and other pettifoggers in dialectic, see Étienne Gilson, *La Philosophie du Moyen Age* (Paris, 1922), I, 70.

[16] *Histoire des Lettres Latines*, p. 70.

[17] *Babio*, 135–36: Nosco tamen logicam; bene premeditando probabo / Quod Socrates Socrates et quod homo sit homo.

[18] *Geta*, 167–77 and 271–394.

[19] *Geta*, 419: Reddidit insanum de me dialectica stulto.

[20] The final episode of this tale has Lidia promising her nervous lover, as the last of four proofs that her husband can be easily fooled, that they can couple with

Afra in Matthew of Vendôme's *Milo*, a poor but lovely girl who is married to Milo, a farm worker. The king seduces her while Milo is working. She turns cold to Milo, who suspects she has been meeting an adulterer. Meanwhile she continues her clandestine meetings with the king. One day Milo returns home unexpectedly; the king flees, but leaves his sandals, which Milo recognizes. He ceases sexual intercourse with Afra, whose brothers arraign him before the king on the grounds that he is not "cultivating the vineyard." Milo shrewdly observes that he has found traces of a lion in it. The king blushes, exonerates him and sends him back to "cultivate his vineyard," happier than ever before in married life. This tale, which Matthew says came from the East, appears in the collection known as *The Seven Sages*. There the wife protects her virtue. In Matthew's version, Afra is a willing partner in adultery. Except for being married, she is little different from Gliscerium in *Pamphilus, Gliscerium, et Birria*, who agrees to her lover's suggestion that they go to an inn, gorge themselves on food, and couple repeatedly until dawn.

The type of female pimp, familiar from Ovid and the fabliaux, is well exemplified by the harridan Baucis in *Baucis et Traso*. This work is about a young gallant, Traso, who wins his girl by the aid of a slave Davus, who works in concert with Baucis. A quarrel between the two pimps livens things up, as do the antics of the girl's slave, Birria, who at one point urinates on Traso. At the end, Baucis "restores" the girl's virginity with a potion concocted of such horrid ingredients as the "whiteness" of a crow, three puffs of wind, the eyes of a blind man, and the sex member of a eunuch. She unites in herself the skills of both *lena* and *strega*.

The coy but willing maidens are best exemplified by the girl in *Ovidius puellarum*, a work so Ovidian in tone that it was sometimes taken to be by Ovid himself, a kind of companion piece from the woman's point of view to his *Ars amatoria*. In it the poet praises himself as a lover and describes a girl whom he hesitates to approach. He describes her as (v. 36–45) of clear complexion, with black eyebrows, bright eyes, chaste-looking lips, white teeth, blond hair, ivory neck; she is dressed in gold, but outshines it, and her hands are brighter than the gems that blaze

---

impunity before his very eyes. She feigns sickness and for a cure goes with her husband to repose under a pear tree. Pirrus goes with them, climbs up to get some pears, then pretends to be scandalized by the husband's conduct below. Nothing is actually going on, but Lidia explains that the tree causes optical illusions. The husband climbs up, and sees his wife and Pirrus making love below—but of course it is an illusion! To prevent exposure as frauds, they persuade him later to have the tree felled. This story reappears in Boccaccio, *Decameron*, VII, 9.

upon them. He stops at the waist, as such portraits often do. They are stylized, and seem to have derived from Maximian's *Elegia* I, 93–98. All of them begin from the head and go progressively lower.[21] He sends her gifts. The messenger, a clever fellow, piques her curiosity about the sender, then praises her beauty, breeding, kindness, pleasant nature, and chastity, and says his master is blameless, lively, versatile, good-looking, noble, modest, sensible, faithful, rich, generous, discreet. The girl says she is too young to hear such heady talk. The messenger finally gets her to agree to see his master (lines 117–130):

MESSENGER: You really did say that you were willing to see the lad. Now you say no. You would praise the thing, if it were done (*actum*).

GIRL: I would praise the deed (factum)? What "deed?" I don't know this "deed." Say what the "deed" is; I think that it's not a nice expression.

MESSENGER: It's nice when it's said, but it would be even better done (actum).

GIRL: What does this word "deed" (factum) mean? Something profane, maybe? I don't know what it means. The meaning of it defeats me. This "deed" you speak of, tell me, is it known to lovers (*amicis*)?

MESSENGER: There are scarcely any called "lovers" alive who can really have a stable relationship without the pact of Venus leading to the "act" (*actum*). This is the "deed" that the pact of Venus implies.

[21] It was commonly believed in the Middle Ages that God first created Adam's head, then the lower parts in order. Hence descriptions followed this order; see also *De tribus puellis*, 32–56 and 255–62. Vital's description of Geta (*Geta*, 336–352) similarly duplicates the plan of Sidonius Appollinaris' description of Theodoric (see Faral, "Le fabliau latin," p. 322, n. 3.)

[22] Dixisti vere puerum te velle videre;
Ecce negas dictum; laudares si foret actum.
—Laudarem factum? quod factum? nescio factum.
Dic quid sit factum; puto quod non sit bene dictum.
—Et bene stat dictum, melius quoque si foret actum.
—Quid vocat hoc "factum"? quoddam fortasse profanum.
Nescio quid dicit. Sua me sententia vicit;
Factum quod dicis, dic notum si sit amicis.
—Vix vivunt aliqui, quicunque vocantur amici,
Qui possint vere sibi firmum fedus habere,
Quin Veneris pactum primum ducatur ad actum.
Est illud "factum" quod vult Veneris sibi pactum.
—Sencio quid queris: me fallere velle videris!

GIRL: I sense what you're getting at: You apparently want to deceive me.[22]

There is more in this vein, but the upshot is success for the lover's suit. In the above exchange, the girl herself introduces the word "factum," a hint that she knows all along what is going on. The *factum* is, of course, sexual intercourse, the celebrated "quatre point" (step four) of the literature of love; the first three are sight (or conversation), touching, then kissing.[23]

All of the "comedies" conform fairly closely to the classical usage in Latin vocabulary, syntax, and versification, if we allow for certain persistent medievalisms.[24] It is rather in the area of rhetorical embellishment that they reveal themselves as "medieval."

Very little use is made of metaphor (*transsumptio*) and the other nine tropes listed by Geoffrey of Vinsauf for using words in a figurative rather than a literal sense.[25] Instead, we find almost all of the thirty-five figures of diction and the nineteen figures of thought which comprised the simple style appropriate to comedy.[26] A full discussion of the rhetorical devices is impossible here,[27] but the commonest may be mentioned.

One of these is *interpretatio* (or *expolitio*), which consists of repeating the same idea in a variety of ways, as in *Miles Gloriosus* 80–88: "Gifts have a deep knowledge of the colors of rhetoric. When money talks, Tully himself is silent. Wealth plays a sweet lyre in the ears of the powerful. The whole of music does not know so gentle a sound. Prayers have

---

[23] Cf. *Baucis et Trasco*, 13: Virginis alloquium, contactus, oscula, factum. Sometimes five stages are mentioned, e.g. in *Carmina Burana*, 62: "Tantum volo ludere, tantum contemplari, / Presens volo tangere, tandem osculari, / Quintum, quod est agere, nolo suspirari." (*Carmina Burana*, ed. J. A. Schmeller [Stuttgart, 1847], p. 151).

[24] Cohen's editors discuss these in their introductions: particularly useful is Dain's discussion of syntax in Cohen II, pp. 112–13. Their treatment of metre is somewhat inadequate; further study of it might be made with the aid of D. Norberg's two books, *Introduction a l'Étude de la Versification Latine Médiévale* (Stockholm, 1958), and *Manuel Pratique de Latin Médiévale* (Paris, 1968).

[25] *Poetria nova*, 765 ff. in E. Faral, *Les Arts Poétiques du XIIe et du XIIIe Siècle* 1637–41:

[26] *Poetria nova*, 1094–1587.

[27] A subject for doctoral research might be the rhetorical procedures of these Latin comic tales in comparison with the recommendations of Geoffrey of Vinsauf in *Poetria Nova* and *Documentum de modo et arte versificandi et dictandi* and Matthew of Vendôme's *Ars versificatoria* (all in Faral, *Les Arts Poétiques*). The *Poetria Nova* is now handily available in English in *Three Medieval Rhetorical Arts*, ed. J. J. Murphy (Berkeley, Los Angeles and London, 1971), pp. 32–108.

no sweetness, if they lack the sweetness that goes with a little profit; only the power of riches makes the strength of prayers efficacious. A speech may be sweet, but if wealth does not flavor it, it turns sour. Holy Giving sees to it that prayers are not in vain."[28] This is a device for "amplifying" the subject matter. Others are *enumeratio* (enumeration), often in triplets, as in *Ovidius puellarum* 84, "You are well brought up, courteous, chaste"; *anaphora*, which consists of beginning a series of clauses with the same word or words, as in *Pamphilus* 455–56, "Hope injured me. . . . Hope has far gone"; minute descriptions[29] such as that of a garden in *Miles Gloriosus* 269–82; and the so-called *attributa negotii*, or commonplaces which generate further ideas to pad out a narrative. The last are best exemplified by *De mercatore*. Faral points out[30] that from the first twenty-six lines alone one could learn all the commonplaces needed for amplification in telling this story: the weakness of female morals, a wife left alone, the persistence of suitors, female vanity, and so on. Lines 23–24 provide a summary of the most important *attributa*: "An absent husband, a place without witnesses, flesh craving satisfaction, gallants paying court, a pleasant appearance."[31] The whole work, in fact, is a series of amplifications; lines 33–44, for example, thoroughly explore the theme of *gaudens dolet*, joy in sadness. In effect, the author took the folktale of the Snow Child (in which a wife bears a bastard boy, tells her husband that

[28] Munera rethoricos penitus novere colores;
    Nummus ubi loquitur, Tullius ipse silet.
Dulci gaza sono citharizat in aure potentum;
    Tam placidum nescit musica tota sonum.
Dulcor abest precibus, si desit dulce lucellum;
    Sola precum vires vis operatur opum.
Sermo licet dulcis, nisi gaza saporet, acescit.
    Non faciunt vanas munera sancta preces.
There is an excellent example of *interpretatio* in Chaucer's *Canterbury Tales*, B[2], 1637–1641:
    "My lady Prioresse, by your leve
    So that I wiste I sholde yow nat greve,
    I wolde demen that ye tellen sholde
    A tale next, if so were that ye wolde.
    Now wol ye vouche sauf, my lady deere?
(quoted in *Three Medieval Rhetorical Arts*, p. 42, n. 23).

[29] Not to be confused with the rhetorical figure *descriptio*, defined by Geoffrey of Vinsauf as that which "describes things that will follow and things that can come to pass as a result of something under discussion" (Kopp's translation in *Three Medieval Rhetorical Arts*, p. 78).

[30] "Le fabliau latin au Moyen Age," p. 370.

[31] Absens vir, sine teste locus, caro prodiga luxus, Instantes proceres et sua forma placens.

she became pregnant by a snowflake; he pretends to believe her, but later disposes of the child and explains his absence by saying that he melted) and turned it into a rhetorical exercise. One must admire his skill in using the *attributa*, but for those familiar with them and the basic story, its rhetorical development is quite predictable.

Sententiae also provide a starting point for amplifications.[32] These are proverbs, or utterances with a proverbial flavor. They are particularly common in *Pamphilus* and *Ovidius puellarum*, and may have been one reason for the enormous appeal of these works.[33] In elegiac verse, *sententiae* are invariably carried by the hexameter, which suits their self-contained, quasi-lapidary nature. They have their origins in traditional wisdom, popular sayings, or folktales. An example of the latter case is *Ovidius puellarum* 151: "If you were the fox, maybe you'd put the hounds to flight."[34] Often they give rise to an *interpretatio*. For instance, *Ovidius puellarum* 107–111 begins, "The kings of this world do not have unlimited power,"[35] then piles *sententia* upon *sententia*, each of which illustrates the first. The device can be overdone, but it does lend a certain weight to the narrative, and many *sententiae* contain reverberations of meaning far beyond their surface one. For example, "Heavy sorrow often comes with an empty laugh"[36] (*Ovidius puellarum* 207) refers in its context to the idea—uncommon in medieval literature—that regret will follow the act of love, but suggests the more generalized one that all joy is merely the obverse of sadness.

Contrast these procedures with that of *dissolutum* or as Geoffrey of Vinsauf calls it, *brevitas*, defined as "compressing a whole topic into a few words." An example is *Miles Gloriosus* 177–78: "He falls silent, the other gives assent; night passes; the next day's light rises; the soldier departs, goes to the citizen's house."[37] This device lends rapidity to the narrative

[32] According to the medieval theoreticians, a writer could use either the "natural order" (chronological) or the "artificial order" in constructing a work. One of the eight ways of using the "artificial" order was by starting from the beginning, middle or end of the story by using an introductory *sententia* (*Poetria Nova*, 87–202). *Sententiae* were also useful for ending a work (*Documentum de arte versificandi*, III, 1). Many collections of *sententiae* were made; e.g. those in Poems 44–72 in *Serlon de Wilton: Poèmes Latins*, ed. J. Öberg (Stockholm, 1965).

[33] Évesque in Cohen II, p. 182–83, lists 25 mss. with a complete text of *Pamphilus* and 17 with incomplete texts or which contain *Proverbia* drawn from *Pamphilus*.

[34] Si vulpes stares, catulos fortasse fugares.

[35] Reges qui vivunt non omnes omnia possunt.

[36] Luctus sepe gravis risu contingit inani.

[37] Hic silet; ille favet: nox transit; crastina surgit / Lampas; abit miles, civica tecta subit.

and is often effective amid much that may strike the reader as unnecessarily detailed or tediously exuberant. The frequent exclamations and short questions also impart a welcome variety, but this can become irritating, as in *De clericis et rustico* which consists of sixty-two lines of rapid question and answer.

Verbal plays abound, such as assonance of word endings (*similitudo desinens*); alliteration, as in *Pamphilus* 194, "Thus many men, trying many times, attempt to tempt many a maid,"[38] an extreme example which Geoffrey of Vinsauf would have condemned;[39] false etymologies of personal names to explain character traits;[40] and above all, *annominatio*, the basic form of which consists of using the same word in a succession of grammatical cases, as in *Miles Gloriosus* 7–8, "Rome (*Roma*) summons him, he goes to Rome (*Romam*), he sees everything worth seeing at Rome (*Rome*)."[41] *Annominatio* may also involve puns, as in *De mercatore* 29, "As the weight of a woman's belly increases, her attractiveness decreases,"[42] which involves plays between *crescit* ("increases") and *decresit* ("decreases"), and *onus* ("weight") and *honos* ("beauty," but also recalling *honor*, "reputation"). This same example illustrates another recurrent figure called *contentio*, in which one or more words are set in opposition, as in *Geta* 63–64, "She may yell, you keep quiet; let her stir, you sleep; let her scurry around, you lie still."[43]

Figures involving arrangements of words are extremely common; for example, the juxtaposition of two words each from the same stem but in different cases (*salute salus*, *Lidia* 278), or belonging to different parts of speech (*non misere miser est*, *Alda* 37), or with different metaphorical meanings (*lumina lumen*, *Pamphilus* 64, where *lumina* means "eyes" and *lumen* "salvation"). But by far the most affected device is that of *versus rapportati*, which might be translated as "convoluted verses." It consists of a violent displacement of words from their natural order, as in *Baucis et Traso* 147, *Verbo, furtive, vi decipis, eripis, aufers*, a jumble until restored to its natural order, *Verbo decipis, furtive eripis, vi aufers* ("You deceive by word, snatch away by stealth, carry off by force"). An even more exquisite example, with chiasmus, occurs at *Lidia* 337–38:

[38] Sic multi multas multo temptamine temptant.
[39] As he condemned *Tu, Tite, tuta te virtute tuente tueris* (Murphy, p. 102).
[40] E.g. Davus dicor, nil dans nisi vana (*Baucis et Traso*, 189)
[41] This is the basic technique in what Peter Dronke calls the *"flos-florem* conceit," exemplified in *Carmina Burana* 147, (Schmeller).
[42] Crescit onus ventris, decrescit honos mulieris.
[43] Clamet licet illa, taceto; / Hec vigilet, dormi; cursitet illa, iace.

Artibus, ingenio, vitiis, fidens, rata, plena
Corda trahit, mentem suscitat, ora ligat

("Full of artifice, using her brains, relying on vices, she allures hearts, stirs emotion, joins lips to lips").

All of the tales are set in a vague past, Graeco-Roman in the cases of *Geta, Aulularia,* and *Alda,* but the Roman names, the allusions to pagan myths, even the intrusion of the "divine machinery" in *Geta,* are but a thin veneer over a medieval canvas. Only the three works just mentioned owe anything to ancient drama, and little at that. Vital's source for *Geta* seems to have been a late Latin adaptation of Act I of Plautus' *Amphitryo.* For *Aulularia* he also used an intermediate source, the anonymous fourth-century *Querolus,*[44] reducing its 1,500 lines to 792. In his prologue he boasts of "curtailing" Plautus and improving him, but we know that he was not using Plautus. For his *Alda* Guillaume de Blois claims to have used a play of Menander "recently done into Latin," which he calls *Mascula virgo.* Probably this was some Latin imitation done in Sicily, where Guillaume lived 1167–69, of Menander's *Androgynos.* All of the other tales in Cohen's collection suggest a French or English locale, owe their poetic inspiration to Ovid, and draw their plots from stories current among the people of their time.

Opinions differ as to whether any of these "comedies" was ever staged. Only *Babio* could have been, as it stands. The rest might have been, but only with substantial changes: the story would have to be carried wholly by the actors' speeches, or else an actor playing the part of narrator would have to step forward from time to time. In either case the text would have to be re-written at many points to accomodate these changes. No such adaptations for stage production have survived in manuscripts. The fact is that no secular theatre existed in the twelfth century that could have staged a comic play in this fashion. Admittedly, from the religious drama there was some conception of what constituted a "scene," and there was an abundance of mimers and other performing artists, but it is impossible to imagine these *histriones, mimi* and *ioculatores* staging a full-length comedy in Latin hexameters or elegiac couplets. On the other hand, it is easy to imagine students taking parts, perhaps with their teacher as narrator, in what we should call a dramatic reading, accompanied by gestures and vocal flourishes. In most cases, however, the read-

[44] *Querolus,* ed. L. Havet (Paris, 1880).

ing was probably done by one person to a limited audience of scholars. His success would mainly depend on two things: the ability of the audience to appreciate the rhetorical embellishments, and his own skill in mimicking different voices, like that of the wheedling Baucis or the whining Querolus. Delivery was an important branch of rhetoric, as Geoffrey of Vinsauf emphasized in the last part of his *Poetria nova*, and it is possible that Vital de Blois' epitaph refers to the kind of solo performance I have suggested: "I feigned the expressions, appearance, and words of speakers, so that you would think many were speaking from one mouth."[45]

Although comedy in the sense of a literary form intended for the stage did not exist in the twelfth century, a sense of "the comic" did, as it always has. It is perhaps impossible to find "objects of universal laughter," but it is possible, within limits, to say what kind of humor seems most prevalent among certain groups of people at certain times in history. We may thus ask what seems to have been "comic" to men like Vital de Blois.

This is harder to answer than it appears. We are hampered at every turn by the lack of an adequate vocabulary for discussing "the comic." The writers of classical antiquity were perplexed by its nature. Democritus said it could not be defined, and indeed there was no ancient theory of the comic except what one can glean from such passages as Quintilian, *Institutio oratoria* VI, 3 and the pseudo-Aristotelian *Tractatus Coislinianus*.

Grammarians of the fourth century after Christ did concern themselves with the nature of tragedy and comedy, but not systematically, and they tended to treat comedy as a branch of romance. The Middle Ages, when so much comic material was written, also produced no theory of comedy. We can, however, begin by considering what a theoretician like Geoffrey of Vinsauf had to say on the subject.

In his prose work *De modo et arte versificandi et dictandi* Geoffrey says, "The principles laid down by Horace about comedy have today completely vanished from court and fallen into disuse. For the moment, then, let us eschew discussion of comedy. But we may say what he himself says about how humorous material should be handled."[46] He then

---

[45] Quoted by R. Peiper, *Die Profane Komödie des Mittelalters* in *Archiv. für Literaturgeschichte*, V (Leipzig, 1876), 511.

[46] Illa quae condidit Horatius de Comoedia hodie penitus recesserunt ab aula et occiderunt in desuetudinem. Ad presens igitur omittamus de comoedia. Sed illa quae ipse dicit, et nos de iocosa materia dicamus qualiter sit tractanda.

cites *De clericis et rustico* as an example of Horace's recommendations well applied. In his *Poetria nova* he quotes the entire *De tribus sociis* as a model of the comic manner.[47] "It is," he says, "sometimes a color to avoid colors, except those that common speech knows or that common usage affords. A comic subject rejects speeches labored at with art: all it requires is the plain style—which fact this joke demonstrates in a few words:

> There are three of us sharing expenses, with no servant. We make this rule, to take turns preparing the meals. The other two have done their stint; it's the third day, and my call to kitchen duty. To make a fire I use my breath for bellows. There's no water, so I have to attend to that. I take a jug and go to a spring. A stone gets in the way, my foot slips, and the jug breaks. The loss has two results: no water and no jug. What now? As I'm wondering, I enter a market place. A merchant is sitting there alone surrounded by jugs. I lift them, handle them, inspect them. Seeing me at it, he fears a penniless thief and curses at me. I leave in confusion, come back, find one of my friends, and tell him what happened. "I'm going back to him," I say, "and you follow and tell me my father's dead." Putting on a show, I return to the place. I lift a jug in either hand. "What are you doing?" my friend yells, "What are you doing here, poor fellow? Your ailing father is dead, and you're still wasting time? You're crazy!" At the word "dead" my hands slap together and smash the jugs. I take off, thus confounding the boor who confounded me, and paying him back for his insults.

By this reasoning is a humorous speech designated 'light': humor proceeds from lightness of heart. And a joke is a youthful thing and is agreeable to those who are in their green years. And a joke is a 'light' thing to which the more sprightly age applies itself easily. And third, the action is light. Therefore let everything to do with it be light. The whole is in harmony with itself throughout if the heart is light, the action light, and the words light."

Geoffrey is here more concerned with style than with content, but it is the content that concerns us. As a "joke" it would fall flat, I think, to most modern readers because of the callous disregard for the merchant's loss and the tasteless use of a father's death—even an imaginary father and an imaginary death—to trigger the climax. Perhaps if the young men

---

[47] The translation of *De tribus sociis* is mine. For the rest I quote Kopp's translation in Murphy, pp. 101–02.

were clerics, this might have amused others of their calling, who seem to have regarded the laity as fair game (as the laity regarded them), but it would be less appreciated today. The fact is that men of the Middle Ages seem to have found great amusement in much that we do not think so jocund: ugliness, obscenity, stupidity, deceit, scatology, even blasphemy. This can only be because of changes in social pressures and values.

Derek Brewer in a recent work has suggested that comedy arises from the juxtaposition of and incongruity between "higher" and "lower" elements in a given culture.[48] In the Middle Ages the "higher elements" are those aspects of social life that aim at order. These constitute the "official culture" that inevitably clashes with some of the facts of human nature. The constant tension between the "official" culture and the "sub-culture" that defies it is productive of the "comic" in society as a whole. In other words, humor springs from the difference between what one does or is and what society "officially" expects one to do or be. This idea goes far in explaining why adultery, deceit, ugliness, stupidity, cowardliness, impersonations, obscenity and baseness of all kinds can be amusing. The more a society condemns such things, the funnier they will seem when they are done in defiance of accepted norms of good behaviour. There are, of course, other kinds of tension, such as that between the longing for proper hygiene and the lack of it; hence perhaps the vast amount of medieval humor that turns on chamber pots and the disposal of their contents, finding places to attend to natural functions, stench generally and farting in particular. It should be noted, however, that in Cohen's collection there is very little scatology. Only one person is urinated upon, and in all 5,720 lines there is no flatulence. Any departure from normal behaviour or normality in general can be expected to cause laughter. For example the increased speed of events at the end of *Geta* is somehow funny in itself; it is the same device that Chaucer uses in the last part of *The Nonne Preestes Tale* and one of the secrets of "Keystone Cops" comedy.

The writers and readers of the Latin "comedies," however, probably derived much of their amusement from a more esoteric source, scholarship. The fascination with verbal humor is everywhere apparent, whether it be puns, incorrect etymologies, or the sheer delight of playing with word-order. Only scholars would find an expression like "he walks

[48] *Medieval Comic Tales* (see n. 6 above). Brewer's *Afterword: Notes Towards a Theory of Medieval Comedy* (pp. 140–49) has suggested the view of comedy I take here.

in iambics"[49] amusing, or relish the parody of the *pastourelle* in *De tribus puellis.*[50]

The above remarks are not intended as a systematic study of the "comic" in these works, but rather as suggestions for more extended treatment.

[49] *Alda* 187, iambicat incedens.
[50] See n. 14 above.

Investigations into the Principles of Fabliau Structure

Roy J. Pearcy
University of Oklahoma

An invitation to discuss the Old French fabliaux as a pre-Shakespearean comic form poses an interesting problem.[1] Is it indeed possible, given the multiplicity and diversity of the fabliaux, to define a form common to them all and capable of accounting for some significant part of the comic effect of any individual tale? Bédier's oft-quoted description, "des contes à rire en vers," certainly stresses humor as the effect universally aimed at in the fabliaux, and identifies their most important formal property, that they are narratives. Bédier may have intended to imply, although he does not explicitly state, that the ideas of humor and narrative structure are essentially interdependent, so that the comic effect common to all the fabliaux is uniquely achieved by manipulating narrative incidents. Chaucer's *Miller's Tale* and *Tale of Sir Thopas* are both "contes à rire en vers," but by this criterion only the former shares essential characteristics with the fabliaux. In practice, Bédier's more detailed examination of fabliau structure, pursued for the purpose of historical comparative studies, proceeded without significant reference to comic effect, and his general pronouncements on humor ignore the concern shown elsewhere for structure. His lead set the pattern for later critics, who have opted either to discuss the genre as a whole and to talk in vague generalities about an informing spirit of humor, the familiar *esprit gaulois*, or alternatively to be more specific, and formally to identify some fabliaux as social satires, or as parodies of the heroic or courtly literature of the period, but at the cost of carefully selecting for discussion only such fabliaux as conform to the type, and of reaching conclusions which

[1] Some of the materials in this article are taken from the first chapter of a forthcoming book on the fabliaux. The methodology was in part worked out during tenure of a fellowship at La Fondation Camargo, Cassis, France in 1974–75, and I would like to take this opportunity to thank the foundation for its generous support.

67

are demonstrably inadequate or totally inappropriate for the majority of tales conventionally accepted as authentic fabliaux.[2]

This study attempts, through a structural approach, to identify the defining characteristics of the genre as a whole, and then to draw some generally valid conclusions about the way in which individual fabliaux function as comic artefacts. Limitation on space dictates that the number of fabliaux discussed in detail will still be small, but hopefully the fact that those chosen for discussion were not selected according to any pre-conceived notions of their effect as comedies will protect the conclusions drawn from being vitiated by the admitted numerical inadequacy of the sampling.

i

I would like to begin with the proposition that comic action in the fabliaux is based on a concern with epistemology, and that fabliau plots evolve in the shadow of uncertainty and misapprehension which falls between perception of the data of sense experience and the knowledge of external reality those data are supposed to generate, through proper inter-pretation, in the mind of the perceiver. This is not to suggest that the authors of fabliaux show any theoretical interest in exploring abstract philosophical problems. On the contrary, such concerns are deliberately eschewed by an intense and exclusive concentration on mundane social activities. When one recognizes, however, that the central comic action in the fabliaux routinely confronts us with a situation where one charac-ter is responsible, in the course of such everyday social life, for proferring to another character a complex of sense data either ambiguous in itself or rendered so by the context of the exchange between them, then it becomes evident that epistemological issues may underlie and coexist with a narra-tive surface texture apparently lacking any abstract philosophical dimension.

Since there is always some character who controls, to a greater or less

---

[2] None of the major critical texts dealing with the fabliaux directly confront the problem of defining the genre as medieval comedy. I refer to Joseph Bédier, *Les Fabliaux: Études de littérature populaire et d'histoire littéraire du moyen âge*, 5th ed. (Paris: Champion, 1925); Per Nykrog, *Les Fabliaux: Étude d'histoire littéraire et de stylistique médiévale*, Diss. Aarhus 1957 (Copenhagen: Munksgaard, 1957); and Jean Rychner, *Contribution à l'Étude des Fabliaux* (Geneva: Droz, 1960). Some attempt to repair this oversight is made in *The Humor of the Fabliaux*, ed. Thomas D. Cooke and Benjamin L. Honeycutt (Columbia, Mo.: Univ. of Missouri Press, 1974), but this is a collaborative effort by ten scholars working independently, and is consequently eclectic in its approach.

degree, the sense data presented to another character for interpretation, the exchange between them may legitimately be conceived as a message conveyed by means of a sign. A very large number of fabliaux depend for their comic plot on conventional, verbal messages, of course, but progress towards an understanding of the structural principles which unite all fabliaux as members of a demonstrably single and closely knit literary genre requires that we extend the concept of a fabliau message to include all exchanges as defined above. When one of the Englishmen in *Les deux Angloys et l'Anel*, seeking something which will tempt the appetite of his sick friend, asks for "un ainel que il velt mengier" (a lamb / a young donkey that he fancied to eat), that is a message in the sense defined, but so is it when a knight disguised as a monk volunteers to hear his wife's deathbed confession (*Le Chevalier qui fist sa Fame confesse*), or when a priest, surprised with the wife of a woodcarver, strips naked and lies arms akimbo in hopes of escaping detection by being mistaken for just another crucifix (*Le Prestre crucefié*). Fabliau messages may be visual, as in these latter instances, or they may be auditory without being verbal, as when the clerk in *Le Meunier et les .ii. clers* tweaks a baby's ear to make him cry and thus confuses the baby's mother about the location of her own bed, or when a wife drops a stone in a well to trick her husband into believing that she is drowning herself (*La Piere au puis*). In certain comparatively rare cases the message may depend on a sense of touch (*Gombert et les .ii. clers*), taste (*La Crote*), and even smell ("Poisson," the first of three stories in the second version of *Les trois Dames qui troverent l'anel au conte*).

If all fabliau messages presuppose a sender and a receiver, and if all are distinctively, by intent or default, ambiguous, then the nature of the comic action may be classified according to whether the sender or the receiver is conscious or ignorant of the ambiguity. A total of four patterns, as set out in the diagram below, will cover every possible permutation.

		Receiver	
		Ignorant	Conscious
Sender	Conscious	I	4
	Ignorant	3	2

All four patterns are realized in the plots of various fabliaux, but the particular nature of the ambiguity dictates which patterns appear in individual instances. It will be appropriate, therefore, to begin an examination of the actual texts with those fabliau episodes which feature a conventional verbal message, and where ambiguity is naturally inherent or artificially created in the meaning of words, since uniquely this type of ambiguity provides examples of all four basic patterns.

Pattern 1 (the sender is conscious of the ambiguity, the receiver ignorant of it) is exemplified in the first episode of the fabliau by Rutebuef entitled *Charlot le Juif qui chia en un pel dou lievre*. The sender, a certain Guillaume, promises a minstrel, Charlot, in payment for his services at the wedding of Guillaume's cousin, "Teil choze . . . qui m'a coutei plus de .c. sous" (something which cost me more than a hundred sous). He then gives him a hare's skin, which he claims did indeed cost the sum stated because he rode his best horse to death hunting the hare. Charlot is naturally not overjoyed with this settlement: "Hom n'en auroit pas samedi, / Fais Charlot, autant au marchié" (One would be hard put, said Charlot, to raise that much on it at Saturday's market).

The verb *couster* as it is used by Guillaume in the message quoted is clearly ambiguous in that it may mean different things in different contexts, and Guillaume makes use of the ambiguity to cheat Charlot of his just reward. The equivocation rests on the fact that *couster* may be used as a term of the market place (see Charlot's disgruntled response to the discovery of the exact nature of his gift), when its meaning is closely related to that of commercial value, and alternatively as a term, for example, of the battlefield, when its meaning may have little or nothing to do with commercial value at all (as would be the case, for instance, in comparing the "cost" of capturing a small area of no-man's-land in WWI with its "value" in real estate terms). Guillaume cunningly plays on this ambiguity to trick Charlot into agreeing to accept something he does not want (the hare's skin) in place of something he had a right to expect (fair payment for his services at the wedding).

The opening episodes of *L'Evesque qui benëi lo con* provide three examples of pattern 2 (the sender is ignorant of the ambiguity, the receiver aware of it). In this story a bishop issues a series of injunctions against a local priest, forbidding him successively to drink wine, eat goose, or sleep on a mattress as long as he continues to maintain a concubine in his house. The *pretresse*, however, teaches the priest to respect the letter of the bishop's prohibitions without suffering any hardship. If forbidden to drink (*buver*) wine, he should sip (*humer*) it instead; in place of goose (*oie*) he should eat gander (*jars*); and if he is denied a mattress (*coute*), she will make him up a comfortable bed with cushions (*cousins*).

In this series of messages it is the receiver rather than the sender who has the higher consciousness about the ambiguity inherent in the sender's signs, discovering (to take just the first message as typical of all three occurring here) that the verb *buver* has two possible meanings, one conventional and intended by the sender, whereby as a general verb to express the idea of drinking it would include the sense of *humer*, and another, as understood in a more specialized and sophistical sense by the receiver, whereby *buver* as one method of drinking is distinguished from *humer* as another.

An example of pattern 3 (both sender and receiver are ignorant of the ambiguity) is provided by the fabliau entitled *La male Honte*, wherein a peasant is entrusted by a dying friend, Honte, with a bag (*male*) containing his worldly goods, to be taken to the English king as the law decreed for anyone dying without an heir. The peasant on three separate occasions accosts the king with: "La male Honte vos aport" (I have brought you Honte's bag / Foul shame to you!), and is lucky to escape alive when a noble of the court forestalls the king's attempts to have him killed by suggesting he might be given a chance to explain his behavior.

Other examples of patterns 1 and 2 will be dealt with in illustration of different kinds of ambiguity, but I deal with only one other example of pattern 3, a story quite closely related by the nature of its ambiguous message to *La male Honte*, so it will be appropriate to introduce it at this point. *La Vielle qui oint la palme au chevalier* tells of an old woman whose cows have been impounded. A neighbor advises her on how best to effect their recovery, by seeking support from a local knight: "Se la paume li avoit ointe, / Ses vaches li feroit avoir" (If she greased his palm, he would have her cows returned to her). The old woman takes the advice quite literally, and finds an opportunity when the knight is standing before his house to smear his hand with bacon fat. The knight is understandably astonished, but when the old woman's motive has been explained to him he takes a tolerant view of her stupidity and restores her cattle without further ado.

The only significant way that *La Vielle qui oint la palme au chevalier* differs from *La male Honte* is that ambiguity in the code does not depend on a pun, a species of the fallacy *aequivocatio*, but on a species of the fallacy *amphibologia*, whereby the same phrase, stated in the same manner, signifies one thing literally and something different meta-phorically. The fallacy is thus illustrated by Thomas Aquinas:

> Litus aratur, principaliter significat litoris scissuram, transumptive vero operis amissionem; et formatur sic paralogismus: Quandocumque litus aratur, tunc terra scinditur, sed quando indocilis docetur litus aratur; ergo quando indocilis docatur, terra scinditur.[3]
> (To plough the seashore literally means to furrow the shore, but meta-phorically to labor in vain; and thus is formed a paralogism: To plough the shore is to furrow the ground, but to teach someone incapable of learning is to plough the shore; therefore to teach someone incapable of learning is to furrow the ground.)

Because of the special circumstances of the story, the exchange between the old woman as receiver and the gossip from whom she has sought advice as sender is broken off after the single message giving this advice. That something has gone wrong is not apparent until the knight is brought into the action, so that his role is partly that of victim, and partly equates in function with that of the king's counsellor in *La male Honte*, that is to say he intervenes from outside to resolve the amphibology on which the comic plot turns.

In pattern 3 the ambiguity which promotes the comic *quid pro quo* must be inherent in the terms used for the message, since the sender is conscious of one valid interpretation of his statement but ignores some inappropriate alternative naturally inferred by the receiver. Interpreta-tions are somewhat more arbitrarily imposed in patterns 1 and 2, where one character is conscious of a potential ambiguity and exploits it for his own purposes. Nevertheless, the victim has to be convinced that there are some grounds for assigning to the verb *couster* the meaning Guillaume chooses to give it, or for recognizing two different possible implications of the verb *buver* in relationship to *humer*, so that here too the ambiguity inherent in the code validates the position of one of the participants in the exchange and inhibits the injured party from contending that he has simply been deceived and cheated. In pattern 4, however, where both the sender and the receiver are conscious of the ambiguity and exploit it for their mutual satisfaction, meanings may be as arbitrary as the protagonists choose, since the society whose standards of conduct are violated has no champion among the *dramatis personae* to challenge the procedures of the solipsists engaged in the exchange.

[3] "De fallaciis ad quosdam nobiles artistas," in *Opuscula Omnia*, ed. Pierre Mandonnet (Paris, 1927), IV, 508–34.

In the latter instance ambiguity in the code may be created simply with a lie which arbitrarily substitutes one term for another. Such is the case, for example, in a second fabliau by Rutebuef entitled *Le Testament de l'Asne*. In this story a rich priest, having buried his donkey in sacred ground, escapes punishment from his outraged bishop by offering him twenty pounds, not as a bribe, which the bishop had indicated he would refuse, but as a legacy, the aggregate of twenty years' service at twenty sous a year willed to the bishop by the donkey for the salvation of his soul! Through his inventiveness, the sender is able to slip the receiver the twenty pounds, to the great satisfaction of both parties.

The same pattern, but in a somewhat more developed form, appears in *La Damoiselle qui n'ot parler de foutre*. An adventurer called David has engineered his way into the bed of a silly young girl who throws a fainting fit whenever she hears scurrilous language. He begins to explore her body, and to a series of questions as to what he is touching she offers a series of identifications: *mes prez* (my meadow), *ma fontaine* (my fountain), and *li cornerres* (the trumpeter), "qui la garde, / . . . / Se beste entroit dedanz mon pre / Por boivre en la fontaine clere" (who is on guard . . . lest any beast should enter my meadow for the purpose of drinking at the clear fountain"). When shortly thereafter the roles are reversed, David identifies *mes polains* (my horse) and *dui mareschal* (two marshalls) "Qui ont a garder mon cheval / Qant pest en autrui conpeignie" (Whose duty it is to protect my charger when he is grazing in some stranger's pasture).

Unless we assume an extraordinary naivety, totally unjustified in the case of David, of course, and hardly born out by future developments in the case of the young girl either, then each false identification constitutes a lie by the sender that is neither meant to deceive nor is misunderstood by the receiver. The cumulative effect of such a series of interdependent false identifications is to create a nonce code in which real and attributed appellations function as ambiguous references, so that it becomes possible for the protagonists to engage in a whole series of equivocal exchanges. For example, to the young man's statement that his "horse" is "dying of thirst" the girl responds in a manner calculated to initiate further equivocations:

> "Va, si l'aboivre a ma fontaine,"
> Fait cele, "mar avras peor."
> "Dame, je dot lo corneor,"
> Fait Daviz, "que il n'en groçast,

Se li polains dedanz entrast."
Cele respont, "S'il en dit mal,
Bien lo batent li mereschal!"[4]

("Go ahead, and water him at my fountain," she said, "you shouldn't be afraid." "Lady, I'm nervous about the trumpeter," said David, "in case he should make a fuss about the horse venturing in." She answered, "If he raises any objection, let the marshalls give him a good beating!").

The pre-established correspondences which impart the intended significance to ambiguous signs are unequivocally understood by both the sender and receiver, who have participated jointly in establishing the code and are therefore fully capable of decoding any of the series of reciprocal messages exchanged between them. This series is capable of almost indefinite extension, and is terminated only when the author intrudes with a blunt and unequivocal pronouncement that the ultimate exchange which the verbal equivocations were meant to effect has been achieved: "A tant li met el con lo vit" (Therewith he stuck his prick in her hole").

The nature of the messages in these four basic patterns is set out spatially in the following diagram, where the r-axis represents material referents forming the basis for mental concepts, the c-axis represents those concepts, and the s-axis is a sign linking concepts in the minds of sender and receiver.

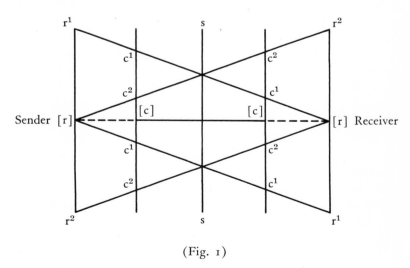

(Fig. 1)

[4] Text from Version B in Rychner, II, 132.

74

Reading from top to bottom, the series of reciprocal messages in *Charlot le Juif* (pattern 1) takes place within the triangular pattern r^1—$[r]$—r^2. Guillaume's statement that he will give Charlot something which cost five pounds is a sign functioning on the axis $[c]$—$[c]$ with referent $[r]$, susceptible to interpretation as either r^2 (goods valued at five pounds) or r^1 (a hare's skin). For the ambiguous concept $[c]$ Charlot substitutes concept c^2 interpreted for the single referent r^2, and he signals his acceptance of the proposed gift accordingly, but Guillaume in turn responds to acceptance of r^2 as though it signified acceptance of r^1 and profers the hare's skin in satisfaction of his original promise.

The reciprocal messages in *L'Evesque qui benëi lo con* take place within the triangular pattern r^2—$[r]$—r^1. In forbidding the priest to drink wine, the bishop intends a message c^1—c^1 with $[r]$ interpreted for a single referent r^1, drinking as an activity which includes and subsumes sipping as one method of drinking. The priest's concubine, however, substitutes the ambiguous concept $[c]$ for concept c^1, so that $[r]$ might be interpreted as either r^1 (drinking *and* sipping) or r^2 (drinking *or* sipping). She then urges the priest to respond on the basis of r^2, so that he obeys the order to stop drinking but goes on sipping wine.

In *La male Honte* the peasant intends a message c^1—c^1 with $[r]$ interpreted for the single referent r^1 (Honte's bag). Because the sign ($[c]$—$[c]$ is ambiguous, however, the king substitutes c^2 for $[c]$ and interprets $[r]$ for a different single referent r^2 (foul shame). The pattern is the same, of course, for *La Vielle qui oint la palme au chevalier*, with the metaphorical and literal significances of "oint la palme" providing interpretations for $[r]$ by the neighbor and the old woman respectively.

In fabliaux conforming to pattern 4 (*Le Testament de l'Asne, La Damoiselle qui n'ot parler de foutre*), messages follow the sequence r^1—c^1—$[c]$—$[c]$—c^1—r^1. The ambiguous message $[c]$—$[c]$ suggests that the referents $[r]$ are interpreted for a single referent r^2 (a legacy in the first tale; a meadow, fountain, etc. in the second), but are in fact interpreted by both the sender and the receiver for alternative single referents r^1 (a bribe; or the sex organs of the girl and young man).

The discussion so far has concerned itself exclusively with signs which are verbal messages, capable of generating concepts susceptible to differing interpretation through association with different referents. Ambiguity in what we may term the metasemiotic function of the message, brought about by some deliberate or inadvertent misinterpretation of the code which renders the message meaningful, is not limited to verbal messages, but occurs in the interpretation of the data of sense experience generally. In order to accommodate fabliaux which incorporate messages of this latter type, we need not move outside the domain of logic, but simply shift our focus from purely linguistic concerns to those dealing with the broader aspects of the reasoning process.

A third fabliau by Rutebuef, *La Dame qui fist trois tors entor le moustier*, provides a simple example of a fabliau of this latter type. The story relates how a wife, whose absence from the house at night to keep a tryst with her lover has been detected by her husband, tells her husband when he accuses her of adultery that she was in fact performing a superstitious ritual at the church to determine the sex of their unborn child. The husband accepts her explanation, and apologizes for his unreasoning suspicion and anger. Initially we seem to be dealing here with an unambiguous message whereby the wife's nocturnal wanderings signify to her husband the fact of her adultery with the local priest. The wife's remarkable equanimity in the face of her husband's accusations is accounted for, however, by her cognizance that the message is not as straightforward as this. A traditional example of the consequence fallacy, repeated in a number of the logical handbooks of the twelfth and thirteenth centuries, has a bearing on the issues raised here. It appears in the *Fallaciae* of Siger of Courtrai in the following form: "Si sit adulter, est comptus et errabundus de nocte, ergo si sit comptus et errabundus de nocte, est adulter"[5] (If a man is an adulterer, he will dress up and wander abroad at night; therefore if he dresses up and wanders abroad at night he is an adulterer). The husband's conclusion, that is to say, while true in this instance, is arrived at by logically invalid means. The wife's lie proposes an alternative explanation, a different referent, which achieves her objective of convincing the husband that the sign of her absence from the house is ambiguous as regards the two possible interpretations now offered. He consequently abandons his projected punishment of the wife, and domestic tranquility is restored.

The fabliau *L'Enfant qui fu remis au soleil* begins in a structurally identical fashion. In this story the telltale sign is provided by a newborn infant a merchant's wife presents to him when he returns after a two-year absence. He accuses her of infidelity, but she pleads that the child was in fact conceived when, standing outdoors on a winter's night, looking at the sky and fondly remembering her absent husband, she acci-

[5] In *Les Oeuvres de Siger de Courtrai*, ed. G. Wallerand, *Les Philosophes belges*, No. 8 (Louvain, 1913), pp. 79–90.

dentally swallowed a snowflake. The husband appears to accept her explanation, and raises the child as his own until he has reached the age of fifteen. Then, under guise of initiating him into the merchant's trade, he sells him into slavery in Lombardy. When he returns alone the wife is distraught, and begs to know what has become of her son. One very hot day, says the husband, crossing a high mountain, the boy melted, a strange fate attributable presumably to the equally extraordinary circumstances of his conception!

The husband in this story initially supposes that the sign provided by the presence of the newborn child is demonstrative proof that his wife has been intimate with another man, but her claim to have been impregnated with a snowflake, in conjunction probably with that tenet of his Christian faith which obliges him to accept the virgin birth of Christ,[6] persuades him of his impotency to refute logically his wife's contentions. To this point the fabliau has followed a pattern exactly parallel to that for *La Dame qui fist trois tors*. But the husband in *L'Enfant qui fu remis au soleil* only pretends, out of expediency, to believe the explanation his wife has volunteered to explain her pregnancy. The ambiguity she created to mediate between alternative explanations of the child's birth is eventually exploited by the husband to mediate between alternative explanations of his disappearance, that he was sold into slavery or that he melted on a mountain top.

The different development in the two stories may be represented using the diagram that appears as Figure 1. In both, the referent $[r]$ for the sender is initially interpreted for one value r^1 (the wife's adultery), conveyed by the sign $[c]—[c]$ (the wife's absence from the house; the presence of the newborn child). That the sign is potentially susceptible to different interpretations is not initially apparent to either husband, and they may assume the message follows the sequence $[r]—c^1—c^1—r^1$, but the machinations of the wives necessitate an adjustment to a sequence $[r]—c^1—[c]—[c]—c^1—r^1$; the interpretation r^1 of $[r]$ happens to be correct, but it is a conclusion reached by a process of deduction and not immediately demonstrable. When the wife in *La Dame qui fist trois tors* tells her husband that her late night excursion was to walk around the church as part of a superstitious ritual, she offers a different interpretation, r^2, of $[r]$. Since this is accepted by her husband, a new sequence $r^2—c^2—[c]—$

[6] The logical issues are explored at some length in my article "Realism and Religious Parody in the Fabliaux," *Revue belge de philologie et d'histoire*, 50 (1972), 744-54.

[c]—c^2—[r] is substituted for the other, and the story acquires some aspects of pattern 3, a single referent known to the sender generating by means of an ambiguous sign a different single referent for the receiver.

In *L'Enfant qui fu remis au soleil*, on the other hand, the husband only pretends to believe his wife's fanciful explanation of her pregnancy, and his response to the wife's proposal of a new referent r^2 (impregnation by a snowflake) follows rather the sequence r^2—c^2—[c]—[c]—c^2—r^2. The new referent is added to, rather than substituted for the old, and so we generate a form exhibiting some aspects of pattern 4, where both the sender and receiver are cognizant of both possible interpretations of [r] but know the truth of one while giving lip service to the other. The net result is to create a nonce logical code having somewhat the same properties as the nonce linguistic code engendered in *La Damoiselle qui n'ot parler de foutre*, and the husband takes advantage of the possibilities thus realized to argue that children conceived from snowflakes melt in the sun. The wife is then trapped by her own duplicity into having to accept without question her husband's preposterous lie that their son's miraculous birth accounts for his equally miraculous demise. *L'Enfant qui fu remis au soleil* just about exhausts the possibilities of a logically contingent sequence of reciprocal messages forming a single, coherent fabliau episode, although the pattern is familiar as that loosely referred to as conforming to the "biter-bit" story type.

We may now proceed to examine in a brief and exemplary fashion some instances where fabliau plots discover potential for comedy in ambiguity occurring elsewhere than in the metasemiotic function of fabliau messages.

Ambiguity at the level of the referential function may conveniently be illustrated with two brief fabliaux from the *Isopet* of Marie de France. They are nos. 44 (*De muliere et proco eius*) and 45 (*Iterum de muliere et proco eius*) in Warnke's edition, *Le Vilain qui vit un autre Home od sa Feme* and *Le Vilain qui od sa Fame vit aler son Dru* respectively in Per Nykrog's nomenclature.

The former relates how a husband looks through the window of his house and sees his wife in *flagrante delicto* with another man. When challenged the wife feigns ignorance of any wrongdoing, declares that her husband is mistaken to believe everything he supposes himself to have witnessed, leads him outside to a water barrel, and asks him to look in and tell her what he sees. He reports that he sees his own reflection, and she triumphantly concludes that the evidence of his senses is clearly untrustworthy, since he is not immersed, fully clothed, in the water.

The pattern of this fabliau follows closely that proposed earlier for *La Dame qui fist trois tors*. The difference depends on the fact that in this latter fabliau the husband inferred his wife's infidelity from the circumstances of her having been absent from the house at night, an interpretation of the logical metasemiotic code which the wife proved to be ambiguous by demonstrating that it was capable of assimilating different referents, one (compromising) which she wants her husband to reject, and the other (non-compromising) which he is led by her guile to accept. But just as ambiguity of the metasemiotic function may mediate between different concepts, so certain phenomena—dreams, illusions, situations which are presented as fictional rather than factual—mediate between different referents, so that even though the husband in Marie's story actually witnessed his wife's infidelity with his own eyes, the wife is still not at a loss to escape the implications of her act.

The wife must persuade her husband that what he has taken as the clear evidence of his senses is unreliable because it ignores the possibility that his senses may have betrayed him, and that what he supposed himself to have seen was actually an ocular illusion. This she does by taking him to the water barrel and pointing out that the sight of his reflection in the water does not prove his physical presence there. This is a genuine instance of ocular illusion, of course, but since its influence on the husband's understanding of what he witnessed is achieved by virtue of a false analogy with the situation there occurring, we may equate it with the wife's lie in *La Dame qui fist trois tors*, so that the total complex of reciprocal messages in the two works would then be brought into precise parallel. They both conform to pattern 1, as does the other fabliau by Marie de France described below, in that each wife creates an ambiguity and then persuades her husband to accept, of the two possible interpretations, that which favors her own interests.

In the second fabliau from Marie de France, *Le Vilain qui od sa Fame vit aler son Dru*, the husband sees his wife disappearing into the woods with her lover. When he gives chase the lover hides himself, and the husband returns in a fury. He accuses his wife of dishonoring him. She feigns astonishment, and wants to know the reason for his displeasure. Because I saw you with a young man, he tells her. If it is really the case that that is what you *thought* you saw, says the wife, then my days are numbered, for the same thing happened just before they died to my grandmother and my mother. Give me my share of our joint possessions, and I will retire to a convent while I still have some time to make provision for my immortal soul. The husband, nonplussed by this unexpected turn of events, admits that he might have been mistaken, and swears to forget the whole matter and never to mention it to a living soul.

The pattern of messages here is clearly identical with that in *Le Vilain qui vit un autre Home od sa Feme*. It is by far the commonest pattern involving ambiguity of the referential function, and recurs in numerous other fabliaux. Few appear in the pure form exemplified by these two fabliaux of Marie de France, however, and they will have to suffice as representatives of the type.

The sophistry of the wives in these two tales of Marie may be compared with one of the six *impossibilia* of the thirteenth-century Averroist Siger of Brabant: "Proponebat secundo quod omnia quae nobis apparent sunt simulacra et sicut somnia, ita quod non simus certi de existentia alicuius rei"[7] (In the second place he proposed that all things which appear to us are phantasmata and dreamlike, so that we cannot be certain of the existence of anything).

Ambiguity in the phatic function,[8] involving the physical contact of sender and receiver which makes communication between them possible, is illustrated in the final episode of *L'Evesque qui benëi lo con*. After the series of messages by which the bishop of the title had vainly attempted to enforce a number of prohibitions on the errant priest, the priest learns that the bishop has arranged a rendezvous with a bourgeoise of his own parish, and he persuades her to hide him in her bedchamber during the bishop's visit. Before making love she insists that the bishop perform the little ceremony indicated by the title of the piece, and, familiar apparently with feminine idiosyncrasies involving *épreuves d'amour*, he is perfectly willing to indulge her fancy in this regard, but is abashed to hear the priest from his place of concealment add a dutiful "Amen" at the conclusion of the benediction. The priest then identifies himself as the wretch whom the bishop has been persecuting for keeping a concubine, and at this point the bishop, tacitly acknowledging that his own lechery and hypocrisy have been somewhat humiliatingly revealed, reassures the priest that the persecution will cease forthwith.

[7] *Die 'Impossibilia' des Sigers von Brabant*, ed. Clemens Baeumker, *Beiträge zur Geschichte der Philosophie des Mittelalters*, Band II, Heft 6 (Münster, 1898), 7.

[8] The terms used to describe the various functions of the act of communication are adapted from an essay by Roman Jakobson, "Linguistics and Poetics," in *The Structuralists from Marx to Levi-Strauss*, ed. Richard and Fernande DeGeorge (New York: Doubleday, 1972), pp. 85–122.

The bishop supposed himself to be giving a sign to the known receiver, the bourgeoise, but was in fact also giving a sign to a hidden and unsuspected receiver, the priest. The presence of two different receivers has the effect of transforming the message, since what to the bishop's mistress in the supposed secret intimacy of the bedroom is a bizarre but apparently innocuous concession to the frivolities of love play, is for the clandestine observer a somewhat blasphemous intimation of amorous dotage. The sign requested by the bishop's mistress, that he bless her *pudendum*, is a single sign rendered ambiguous by the circumstances under which it was solicited. *L'Evesque qui benëi lo con* conforms to pattern 2, since the sender is ignorant of the presence of a second receiver and ignorant consequently of the double significance of the sign he has been persuaded to give by the unsuspected receiver's co-conspirator.

An identical series of messages begins the well-known fabliau by Henri d'Andeli entitled *Le Lai d'Aristote*, wherein Alexander plays the role of hidden observer, and it is Alexander's Indian mistress who elicits from the philosopher the sign produced when she persuades him to allow himself to be saddled and bridled and ridden by her around the garden. While the bishop in *L'Evesque qui benëi lo con* accepts his exposure when the priest reveals his presence, Aristotle, true to his image, at least attempts to mitigate the apparently compromising evidence witnessed by Alexander. Aristotle does not actually deny that he has been fooled by Phyllis into revealing his own vulnerability to behave as a foolishly doting lover, but he does hint at his ability to turn the situation to his own advantage had he so desired, because he *might* have merely pretended to go along with Phyllis' attempt to deceive him as a means of proving to Alexander that if an aged philosopher is capable of being so exploited, a young blade such as Alexander himself would be so much the more vulnerable. Such a reversal would only be possible if Aristotle had somehow become aware of Alexander's presence at the window overlooking the garden, and the story gives no hint that this was in fact the case. Had it been, then we would have had a reversal pattern parallel to that in *L'Enfant qui fu remis au soleil*. Aristotle's agreement to the "petit chevauchier" would then have been a deliberate display of foolish behavior intended as an object lesson for the anticipated receiver Alexander.

The foregoing analysis has dealt with eleven complete fabliaux. This number could be augmented slightly because Nykrog's total count of 160 fabliaux included three versions of *La Damoiselle qui n'ot parler de foutre* and two of *La male Honte*, all of which are identical from the point of view of the structural level at which we have been working. I have defined a fabliau episode as a special kind of message, or a logically contingent, reciprocal sequence of such messages, and according to such a definition most of the fabliaux chosen for discussion, even including such a comparatively complex fabliau as *L'Enfant qui fu remis au soleil*, are comprised of a single episode. Many fabliaux, however, are episodic in structure—that is to say the complete plot combines two or more episodes—and in order to make our survey as complete as possible these episodic fabliaux must also be taken into account. We have already analysed the two separate, pattern 2 episodes which combine to form the complete plot of *L'Evesque qui benëi lo con*.

A different kind of combination of episodes appears in *Charlot le Juif qui chia en un pel dou lievre*, which concludes, as the title itself indicates, with an additional episode to the one already examined. Charlot is disconcerted with his payment from Guillaume, and determines to be revenged on him. He takes the hare's skin he has been given and clandestinely shits in it, and then returns to ask Guillaume: "Biau sire / Se ci a riens, si le preneiz" (Good sir, if there is anything in here, would you want it). This time it is Guillaume who is ensnared by the phrasing of Charlot's question, supposing that the "riens" Charlot enquires about may be something of value inadvertently left in the skin which he, Guillaume, would not want to relinquish:

> Je cuit c'est la coiffe ma fame,
> Ou sa toaille, ou son chapel;
> Je ne t'ai donei que la pel."
> Lors a boutei sa main dedens;
> Eiz vos l'escuier qui ot gans.[9]

("I imagine it's my wife's headdress, or her napkin, or her hat; I gave you only the pelt." Then he stuck his hand inside, and, behold, the squire has gloves.)

The pattern produced is that familiar for ambiguity in the code, since, like Guillaume's original offer of "something that cost one hundred sous," or the priest's offer in *Le Vescie a Prestre* of "something for which he would not accept a thousand marks," the single referent generated in the mind of the receiver corresponds with diverse referents in the minds of the senders, a gift worth five pounds or a valueless hare's skin, a jewel

---

[9] Text in *Recueil Général et Complet des Fabliaux des XIIIᵉ et XIVᵉ siècles*, ed. Anatole de Montaiglon and Gaston Raynaud (Paris, 1872–90), III, 226.

worth a thousand marks or the priest's bladder, Guillaume's wife's *coiffe*, *toaille*, *chapel*, or a handful of feces. Guillaume is misled by the ambiguity of the "riens" to reach for an anticipated referent (unidentified, but carefully delimitated as something valuable for which his wife might have used the hare's skin as a repository), and discovers that the ambiguous sign embraces a referent he had not anticipated.

The complete plot for *Charlot le Juif* therefore combines two identical messages of the pattern 1 type. Unlike the episodes of *E'vesque qui benëi lo con*, however, where the priest triumphs in both episodes as receiver, and where the effect of combining episodes is simply cumulative, the plot of *Charlot le Juif* contains a reversal, Guillaume triumphing as sender in the first episode, and Charlot as sender in the second. When combining these episodes, therefore, we must indicate in some manner that the roles of sender and receiver have been reversed.

ii

I have been concerned up to this point with the identification of certain elements which, in their various transformations and through various processes of combination, constitute the structural features of those fabliau plots selected as exemplary of the genre as a whole. The next question which presents itself for discussion is the relationship between these elements and the specifically comic structure which is a definitive characteristic of the plots they generate.

We may begin by enumerating some pertinent attributes of the constituent elements themselves which may be deduced from their function within the fabliau plots summarized. All four patterns, as exemplified throughout the foregoing discussion, describe a dyadic relationship between a sender and a receiver. All also involve some sense of conflict, and an adversary relationship between individuals for whom we may appropriate the traditional designations *duper* and *dupe*. It should be immediately apparent that in patterns 1 and 2 the adversary relationship is between the sender and the receiver, and that the roles are reversed in the two patterns, so that pattern 1 identifies the sender as fulfilling the duper role and triumphing in some fashion over the receiver, and pattern 2 identifies the receiver as duper outwitting the sender. In the remaining two patterns the adversary relationship is not between sender and receiver acting in opposition to one another, but some sender and receiver acting in consort in opposition to some outside agency, which may be vaguely determined as society at large, or more specifically as some narrowly defined segment thereof. In pattern 3 both sender and receiver may be considered dupes, and consequently some outside agency as duper, although the nature of the episodes where this pattern is manifested requires that the sender and receiver as active participants dupe themselves, and the role of the outside agency is relatively passive. In pattern 4 both sender and receiver are actively dupers, and it is the outside agency, society at large, which is duped.

It follows from what has been said that all fabliau plots involve some instance of a comic peripety, or change of fortune. In pattern 3 both sender and receiver begin in a state of neutrality as regards fortune, or in comparative good fortune, and end in a state of misfortune. In pattern 4 both protagonists begin in a state of misfortune and end in good fortune. In pattern 1 the sender begins in a state of comparative misfortune and ends in good fortune, or the receiver begins in a state of good fortune and ends in misfortune, or, of course, both of these changes may occur simultaneously. Pattern 2 simply reverses these relationships. This general distribution of protagonists on an axis of comparative good or bad fortune will hold good for more complicated patterns such as that exemplified in *L'Enfant qui fu remis au soleil* (or in *Le Prestre crucefié, La Borgoise d'Orliens*, and other examples of the type) where a reversal occurs, but it should be noted in these instances that adversary relationships are established by the extreme initial and final patterns (1 and 2 in the case of the example cited), and are not changed by the possible generation of patterns 3 or 4 medially.

It is an axiom of the genre that audience sympathy in the fabliaux is always solicited for the duper figure (a fact of the general moral ambiance of the genre to be discussed in the concluding statements), so that all fabliaux, in the very restricted sense implied by the foregoing discussion, end "happily," and impart something of the comic enjoyment of witnessing the triumph over adversity of a favored, sympathetic figure, whose "goodness" however is also narrowly and uniquely defined by the literary context and may seem ambiguous or even perverse by conventional Christian-moral standards.

The fabliaux, that is to say, conform to the Knight's general description of comedy, or the "contrarie" of the Monk's tragedies, in dealing with

> "joye and greet solas,
> As whan a man hath been in povre estaat,

And clymbeth up and wexeth fortunat."[10]

Such a description, however, clearly leaves much of the special flavor of fabliau comedy unaccounted for, and provides us no criteria for discriminating between the different kinds and degrees of comic satisfaction which individual fabliaux provide the reader. Each fabliau is, of course, both a member of the fabliau genre and also an individual comic artefact whose individuality can ultimately be expressed only by an exhaustive analysis which would account for every nuance of meaning influencing comic effect, an endeavor clearly beyond the scope of this study or any other aiming in some measure to be synoptic.

iii

A significant step may be made toward establishing some criteria for assessing comic effect, however, if we return to consider in more detail the context for fabliau messages, what it is that the ambiguous messages are about as subject matter. To accomplish this will require a set of symbols not previously introduced. These deal with the attitudes of the sender (S) and the receiver (R) towards what we will designate an "item of exchange," whose exact nature will be established as we proceed. The symbols are as follows:

$$s \overset{\rightarrow}{\not\leftarrow} r \equiv \text{def. desired by S and opposed by R}$$
$$s \overset{\leftarrow}{\not\rightarrow} r \equiv \text{def. opposed by S and desired by R}$$
$$s \leftrightarrow r \equiv \text{def. unopposed by both S and R}$$
$$s \nleftrightarrow r \equiv \text{def. opposed by both S and R}$$

We will begin with the group of fabliaux conforming to message pattern 1, the largest single group of comparatively simple forms among those analysed, and specifically with *Le Vescie a Prestre* (or either episode of *Charlot le Juif*, it does not matter which) where some material exchange evidently takes place. What the dying priest wants to bequeath to the importunate Jacobin friars in the former fabliau is actually his bladder, a worthless and indeed even repellent gift which under normal circumstances they could obviously be expected to reject with disdain. What he actually offers them is "something for which he would not accept a thousand marks," and this offer they accept with jubilation. Once they have accepted, the true nature of the gift is revealed to them.

[10] *The Works of Geoffrey Chaucer*, ed. F. N. Robinson, 2nd ed. (Cambridge, Mass.: Houghton Mifflin, 1957), p. 198.

Let us now imagine a class of objects, *A*, such that its constituent members all exhibit the property (s$\overset{\rightarrow}{\ne}$r), i.e., they are such that the sender wishes to convey them to the receiver, but the receiver opposes the exchange. The item of exchange, *x*, as envisaged by the priest (his bladder) will clearly belong to this class (x ϵ A). If we take a second class of objects, *B*, such that its constituent elements all exhibit the property (s$\overset{\leftarrow}{\ne}$r), i.e., they are such that the idea of their transfer from sender to receiver is opposed by the former and favored by the latter, then the "jewel" which the Jacobins expect to get from the priest would belong to this class (x ϵ B). Finally, we can imagine a third class, *K*, which is the sum of the two classes *A* and *B*. Since x ϵ A, and (A+B)<K, then it follows that *x* is also a member of class K (x ϵ K). As a class of objects, however, *K* cannot be said to exhibit either of the properties (s$\overset{\rightarrow}{\ne}$r) or (s$\overset{\leftarrow}{\ne}$r), since its constituent members may possess either one or the other, depending on whether they belong to class *A* or class *B*, of which *K* is the sum. The "something for which he would not accept a thousand marks" which the priest initially offers the Jacobins exactly fits this description of *K*, since the attributes hold true both for the class of objects *B* (by a natural and immediate interpretation within the context of a deathbed legacy), but also for the class of objects *A* (by the special circumstance that parts of a man's body, invaluable to him while he is still alive, will be worthless and expendable after his death).

Using this new set of symbols, we could therefore represent the plot of *Le Vescie a Prestre* (or either episode of *Charlot le Juif*), previously designated as pattern 1, by the formula:

$$S·x\epsilon\; K(\; [A+B]<K):R·x\epsilon\; B(s\overset{\leftarrow}{\ne}r):S·x\epsilon\; A(s\overset{\rightarrow}{\ne}r):R·x\epsilon\; K([A+B]<K).$$

to depict, respectively, the action of the priest in making his offer to the Jacobins, their interpretation of the nature of the gift offered, the presentation of the gift by the priest which reveals its true nature, and final recognition by the Jacobins of the logical relations which had confused them. This seems a cumbersome substitution, but it clearly tells us much more about what specifically is going on in the story, and its comparatively greater power as a representational system will become apparent as we proceed.

If all fabliau messages exhibiting some variant of the basic pattern 1 are genuinely alike in their structure, it should be possible to show relationships between them in terms of formulae such as that given above. Let us consider in this respect *La Dame qui fist trois tors*. It contains no material exchange of the kind found in *Le Vescie a Prestre*. However, if we broaden our concept of the exchange to include not only such material objects as priest's bladders or hare's skins but also such intangibles as knowledge about a wife's adultery, then Rutebuef's fabliau will also be seen to fit the pattern. The wife's adultery belongs to a class of actions B having the property ($s \leftarrow r$), i.e., it is knowledge which the husband (R) would like to have concerning his wife (S) but which she would like to withhold. Her statement that the action in which she was engaged was in fact a superstitious ritual to determine the sex of their unborn child places it in the class of actions A having the property ($s \rightarrow r$), i.e., it is a piece of information whose exchange is favored by the sender but which is prejudicial to the receiver. What the husband realises finally is that the sole piece of information which he has, that his wife secretly left the house and was unaccountably absent for a brief period of time, is not sufficient to resolve whether the action in fact belongs in class A as he had originally supposed, or in class B as his wife maintains, since it is a common property of them both. All he knows is that the action belongs in the more extensive class which is their sum, K, such that $K([A+B]<K)$. The plot of *La Dame qui fist trois tors* may therefore be represented as:

$$R \cdot x\epsilon\, A(s \underset{\not\to}{\leftarrow} r):S \cdot x\epsilon\, K([A+B]<K):S \cdot x\epsilon\, B(s \underset{\not\to}{\to} r):R \cdot x\epsilon\, K([A+B]<K).$$

to depict, respectively, the action of the husband in suspecting his wife of adultery, the wife's realization that the sign causing her husband to accuse her is potentially ambiguous, her lie to the effect that she was out walking around the church, and the husband's realization that since what he knows of his wife's activities could as adequately be explained by the one set of circumstances as the other, he has no way of determining which is true and which false, the common class K to which he can assign her action exhibiting the opposed properties of both classes comprising it.

A little thought will disclose that the formula given above for *La Dame qui fist trois tors* will also hold good for the two fabliaux cited from the works of Marie de France. Clearly too the formula for these three fabliaux is closely related to that given for *Le Vescie a Prestre* and both episodes of *Charlot le Juif*, since all incorporate the same number of similar elements differently distributed.

In the first episode of *L'Evesque qui benëi lo con* the exchange may be conceived in terms of the bishop's injunction that the priest should drink no wine. In issuing his prohibition, the bishop supposes that its range of possible interpretations will be confined to a class *A* with property (s$\overset{\rightarrow}{4}$r). The priest, by interpreting the sense of *buver* (to drink) as meaning something distinct from, and not including, the sense of *humer* (to sip), changes the class affiliation to *B* with property (s$\overset{\leftarrow}{4}$r), and the bishop, on being informed that the priest is continuing to consume wine, realizes that his prohibition, to be effective, would need to have been directed against both drinking and sipping, classes *A* and *B*, or, in the terms which we have been using throughout, the class *K* representing the sum of *A* and *B*. The first episode of *L'Evesque qui benëi lo con* may therefore be represented by the formula:

$$S\cdot x\epsilon\ A(s\overset{\rightarrow}{4}r):R\cdot x\epsilon\ K([A+B]<K):R\cdot x\epsilon\ B(s\overset{\leftarrow}{4}r):S\cdot x\epsilon\ K([A+B]<K).$$

We have so far dealt with fabliaux exploiting ambiguity in the meta-semiotic and referential functions. To complete the survey let us consider the second episode of *L'Evesque qui benëi lo con*, which involved ambiguity in the phatic function. The exchange in this instance concerns the sign given by the bishop in blessing the *pudendum* of his mistress, a sign rendered ambiguous by the presence of an unsuspected witness. The two classes *A* and *B* will be furnished by *épreuves d' amour* on the one hand, with property (s$\overset{\rightarrow}{4}$r), and "exhibitions of amorous folly" or some such on the other, with property (s$\overset{\leftarrow}{4}$r). The hidden observer knows from the start that his presence will impart a double implication to the sender's activities. The bishop initially believes himself to be giving a private proof of love, the presence of the priest in the bedchamber transforms it into a compromising public display, and when the priest indicates with his "Amen" that he has witnessed the ceremony, the bishop realizes that his action has in fact had both significances. The fabliau episode therefore follows the pattern:

$$R\cdot x\epsilon\ K([A+B]<K):S\cdot x\epsilon\ A(s\overset{\rightarrow}{4}r):R\cdot x\epsilon\ B(s\overset{\leftarrow}{4}r):S\cdot x\epsilon\ K([A+B]<K).$$

The truncated form of *Le Lai d'Aristote* (the action up to the point of the philosopher's cavilling about the conclusions to be drawn from it) will clearly conform precisely to this same pattern.

Now that all the examples of patterns 1 and 2 in the sample have been dealt with, it will be profitable to examine them together as a group to see what precisely are the relationships between the different formulae generated by the episodes analysed.

Le Vescie a Prestre
Charlot le Juif (1) S·x∈ K([A+B]<K):R·x∈ B(s ⇆r):S·x∈ A(s ⇉r):
Charlot le Juif (2) R·x∈ K([A+B]<K)
La Dame qui fist
Le Vilain qui vit R·x∈ B(s ⇆r):S·x∈ K([A+B]<K):S·x∈ A(s ⇉r):
Le Vilain qui od R·x∈ K([A+B]<K)
L'Evesque (1) S·x∈ A(s ⇉r):R·x∈ K([A+B]<K): R·x∈ B(s ⇆r):
  S·x∈ K([A+B]<K)
L'Evesque (2) R·x∈K([A+B]<K):S·x∈ A(s ⇉r):R·x∈ B(s ⇆r):
Le Lai d'Aristote S·x∈ K([A+B]<K)

The formulae as given above are evidently susceptible to some simplification, since a small number of identical elements recur throughout.
By introducing three new symbols, Ω, a, and β, such that $\Omega \equiv$ def.
x∈ K([A+B]<K); $a \equiv$ def. x∈ A(s ⇉r); and $\beta \equiv$ def. x∈ B(s ⇆r), these
formulae could be rewritten:

$$(1) \quad S\cdot \Omega : R\cdot \beta \ :S\cdot a \ :R\cdot \Omega$$
$$(2) \quad R\cdot \beta \ :S\cdot \Omega :S\cdot a \ :R\cdot \Omega$$
$$(3) \quad S\cdot a \ :R\cdot \Omega :R\cdot \beta \ :S\cdot \Omega$$
$$(4) \quad R\cdot \Omega :S\cdot a \ :R\cdot \beta \ :S\cdot \Omega$$

thereby producing for the nine quite diverse fabliau episodes analysed
an elegant reduction to four simple and clearly interrelated formulae.

Having dealt with the seven fabliaux whose nine episodes all reflect
some variant of patterns 1 and 2, let us turn briefly to examine the remaining eight fabliaux in our original sample, the two versions of *La male
Honte* with *La Vielle qui oint la palme au chevalier* (pattern 3), *Le
Testament de l'Asne* with the three versions of *La Damoiselle qui n'ot
parler de foutre* (pattern 4), and *L'Enfant qui fu remis au soleil*.

The notation in terms of class relationships already employed for
patterns 1 and 2 will work perfectly well for patterns 3 and 4 with only
minor adaptations. We shall need to introduce the two alternative s—r
relationships enumerated earlier

  s ⟷ r ≡ def. unopposed by both S and R
  and s ⟷ r ≡ def. opposed by both S and R

which have not figured in any of the formulae so far devised. Also, as was
noted earlier, adversary relationships in patterns 3 and 4 are not between
sender and receiver acting in opposition to one another, but between them

acting together on the one hand and some outside agency on the other, so that to the symbols S and R representing sender and receiver acting individually we will add two new symbols, SR to represent sender and receiver acting jointly, and O to represent the outside agency.

In the case of *La male Honte* we have the rather special case of two classes A and B with only one constituent member in each class, *male honte* meaning "foul shame" in one instance, and *male Honte* meaning "Honte's bag" in the other, and a composite class K which is the sum of these two classes and comprised consequently of just two elements. From the circumstances of the story, it is easy to deduce that Class A has the property (s ↮ r), that is to say the peasant has no more desire to insult the king than the king has to be insulted. Equally class B has the property (s ↔ r), conveyance of the bag from sender to receiver being desired by both parties, the sender in fulfillment of his acknowledged obligation to his dead friend Honte, and the king in receiving his due in accordance with the law of the land. When the peasant accosts the king with his offer, "La male Honte vos aport," we may therefore represent what happens with the notation

$$S \cdot x\epsilon \ B(s \leftrightarrow r) : R \cdot x\epsilon \ A(s \nleftrightarrow r).$$

Since neither party to the exchange has any cognizance of the interpretation being given x by the other, the result is an impasse which requires the intervention of some outside agency for its resolution. Now the fact that *male honte* is susceptible to diverse interpretations is known to the reader from the start, because the author has carefully articulated the circumstances giving rise to the equivocation. The audience knows, that is to say, that x ϵ K([A+B]<K). Eventually, through the intercession of the king's courtier, this relationship is also explained to the protagonists, and the animosity between them dispelled. The complete plot of *La male Honte*, and of *La Vielle qui oint la palme au chevalier*, which follows the same pattern, may therefore be represented by the formula:

$$O \cdot x\epsilon \ K([A+B]<K) : S \cdot x\epsilon \ B(s \leftrightarrow r) : R \cdot x\epsilon \ A(s \nleftrightarrow r) :$$
$$SR \cdot x\epsilon \ K([A+B]<K).$$

If we consider next the plot of *Le Testament de l'Asne*, it will be seen to employ the same constituent elements as *La male Honte*. The classes A and B in this instance will represent respectively the class "bribes" having the property (s ↮ r), and the class "legacies" with property (s ↔ r). In *Le Testament de l'Asne*, however, it is the protagonists who from the start are conscious of the relationship $x \in K([A+B]<K)$, i.e., the same twenty-pound gift which the priest wants conveyed to the bishop to exculpate himself for his sacrilegious act may be *either* a bribe or a legacy, and the priest and the bishop together recognize their ability to transform the one into the other. The audience, or society at large, who are responsible for the moral and social standards by which bribes and legacies are differentiated, discover at the conclusion that they have been outwitted, the sender and receiver having conspired together to exchange in the guise of a legacy what in any but the sophistic minds of the protagonists would be a sordid bribe. The audience in pattern 4 episodes is therefore forced into an interestingly ambivalent response to the outcome of the events, since it functions in the role of dupe while still being inveigled into the mandatory sympathetic response to the fabliau dupers. The plot of *La Damoiselle qui n'ot parler de foutre* may readily be recognized as structurally identical with that of *Le Testament de l'Asne*, the only difference being that while the latter deals with the circumvention of conventional strictures against ecclesiastic venality, the former deals with similar strictures against sexual promiscuity. The plots of both may be represented by the formula:

$$SR \cdot x \in K([A+B]<K):S \cdot x \in B(s \leftrightarrow r):R \cdot x \in B(s \leftrightarrow r):$$
$$O \cdot x \in A(s \nleftrightarrow r).$$

Juxtaposing these formulae will indicate that they too are susceptible to the kind of simplification already practiced in the case of patterns 1 and 2.

La male Honte	$O \cdot x \in K([A+B]<K):S \cdot x \in B(s \leftrightarrow r):$
La Vielle qui oint	$R \cdot x \in A(s \nleftrightarrow):SR \cdot x \in K([A+B]<K)$
Le Testament	$SR \cdot x \in K([A+B]<K): S \cdot x \in B(s \leftrightarrow r):$
La Damoiselle	$R \cdot x \in B(s \leftrightarrow r):O \cdot x \in A(s \nleftrightarrow r)$

The formula $x \in K([A+B]<K)$, invariable in the four formulae examined earlier, has exactly the same form here, so we can substitute for it the same symbol, Ω. For the formulae $x \in B(s \leftrightarrow r)$ and $x \in A(s \nleftrightarrow r)$ we require two new symbols, since classes having these specific properties have not previously appeared. In the formulae now being examined, classes *A* and *B* are also invariable in their occurences, however, so if we introduce two new symbols γ and δ, such that $\gamma \equiv$ def. $x \in B(s \leftrightarrow r)$, and $\delta \equiv$ def. $x \in A(s \nleftrightarrow r)$, then we may substitute γ or δ for all occurrences of the class notations above. Our two formulae may therefore be rewritten:

$$(5) \quad O \cdot \Omega : S \cdot \gamma \quad : R \cdot \delta \quad : SR \cdot \Omega$$
$$\text{and} \quad (6) \quad SR \cdot \Omega : S \cdot \gamma \quad : R \cdot \gamma \quad : O \cdot \delta$$

To complete the survey, something must be said about *L'Enfant qui fu remis au soleil*. Doing so will demonstrate the flexibility of the system being used, although at the price of demonstrating a commensurate complexity. The fabliau begins with an exchange exactly parallel to that occurring in *La Dame qui fist trois tors*, which may consequently be represented with an identical formula:

$$R \cdot x_\epsilon \, B(s \overset{\leftarrow}{\twoheadrightarrow} r) : S.x_\epsilon \, K([A+B]<K) : S \cdot x_\epsilon \, A(s \overset{\rightarrow}{\twoheadrightarrow} r) : R \cdot x_\epsilon \, K([A+B]<K).$$

The classes A and B will here be interpreted as "children conceived by swallowing snowflakes" and "children conceived in adultery" respectively. Unlike the husband in *La Dame qui fist trois tors*, the husband in *L'Enfant qui fu remis au soleil*, however, is not nonplussed by his inability to disprove his wife's lie, and the fabliau does not end here. Instead he responds to his wife's lie with a lie of his own, that their son melted on a mountain top. To represent this symbolically we may posit a new class, C, with property $(s \overset{\leftarrow}{\twoheadrightarrow} r)$, such that C is interpreted as "children who melt in the sun." Finally, she has to acknowledge *her* inability to dispute the proposition that the class of children conceived from snowflakes is identical to the class of children who melt in the sun, i.e., that $x \, \epsilon \, K([B \times C]<K)$. *L'Enfant qui fu remis au soleil* therefore differs from all the other examples of fabliaux investigated in juggling three class terms instead of two, and in introducing a new class concept K which is the product rather than the sum of two sub-classes. The complete formula for *L'Enfant qui fu remis au soleil* will also have six constituent elements rather than four:

$$R \cdot x_\epsilon \, B(s \overset{\leftarrow}{\twoheadrightarrow} r) : S \cdot x_\epsilon \, K^1([A+B]<K) : S \cdot x_\epsilon \, A(s \overset{\rightarrow}{\twoheadrightarrow} r) :$$
$$R \cdot x_\epsilon K^1([A+B]<K) : R \cdot x_\epsilon \, C(s \overset{\leftarrow}{\twoheadrightarrow} r) : S \cdot x_\epsilon \, K^2([B \times C]<K).$$

Since we are dealing with just one example of the pattern there is no point in pursuing further any generalization of the constituent elements here, but evidently the formula given above presents no threat to the comprehensiveness of the system because it may be generated from formula (2) by the addition of related constituent elements.

We have now dealt with thirteen distinct fabliau episodes, and, counting minor variants but leaving out *L'Enfant qui fu remis au soleil*, fourteen complete fabliau plots. These have been expressed in six formulae containing a total of nine variables. Formulae (1)–(4) contain only five variables, and could readily be generated as manifestations of a single fabliau type using a simple, context-sensitive, phrase structure grammar. Formulae (5) and (6) clearly are also closely related to one another, but form a distinct, transformed sub-group by comparison with formulae (1)–(4).

iv

The thrust of the foregoing discussion has been towards demonstrating the essential identity, as members of the fabliau genre, of the various stories analysed, and this has been achieved by a process of increasing abstraction. It is now time to reverse this direction to determine, by a return to specificity through interpretation, how what has been learned may be used to tell us something more about the individual fabliaux and their discreteness as comic artefacts.

From our analysis using the basic concept of a fabliau "message" we discovered something of the nature of adversary relationships in the fabliaux, and determined that all fabliaux exhibit some quality of the comic equivalent of *peripety*, or reversal of fortune. Working with the basic concept of a fabliau "exchange" reveals that all fabliaux also exhibit some quality of the comic equivalent of *anagnorisis*, or discovery. At the conclusion of every exchange dupe figures are precipitated into a reassessment and adjustment of their understanding of some logical relationship which turns out to be considerably different from what they had casually and erroneously supposed it to be. When adversary relationships are between duper and dupe figures who are the sole protagonists in the comic action, this discovery is concomitant with and contributes to the dupe's discomfiture, and the audience's role is that of partisan witness to the proceedings. In fabliaux following the pattern of *La male Honte* it is the audience themselves who from the beginning are fully informed of the logical relationships involved, and both protagonists who experience *anagnorisis* at the conclusion of the story. In fabliaux following the pattern of *Le Testament de l'Asne* the protagonists jointly are fully cognizant of the logical complexities of their machinations, and it is the audience, as tacit supporters of the conventional moral and social standards of behavior, who experienced *anagnorisis* in witnessing those standards circumvented and mocked.

This is certainly a helpful observation in assessing and explicating something of the different kinds of comic satisfaction to be derived from reading fabliaux which belong to different sub-species of the genre, but its usefulness is not limited to just this particular issue. Of the fabliaux for which a précis of the plot has been given here, most readers would concur I suppose with the general critical opinion that *Le Vescie a Prestre* is a better fabliau than *La Dame qui fist trois tors*. Such a judgment may of course rest on any number of factors which contribute to making Jacques de Baisieu a more competent literary artist than Rutebuef, although no one would seriously dismiss Rutebuef as an incompetent literary hack. If, therefore, the significant differences should be attributable to questions of "style" in the narrow sense of skill in handling surface details of the narrative, an issue for which the approach followed here clearly contributes no criteria for judgment, then those questions are likely to be resolved only through some rather fine discriminations in literary taste.

But I think the differences between the two works cited are more fundamental—function at a deeper structural level—than this, and that the works can be meaningfully differentiated on the basis of structural features that have been subjected to analysis.

Now it is true, and significant, that the plot of *Le Vescie a Prestre* functions in a moral framework which reinforces conventional moral judgments, while *La Dame qui fist trois tors* violates them, and this fact definitely contributes to the reader's enjoyment in identifying with the duper figure and taking pleasure in the discomfiture suffered by the dupes. The dying priest in *Le Vescie a Prestre* is portrayed as an ideal shepherd of his flock. He exemplifies Christian charity in his evident wish to dispense his modest worldly possessions with compassionate impartiality to the poor and needy of his parish and to deserving religious institutions. The Jacobins, on the other hand, are greedy, selfish, and importunate. That their behavior should be such as to provoke so mild-mannered and considerate a character as the priest to seek the means he devises to humiliate them is a damning commentary on their personalities in itself. By contrast, the wife in *La Dame qui fist trois tors* is a shameless adulteress. No justification is offered in the story for her betrayal of her husband with a lecherous priest, and the only moral trait the husband shares with the Jacobins is to be guilty like them of what for the fabliau ethos is a fatal gullibility. Conventional moral concerns therefore evidently influence significantly the comic effect of the two stories. But generically such issues are accidental rather than structurally essential, a kind of moral icing on Jacques de Baisieu's cake. That this is so is evident from the fact that, as structurally defined, all fabliaux conforming to pattern 4 necessarily violate conventional moral standards, since in these stories the audience as champion of such standards is routinely victimised by the protagonists who defy or ignore them. Conformity to the dictates of a traditional Christian morality is a variable in the fabliaux. Its services may be enlisted to sharpen the comic denouement by certain authors, but it may as readily be left in abeyance, or its contravention may be deliberately flaunted.

If we exclude conformity to conventional morality as a criterion, what then remains from our analysis which may be used to help explain the apprehended superiority of the one fabliau over the other? Something very important and readily perceivable in terms of the method of analysis employed. *Le Vescie a Prestre*, as the foregoing analysis demonstrates, begins with the greatest degree of abstraction, while *La Dame qui fist trois tors* begins with the greatest degree of specificity. In one story we witness intellectual ingenuity crystallize into surprising but irrefutable fact, while in the other we witness apparently irrefutable fact dissolve into intellectual uncertainty. In *Le Vescie a Prestre* the priest creates a "universe of discourse" which rigorously controls the development of the comic action so that it proceeds inevitably towards a foreordained conclusion. In *La Dame qui fist trois tors* the wife attempts in an impromptu and comparatively haphazard manner to subsume the fact of her adultery in a universe of discourse that effectively clouds its adverse implications. The analogy will not bear much elaboration, but as comic artefacts *Le Vescie a Prestre* is related to *La Dame qui fist trois tors* in somewhat the same way as tragedy is related to melodrama. It follows from what has been said that if the comic effect of *La Dame qui fist trois tors* is, in the manner described, different from that of *Le Vescie a Prestre*, it should be exactly similar to that of the two pieces by Marie de France. Whether this is the case, as I believe it to be, I will leave to the reader's judgment to decide.

That the impromptu and haphazard quality attributed to the wife's actions in *La Dame qui fist trois tors* reflects a genuine structural deficiency in the plot may be inferred from the fact that, unlike the plot of *Le Vescie a Prestre*, it is susceptible to the kind of anomalous elaboration exemplified in *L'Enfant qui fu remis au soleil*. The husband in this latter story asserts control over the universe of discourse tentatively established by his wife because he is able to recognize and exploit its logical loose ends. Peripety and anagnorisis are reduplicated in *L'Enfant qui fu*

95

remis au soleil, and correspond to two shifts from specifics to abstractions. But something of the satisfaction to be derived from witnessing events unroll in this story is to be explained by the fact that overall, and at the level of class relationships, something of the quality of a movement from abstraction to specificity is achieved by the shift from a general class which is the sum to a general class which is the product of two other classes. The effectiveness of the comic structure thus generated is manifest in the great popularity of the story during the Middle Ages following its first known appearance in the late eleventh-century *Modus Liebinc.* It is evident that this effectiveness is indeed attributable to the fundamental comic structure as represented in the formula given earlier, and not to stylistic ornamentation, character development, or evoked relationship to any conventional moral code, from the three treatments of the story included in the *Poetria Nova* of Geoffroi de Vinsauf, where it is cited in illustration of the techniques of *abbreviatio* and presented in one version occupying just five lines of the text and two versions occupying just two lines each:

> Vir, quia quem peperit genitum nive femina fingit,
> Vendit et a simili liquefactum sole refingit.[11]

(Because his wife pretended that the son she had born was conceived from a snowflake, the husband sold him, and in like fashion pretended in his turn that the boy had been melted by the sun.)

This is not to suggest, of course, that the comic effect of a story may not be heightened, modified, or indeed radically changed by the introduction of any of the concerns necessarily excluded from so skeletal a summary of the plot as that offered by Geoffroi de Vinsauf. Ultimately, as I stipulated earlier, explication of the full comic flavor of any individual fabliau requires consideration of all the details of the surface narrative which can be assimilated to the perceived comic effect of the artefact as an integrated whole. The aim of this study has been rather to establish a point of departure for any such more detailed and specialized investigations, to determine which concerns are essential and universally present in all fabliaux, and which are, by comparison, merely accidental, fortuitous, and sporadic. The tentative conclusion reached here—tentative because evidently the examples of the genre examined constitute too small a proportion of the total corpus to render firm judgments about the

---

[11] Edmond Faral, *Les Arts poétiques du XIIᵉ et du XIIIᵉ siècle* (Paris: Champion, 1958), p. 220.

genre as a whole—is that the essential, definitive characteristic of the fabliaux is a comic structure founded on logical relationships.

v

Whether or not, as one commentator on the origin of language maintained, human speech began in response to an apprehended need to deceive,[12] the fabliaux clearly exploit potentialities present in the act of human communication from its inception. It is not surprising, therefore, that narrative episodes of the fabliau type appear contemporaneously with the earliest known examples of other narrative forms, and recur sporadically throughout the literary histories of numerous societies prior to the appearance of the fabliaux proper in the French-speaking communities of Northern Europe during, approximately, the thirteenth century.

Even if we were to disregard the arbitrary distinctions whereby the Old French fabliaux have traditionally been defined (that they be relatively brief, humorous tales in verse, in the French language, and written during the medieval period), and viewed them simply as exemplary of a genre determined according to broader linguistic, chronological, and formal criteria, their appearance would still require some explanation. This is so in part because of their multiplicity. Some one hundred and sixty examples of the genre survive from the comparatively brief period of their flourishing within the narrow geographical limits of their dissemination, a number which far exceeds not only that produced earlier within any comparable time and space, but indeed all extant prior examples of the genre from any source whatsoever. More importantly, as I hope this study will have helped demonstrate, the consistency and subtlety with which authors of the Old French fabliaux generate a wide variety of humorous episodes on the basis of a very limited number of gross constituent elements presupposes that those authors shared a higher degree of artistic consciousness about the definitive characteristics of the genre to which they were contributing than is evidenced anywhere before their time.

Although stories analogous to the fabliaux exist in sources as diverse as the *Panchatantra*, the *Thesmophoriazusae* of Aristophanes, the *Golden Ass* of Apuleius, or the *Fables* of Phaedrus, there is therefore some reason

---

[12] Edgar H. Sturtevant, *An Introduction to Linguistic Science* (New Haven: Yale Univ. Press, 1947), p. 48.

to regard the Old French fabliaux as a uniquely medieval literary phenomenon. In conclusion it will be appropriate to discuss briefly how the analysis of a number of fabliau plots in terms of a comedic manipulation of logical relationships may be used to support such a judgment. It scarcely needs to be stressed, certainly, how prominent a role logic played in the intellectual life of the Middle Ages, from the beginning of the twelfth century when Peter Abelard reached maturity, throughout the thirteenth and early fourteenth centuries when the fabliaux flourished, and on into the dawn of the Renaissance. Writers such as Hugh of St. Victor (*The Didascalicon*), John of Salisbury (*The Metalogicon*), and Alexander Neckham (*De Naturis Rerum*) laud the virtues of the discipline of logic to sharpen the intellect, advance the cause of knowledge, and confirm the truths of Christian theology, and excoriate the delinquent sophists of their time who trivialised its methods and vitiated its ends. Henri d'Andeli, the author of *Le Lai d'Aristote*, lamented in the farcical allegory of *La Bataille des Sept Arts* what he perceived as a regrettable predominance of logical studies in the schools at the expense of the traditional humanistic disciplines of grammar and rhetoric. Even in Chaucer's England of the late fourteenth century it is automatic for Harry Bailly to assume that the Clerk's quiet reticence is to be explained by the fact that he is immersed in "studie aboute som sophyme."

If true, the assumption may reflect adversely on the Clerk's sociability, but not on his dedication to serious scholarship. For, in the tradition of the *Sophistici Elenchi* of Aristotle, treatises on sophistic made an important and positive contribution to logical studies. In the course of this essay I have had occasion to refer to the *Fallaciae* of Siger of Courtrai and the *De fallaciis ad quosdam nobiles artistas* of Thomas Aquinas. Of the popular logical handbooks of the early thirteenth century, the *Summulae Logicales* of Peter of Spain and the *Introductiones in Logicam* of William of Sherwood contain extensive treatments of fallacies, derived from Aristotle but systematized, subdivided, and copiously illustrated in typical scholastic fashion. The illustrations take the form of indicating the sophisms to which different fallacies might give rise, and this practice in turn generated another important set of medieval logical texts, given the general title *sophismata*, which were collections of sophisms embodying some hidden fallacy or logical difficulty together with an explanation of their composition and a solution of the problem. These latter texts were used as basis for the pedagogically popular and widely practiced *disputationes*, in which the students were given an opportunity to debate among themselves, under supervision of the master, questions of logical interest. At the university of Paris in the mid-thirteenth century all students presenting themselves for an Arts degree were required to prove that they had heard Aristotle's *Sophistical Refutations* discussed twice in ordinary lectures and at least once cursorily, and that they had attended compulsory disputations for a period of at least two years. An intensive concern with sophistic evidently contributed significantly to the intellectual climate of Northern Europe from the twelfth at least through the fourteenth centuries.

All those who attended the universities of the area for however brief a period, and there is good reason to suppose that numerous authors of fabliaux may have been included in this group, could hardly have escaped some exposure to the influence of sophistic. Any of the various treatments of fallacies might in certain respects be regarded as a kind of blueprint for the fabliaux. A majority both of the six Aristotelian *fallaciae in dictione* and of the seven *fallaciae extra dictionem* are illustrated in the fabliaux, some, as we have already noted, very specifically so, and this fact may be used to substantiate and perhaps in part explain the contention of Guerlin de Guer that the laughter provoked by the fabliaux is "le rire de mots et de situations."[13]

But between the treatment of fallacies in the logical handbooks, or in the serious didactic literature of the Middle Ages, and their appearance in the fabliaux there is one fundamental and extremely significant difference. In the former, fallacies are identified and examined for the sole purpose of purging logical discourse of their pernicious influence, so that the search for truth through the exercise of right reason might not be subverted. In the fabliaux, by contrast, fallacies are deliberately introduced into discourse by duplicitous characters with the intent to confuse and deceive, and as a means to ends which are at best mundane and appetitive and at worst flagrantly base and immoral. Just as Pope credited Homer with having discovered, but not devised, the natural, transcendent form for epic poetry, so the Middle Ages credited Aristotle with discovering the laws of logical argument, but piety viewed their devising as an action appropriate to the Godhead, and the perfect system they exemplified as analogical intimation of a divinely ordered universe. The near-hysteria of some of the fulminations against sophistry is explained by the fact that, for writers who perceived this analogy, abuse of logic was

[13] "Le Comique et l'Humour à Travers les Ages: Les Fabliaux," *Revue des Cours et Conferences*, 28 (1927), 325–50.

not only an affront to right reason, but an affront tainted with sacrilege. Alexander Neckham viewed the devil as a sophist.

Now the fabliaux are not exactly sophisms, and the relationship between them and the tractates on fallacies is not, in the vast majority of cases, an affiliation in the sense that one is derived from or even directly influenced by the other. But the two groups of works taken in conjunction do certainly reflect a "community of interest," and are mutually illuminating, and this fact tells us something profoundly important for an understanding of the nature of the fabliaux as comedy. Sophistry is a tear in the intellectual fabric of the age, and when characters in the fabliaux consistently and successfully exploit fallacies for the achievement of ends which challenge the moral presuppositions of their time, one recognizes that considered *in toto* the genre acquires significant intellectual implication, and opens a vista on a subverted, anarchic, comedic world where expediency is the only virtue and gullibility the only vice.

The Grotesque in French Medieval Literature: A Study in Forms and Meanings

Guy Mermier
University of Michigan

> "No matter how often we hear and use the word 'grotesque' . . . it is certainly not a well-defined category of scientific thinking."
>
> Wolfgang Kayser,
> *The Grotesque*, pp. 16–17.

A study of 'the Grotesque' is as frustrating and as fascinating an experience as the study of laughter or of comedy for they all encompass so much of man's intelligence and creativity that, robed in their abstract entities, they are almost ungraspable. Indeed, they are pirandellian characters playing on several stages and constantly shifting in nature and purpose. Their nature is in essence motion, *le mouvant, le mouvant humain.*

i

> "The present study does not aim at being a history of the grotesque. It is impossible to write such a history as it is to compose one of the tragic or comic elements in the arts."
>
> Wolfgang Kayser,
> *The Grotesque*, p. 10.

As we reflected upon an approach to the study of the grotesque in French medieval literature, we found several avenues of investigation: the first one would make us start from a precise definition of the word 'grotesque,' but we soon discovered that would make us retrace the steps of previous scholars[1] and that we would unavoidably end up, like

[1] Wolfgang Kayser, *The Grotesque in Art and Literature* (Bloomington: In-

Barasch, with an unsatisfactory multiple definition. In his introduction, Barasch writes: "In the course of five centuries the word 'grotesque' has acquired a wide variety of meanings. . . . It has been used in the past to classify themes, genres, writers, characters, styles, a stylistic tradition, and writing techniques. It now identifies a school of modern drama and is a critical term, which in addition to the above denotations, connotes pleasure in what was once painfully coarse, barbarous, immoral, incongruous, and extravagant. Its connotations are manifold, its denotations not always clear."[2]

Obviously, if we wanted precision, we would not find it in a definition of the grotesque; we definitely had to look elsewhere; perhaps we could seek some concrete examples of the grotesque, particularly in art. This seemed an excellent approach because of the profound connections which exist between art and literature. But right then we were confronted with the dialectical essence of our world[3] and we quickly came to this conclusion best expressed by Kayser, that "the true depth of the grotesque is revealed only by its confrontation with its opposite, the sublime. For just as the sublime (in contrast with the beautiful) guides our view toward a loftier supernatural world, the ridiculously distorted and monstrously horrible ingredients of the grotesque point to an inhuman, nocturnal and abysmal realm. . . ."[4] It is true that no two concepts are more basic, more quintessential than the dialectics of the sublime and the grotesque, particularly perhaps in the western world and in its art. Christianity reigned supreme and it represented cosmic unity and an ideal order of perfection. And since each work of art—manuscripts, sculptures, stained glass windows and architecture as a whole—were to represent the will and word of God, every conceivable effort was made to give these works the most sacred, the most sublime character possible. Art, in all its forms, was a way to worship God and a way to inspire His worship. The notion of the sublime, therefore, could not exist without its counterpart the

---

diana University Press, 1957). See the notes for an extensive bibliography; Lee Byron Jennings, *The Ludicrous Demon*; *Aspects of the Grotesque in German Post-Romantic Prose* (Berkeley and Los Angeles: University of California Publications in Modern Philology, Vol. 71, 1963). The volume includes an extensive bibliography; Frances K. Barash, *The Grotesque: A Study in Meanings* (The Hague-Paris: Mouton, 1971), includes an important bibliography.

[2] F. K. Barash, Introduction, p. 9.

[3] "The world is a mad house. But the reverse is equally true." Kayser, *The Grotesque*, p. 61.

[4] Kayser, *The Grotesque*, p. 58.

grotesque, that is the representation of the dark world, of the chaotic, monstrous and cruel world of the devil, of Hell, to which the pagans and all non-Christians were without remission condemned.

Now, if we look at as early a work of art as the seventh-century *Book of Durrow*,[5] we notice at the center of the page a perfect circle with a simple small cross while the wide frame represents a horde of fighting grotesque monsters, native animals symbolizing the chaos of the world without Christ. But a better example, perhaps, of the medieval dialectics of the sublime and the grotesque is to be found in Hubert (or Jan) van Eyck's scene of the *Last Judgement*.[6] In a high and narrow frame the picture represents the Lord above in His sublime glory and surrounded by the blessed souls who are being admitted to Paradise. Down below, in the lower half of the picture, the sinners condemned to Hell are tortured by devilish monsters. The grotesque of Hell is underscored by nightmarish colors; enough to give a fantastic scene the frightening and believable illusion of reality. This *Last Judgement* scene, sublime in its totality, gives an equal role to the grotesque. Such duality, this reciprocity of roles between the sublime and the grotesque, is found again and again in the arts, but also in literature. As far as medieval literature is concerned, this feature will be found in hagiography and in the theatre, but also in romance as well as in epic, as we shall see.

At times, however, the grotesque does not have to depend on the sublime to perform its role and achieve its meaning. In fact, in rare cases it is true, the grotesque will stand by itself. Such is the case, for instance, in the *Last Judgement* scene of Jerome Bosch.[7] Through the depiction of grotesque characters, Bosch shows us Hell, the Hell of man's making. The picture tells us that the world of men is full of fools who seek nothing but their pleasure and their leisure instead of being ready for God's Judgement. Such men go about their lives as if they were on a ship adrift without pilot or compass: a ship of fools. Fools and grotesque they are, and grotesque not only because they are fools, but because while indulging every excess, overdrinking, overeating and fighting, they are not happy; they are the very image of dislocated harmony: they are grotesque. The fool, indeed, is an important index of the grotesque and we would commit a grave omission if we did not mention here the art of Pieter Bruegel. In his *Land of Cockayne*[8] Bruegel represents a kind of

[5] In Trinity College, Dublin.

[6] About 1420. Metropolitan Museum of Art, New York.

[7] About 1500. Louvre, Paris. Inspired by the *Ship of Fools*.

[8] 1567. Pinakothek, München.

fool's paradise without religious context. In the picture we see fools lazily stretched on the ground: they are not Bosch's doomed sinners; they are regular men who have become slaves of their own weaknesses. The scholar-clerk has given up all ambition, the knight has abandoned all self-respect and the farmer has dropped his flail: they are all enjoying a kind of grotesque animal happiness, but the moral lesson is clear: Beware! This paradise of fools is dangerous for you are likely to take a liking to it!

Now if we should turn to Church architecture we would find an even more obvious confrontation of the sublime and the grotesque. After admiring the sublime forms of the medieval cathedral, with its statues, its stained glass windows, its tympanum exalting the glory of Christ, the attentive observer discovers next to the Lord and his angels a horde of ugly devils and of grotesque sneering faces. This coexistence of God and devils is symbolic of the form of dialectics which is at the very core of medieval thinking. The middle ages, age of faith, naturally wanted to triumph over the devil, but the age accepted the devil's existence and thought that it was infinitely better to look at the enemy in the eye under the roof of the Church rather than to let him run rampant. Thus we cannot be surprised to discover Reynard-the-fox on the facade of the Cathedral of Bourges.[9] To understand the middle ages one must accept its dualistic view of life, a life spanning and scanning ceaselessly the wide spectrum of the sublime and the grotesque.

But then we have to accept also that each genre, each text in literature has its own form of sublime and/or grotesque. Therefore both must be defined, if at all, in the broadest terms. To get a grasp at our evasive and diffuse subject we must seek it within the widest contextual diversity, with art, style and thought in motion. Our analysis will show that one of the reasons for the failures of previous studies of the grotesque was that critics insisted on looking at it as a single describable form and to compare it with associated forms such as humor, satire, caricature, the fantastic or parody, when, in reality, all the above are, according to the context, the very elements which make up the grotesque. We will show that in the frequent exchange between the sublime and the grotesque, the grotesque is rarely set for its own purpose and unfrequently equal to the sublime. In fact the grotesque is most frequently at the service of the sublime. In a sense Chamfleury in his *Histoire de la caricature* and Thomas Wright in

---

[9] Robert Bossuat, *Le Moyen Age* (Paris, 1962), p. 112.

his *History of Caricature and the Grotesque*[10] who used no specific definition of the grotesque were closer to the truth than critics who, like Heinrich Schneegans,[11] searched for a specific definition of the term. But, if attempting to reach an encompassing definition of the grotesque is as utopic and futile an exercise as to attempt to understand the complex mixture of order and disorder which make up our cosmos, the quest of the grotesque, the contemplation of its multifarious forms are nonetheless an esthetic experience, a kaleidoscopic vision and in short an eternal device used by man to protect himself from his anguish, his fears and weaknesses in his confrontation with the irrational forms of human condition.

ii

Our study of the grotesque in French medieval literature will examine five different areas in which the grotesque has a function. First we shall look at the grotesque in hagiography, then we shall examine the grotesque in epic, in narrative literature, in the fabliaux and late medieval prose, and finally we shall consider the expression of the grotesque in the medieval drama. At first it would seem that a better approach would be to study the different types which express the grotesque, such as the fool, the dwarf, but by doing that we would run the risk of setting up infinitely long or narrow lists of types. The classification we have adopted, perhaps for not being perfect, has the advantage of being logical, of respecting chronology in most cases, and of preventing hasty judgements on a group of widely disparate works.

The Grotesque in Hagiography.

There can be no doubt that the sublime is at the very heart of hagiography; its purpose is to lift men's hearts and minds, to inspire them and to give striking examples of Christian faith. With this goal in mind, hagiographers made use of a great deal of pathetic scenes, of realistic, even bloody scenes of martyrdom. The very word 'passion' involves both the grotesque of the torments and the sublime of the cause in the name of which they were supported. Our examples will be taken from the most important and beautiful saints' lives of French literature.

The *Cantilène de sainte Eulalie*[12] is, in its briefness, probably the finest

[10] Chamfleury (Paris, 1867); Thomas Wright (London, 1865).

[11] In his *Geschichte der Grotesken Satire*, 1894.

[12] About 880. Text in A. Ewert, *The French Language* (London, 1943), pp. 353–54.

model of hagiography; it is a passion story depicting with admirable conciseness the sublime ascent of a young *pucelle*, Eulalie, to sanctity through the grotesque scenes of her persecution by the pagans and of her decapitation at the command of the *rex pagiens* Maximien. In this cantilène the grotesque is as tuned down as the sublime is kept on a low key; the poem gets its power from the interweaving of the grotesque and the sublime.

During the second half of the eleventh century a Provençal life of a saint was composed under the name of the *Chanson de sainte Foy*.[13] Here again the poem's purpose is to inspire the faithful and to bring the spirit of joy to their faith, but this is done through the depiction of grim scenes of torture and of the decapitation of a child. There is perhaps no better proof that the middle ages accepted both the sublime and the grotesque as parts of life, as one thing, than lines 14 to 19 of the *Song of sainte Foy*:

> Canczon audi q'es bella'n tresca
> Que fo de razo Espanesca;
> Non fo de paraulla Grezesca
> Ne de lengua Serrazinesca
> Dolz'e suaus es plus que bresca
> E plus qe nulz pimentz q'om mesca. . . .[14]

This claim that the *Chanson* is a joyful song seems to disregard the violence which makes the song, but that is how the grotesque is supposed to serve the sublime in hagiography.

The *Vie de saint Alexis* is rightfully considered as a gem among saints' lives.[15] Here again the interest of the story is built upon the grotesque forms of Alexis' martyrdom, his beggar's disguise and the mistreatments he endures:

> Tuz l'escarnissent sil tenent pur bricun;
> L'egua li getent si moilent sun liçon.   (ll. 266–67)

The tortures, self-inflicted or inflicted by others are only one form of the grotesque in this *Vie de saint Alexis*. Another form of the grotesque is to be found in the different instances of secular mourning and grief by the

[13] E. Hoepffner et Alfaric, eds., 2 vols. (Paris, 1926).

[14] Some have advanced that this allusion to *canczon* and *tresca* was an addition from a secular source. Quite to the contrary, we believe that it fits the medieval conception of life.

[15] C. Storey, ed., *La Vie de Saint Alexis* (Geneva, Paris, 1968). Modern French translation: Guy Mermier et Sarah M. White, *La Vie de Saint Alexis* (Paris: Champion, 1972).

spouse but mostly by the mother which in the end serve the sublime ending. A typically vivid grotesque/sublime scene is enacted by the mother upon finding Alexis' body:

> Chi dunt li vit sun grant dol demener,
> Sum piz debatre e sun cors dejeter,
> Ses crins derumpre et sen vis maiseler,
> Sun mort amfant detraire ed acoler,
> Mult fust il dur ki n'estoüst plurer.   (ll. 426–30)

Even before his death, upon learning of her son's disappearance, the mother loses all her noble composure; the words *dolenta* (l.396), *dolurs* (l.397), *dol* (l.145), *doilet* (l.503) are preparatory counterparts to the Christian ending of joy (*goie*, l.503) when Alexis becomes l'*Ume Deu*. In this context the scene of the mother stripping Alexis' room and dressing it all up in black is grotesque and grotesque are the words "Pechet me l'at tolut" (l.108) if we bear in mind the high Christian tone of the poem. The word 'Pechet' more than any other in the whole text represents the grotesque of secular world thinking, the grotesque which must be "maté."[16]

Rutebeuf's *Vie de sainte Marie l'Egyptienne* provides another example of the grotesque at the service of the sublime in hagiography. Here the poet increases the pathos of his story by describing Marie's former life of a prostitute and how she now deliberately destroys her physical attractiveness. The following lines underscore the grotesque/sublime contrast in appearances of the saint-to-be:

> A paine deïst ce fust ele
> Qui l'eüst veü damoisele,
> Quar ne paroit en li nul signe.
> Char ot noire com pié de cigne;
> Sa poitrine devint mossue,
> Tant fu de pluie debatue.
> Les braz, les lons dois et les mains
> Avoit plus noirs, et c'ert du mains,
> Que n'estoit pois ne arremenz.   (ll. 449–57)

A similar use of the grotesque for the sake of the sublime is found in the *Vie de saint Thomas* by Guernes de Ponte Sainte Maxence, and particularly in the description of Thomas' martyrdom:

[16] See Moshé Lazar, "Satan et Nostre Dame . . .," *Medieval French Miscellany*, University of Kansas Humanistic Studies, No. 42 (1972), 1–14.

> Car mult plus grief martyre suffri, tant cum fu vis,
> Que ne fist el mustier, la u il fu ocis:
> Car erramment transi e en joie fu mis;
> Mais cele grant vermine dunt il esteit purpris,
> Le quivra plusurs anz, e les nuiz e les dis.   (ll. 5811–15)

The description of Thomas scourging himself is no less grotesque a scene:

> Il meïsmes perneit sun cors a depescier,
> A l'une de ses mains sa char a detrengier.   (ll. 3963–64)

Obviously the grotesque appears whenever there is something unnatural occurring: a young man letting vermin cover his body, or tearing at his own body or ripping up his flesh, for instance.

But the grotesque in hagiography or in quest literature does not need to be restricted to persons. In some cases the grotesque is represented by the supernatural or the fantastic. One outstanding example is to be found in the *Vie de saint Brendan*[17] where we have not only the grotesque narration of the suffering of Judas which will move Brendan's pity, but also the phantasmagoria of fire-breathing sea-serpents, griffins, monstrous fish, birds with human voices, somber depths and caves leading to hell. Wonders like the fight of the sea-serpents or the description of hell's smithy contribute to the grotesque fantasy which is set as a counterpoint to the sweet smelling Garden of Paradise:

The sea serpents fighting:

> Justedes sunt les dous bestes;
> Drechent forment halt les testes;
> Des narines li fous lur salt,
> Desque as nües qui volet halt;
> Colps se dunent de lur noës,
> Tels cum escuz, e des podes.
> A denz mordanz se nafrerent,
> Qui cum espez trenchant erent;
> Salt en li sanz as aigres mors
> Que funt li dent en cez granz cors;
> Les plaies sunt mult parfundes,
> Dun senglantes sunt les undes. (ll. 937–48)

Smithy the giant of hell:

[17] E. G. R. Waters, ed., *The Anglo Norman Voyage of St Brendan* (Oxford, 1928).

> Jetant flammes de sa gorge,
> A grant salz curt en sa forge.
> Revint mult tost od sa lamme
> Tute rouge cume flamme;
> Es tenailes dunt la teneit
> Fais a dis bofs bien i aveit.
> Halcet la sus vers la nue,
> E dreit vers eals puis la rue;
> Esturbeiluns plus tost ne vait,
> Quant sus en l'air li vent le trait,
> Ne li quarels d'arbaleste,
> Ne de funde la galeste. (ll. 1145–56)

In both cases the grotesque is expressed by the fantastic and supernatural: the violence of the blows of the two beasts clawing at each other, the wounds and the blood or the spurting flames from the giant's throat, his supernatural strength. Obviously the grotesqueness of the scenes augments fear for the sailors thus reinforcing the nature of their faith in the mind of listeners. In fact much more space is dedicated to the description of the perils and of the marvelous than to the actual evocation of the men's faith.

The *Vie de saint Gilles* (c. 1170) offers another example of the use of the fantastic-grotesque in hagiography. Guillaume de Berneville sketches a vivid picture of Gilles' storm-tossed voyage:

> Esclaire e tone e plot e vente.
> Tant de la mer tant del grant vent
> Pur poi ke cele nef ne fent;
> L'unde la porte cuntre munt,
> L'autre la treit vers le parfunt,
> L'une la peint, l'autre la bute,
> Pur poi k'ele ne desront tute. (ll. 786–92)

Whenever the harmony of nature is menaced or destroyed the grotesque is the new form nature assumes in danger. The fantastic scene of the storm is also offered as a counterpoint to the sublime and static life of Gilles as an hermit.

But hagiography is only one area in which the tension grotesque/sublime is experienced. Let us now turn to an examination of the grotesque in epic literature.

The Grotesque in Epic.

The *chansons de gestes* are songs of heroic exploits, of sublime performances of knights or of noble men and women, just as hagiography represented sublime episodes of saints. In epic, the grotesque generally intervenes to stress or increase the values of the feudal system (valor, bravery, or *largesse*) and to augment fear and pathos.

In the *Chanson de Roland* the sublime may be said to be dominant as much as we consider the actions and motivations of Charlemagne and his crusaders. However, under this overall sublime appearance the grotesque is present under various forms. Because epic involves so many participants the grotesque will have singular as well as plural faces: it will be on the one hand the hatred of the pagans against the Christians or, on the other hand, individual feelings of revenge, of anger, of pride as experienced both by Ganelon and Roland. The plotting of Blancandrin and the vicious cooperation of Ganelon in the attack of Charlemagne's rearguard are examples of the grotesque of thoughts, ideas or feelings. Roland's and Ganelon's *hamartia* are clear forms of the grotesque inasmuch as they endanger the sublime harmony of Christianity. The *Chanson de Roland* offers also several examples of the grotesque in supernatural events or things: the intervention of wild animals, the fiercesome storm hanging over the land, the insuing darkness, the 'marvelous' drowning of the infidels in the Ebro or the realistic scenes of massacre of the battles. But there is another form of the grotesque, the grotesque ending of Ganelon: he is chained and given to army cooks until his trial and finally quartered. The grotesque here is made up by the sudden shift of Ganelon's condition; he, a noble baron of Charlemagne, is suddenly given to villains and he, a noble baron formerly equal to Roland, ends up shamefully quartered while Roland, his peer, is at the right side of God.

The *Chanson de Roland* illustrates clearly the fact that for the middle ages the grotesque was not a separate entity and that, in fact, it was a part of the oneness of life so essential to the medieval world.[18] It would be wrong, however, to think that the *Chanson de Roland* is a model for all French medieval epic. In reality few epic texts have the remarkable simplicity and equilibrium of the *Roland*. We must therefore look elsewhere to discover other forms of the grotesque in epic.

In the *Couronnement de Louis* the grotesque again functions with the sublime. A famous example of this interaction is Guillaume's interven-

[18] Realism and idealism, good and bad, hell and Paradise, God and the devil. This oneness of life is strongly depicted in a twentieth-century play of Ionesco *Les Chaises* which offers a perfect blend of the sublime and of the grotesque as we have been able to perceive so far in our essay.

tion to protect the interests of the young king Louis menaced by Arneïs: Guillaume grabs the crown which was about to be put on Arneïs' head and he deals the traitor a mighty blow with his fist on the back of his neck, casting him to his feet. The collapse of Arneïs at the very moment he was to be crowned is grotesque, and Guillaume's violent behavior is also grotesque if we keep in mind that the blows were served in a church and that Guillaume uses rather excessive forms of disagreement in front of the Court. However, in the *Couronnement* nothing is as simple or as pure as in the *Roland*; for instance Guillaume is not the superhuman hero that Roland was, he is rather crude at times and at best he is a human hero, full of color, a sort of folk hero type.

Impressively grotesque is also the mighty giant Corsolt representing both a grotesquely exaggerated human form as well as representing the supernatural, myth and folklore. In the long run both Guillaume and Corsolt are 'salvaged' for the cause of the sublime, of God, but their grotesqueness assumes at times caricatural and humorous forms which we had not met previously in hagiography or in the *Roland*.

Better yet than the *Couronnement*, the *Charroi de Nîmes* illustrates the natural bent of medieval literature to mix the serious with the humorous or the burlesque without losing effectiveness. The Guillaume of the *Charroi* is both the servant of the sublime as a fighter of the Saracens and a grotesque figure. For instance Guillaume runs toward the king and breaks his gaiters' leather straps; later he shatters his bow while leaning on it in the king's presence. When he is not agitated he is clumsy or simply a buffoon. At a point he dons a peasant's bonnet and mounts a most feeble mare. Even the Saracens make fun of Guillaume's ridiculous attire. Guillaume is also a grotesque lover; when a fair maiden asks him to accompany her to her bedroom clumsy Guillaume is scared; he says: "Cuidai, beau sire, qu'el queïst amistiez / Ou itel chose que fame a home quiert" (ll. 561–62). This is hardly the reaction of the hearty Guillaume whose "ris geté" resounds so loudly. Such discordances in moods or behavior naturally give birth to their own form of grotesque.

Now if we turn to the *Prise d'Orange* we encounter another form of grotesque, a grotesque made up of cloak and dagger exploits, of melodramatic swashbuckling scenes and, importantly, of parody.[19] Though not devoid of sublime moments, the *Prise d'Orange* mixes with less regularity the grotesque with the sublime and thus anticipates the greater diversity to be found in the novel.

[19] C. Régnier, ed., *La Prise d'Orange* (Paris, 1967).

As a last example for the epic we must choose the Anglo-Norman *Chanson de Guillaume* for it reveals "that medieval propensity for passing from the sublime to the ridiculous in a manner which the modern reader can only find disconcerting."[20] The theme of the *Chanson* is sublime for it serves the Christian cause and ideals, but the text is strewn with grotesque episodes: At the beginning a messenger arrives in Bourges to announce the attack of the Saracen king Deramed. While such tragic event is taking place Tedbald is completely drunk and reeling from side to side incapable of standing up. Later on, during the battle, Tedbald while riding by some gallows touches one of the hanging corpses; he is so frightened that he becomes incontinent. Still terrified, Tedbald rides through a flock of sheep and cuts off the head of one of the animals and enters the city of Bourges with the bloody head still caught in his stirrups. At this point we notice a drift in the presence of the grotesque; it hardly is at the service of the sublime; it already seems to be independent. Another scene of the grotesque illustrating this new feature may be found in the last third of the epic, when Girard who is starved is served a huge meal by Guibourc. As a true descendant of Guillaume, Girard grotesquely gulps down a whole gallon of wine and eats like an ogre. Little is the contribution of such scenes to the sublime!

In the *Chanson de Guillaume* grotesque scenes of massacres are depicted, but with infinitely more violence and realism than in the *Chanson de Roland*. Blood, instead of being a thread of red on the green grass, is everywhere, on the wounded as well as on their gear. Here some are holding their intestines to prevent them from being trampled underfoot by horses. The fantastic forces of nature also contribute to the grotesque: as the Saracen advance toward the forest, the ground trembles and the sun rays striking a thousand armours light up the scene about; the eeriness of the scene is a mighty foreboding of the grotesque death of thousands of Frenchmen. The fantastic and the marvelous belong to the grotesque.

But our survey of the grotesque in the *Chanson de Guillaume* would be much incomplete if we did not present the two characters who are perhaps the most outstanding grotesque figures of this epic, Gui the dwarf, a mean and powerful ally of the Christians and the giant Raynouard and his *tinel*. Of the two, Raynouard is certainly the most grotesque in character and action: he slaughters at whim and with a catchy joy hundreds of Saracens with his mighty club or with his bare fists. We notice here how the grotesque changes in nature from one text or even

[20] John Fox, *The Middle Ages* (London, N.Y., 1974), p. 95.

context to another; we could hardly imagine a Roland fighting with a *tinel* or with his fists; however Raynouard's grotesque is no less a part of the sublime than Roland's, for both assure victory for the Christians against the Saracens.[21] But we must now pursue our investigation in other domains. Next we shall examine Narrative Literature.

The Grotesque in Narrative Literature.

In the Roman d'Antiquité the basic principle is also the evocation of the sublime, but contrary to the epic, the sublime is less encompassing and often limited to individual characters or episodes. This fragmentation of the sublime and therefore of the grotesque occurs when the story tends to take precedent over the (didactic) purpose. In the case of the *Roman d'Alexandre*, for instance, the sublime is centered on the figure of Alexandre. The portrait of the hero is carefully drawn, but in a style "rompant délibérément avec le style des chansons de geste qui préféraient une indication générale à l'analyse des caractères individuels."[22] Contrary to hagiography and epic, in the roman d'antiquité the focus of the sublime is the telling of a charming story in which love plays the "epic" role. The expression of the grotesque will therefore more likely be a form of love or a state created by love.

In *Piramus et Tisbé*[23] the grotesque lies mostly in the melodramatic tone of the complaints of the adolescent in love. The expression of his love is grotesque in the sense that it assumes an unnatural form; it appears more like a sickness than love. And we have seen before that the grotesque feeds on the unnatural. The following lines are typical of the grotesque caused by love:

> Las, cheitif, tristes et dolent,
> Soufferai longues cest tourment?
> Tous tens ai duel, joie noient,
> Et plus me dueil et plus m'esprent Amour.
> Amour la nom? Mes est ardour,
> Qui einsi vient de jour en jour.
> Fletrist ma face et ma colour,
> Com fait gelee tenre flour. Hé las! (ll. 150–59)

The grotesque in the above monologue does not lack a certain innocence

---

21 John Fox, pp. 96–97.
22 Bossuat, *Le Moyen Age*, p. 48.
23 C. de Boer, ed., *Piramus et Tisbé, poème du XIIe siècle* (Paris: CFMA, 1921).

which touches our hearts. The grotesque at times may be noble as it is frequently *vilain*.

In *Eneas*[24] we learn at length that Lavinia has been smitten with love. The expression of this love which consumes her assumes at times grotesque forms, here again in the unusual, unnatural attitude of the character:

> Ele comance a tressüer,
> A refroidir et a tranbler,
> Sovant se pasme et tressalt,
> Sanglot, fremist, li cuers li falt,
> Degiete soi, sofle, baaille: (ll. 8073–78)

Similar traces of the grotesque, but more subdued perhaps, may be found in the *Roman de Troie*,[25] mostly in lines 17606–10 when Achilles reacts to his first encounter with Polyxena:

> Sovent mue color sa face:
> Sovent l'a pale, et puis vermeille.
> A se meïsme se conseille
> Que ço puet estre que il sent,
> Qu'ensi freidist et puis resprent....

Here we have to recognize one of the problems posed by the grotesque in narrative literature: As soon as the scene which is individually grotesque within a certain context becomes crystallized into a particular style and vocabulary, this very typification assigns it to a specific genre, thus depriving it of its "social" impact as grotesque. The lengthy deliberations of Achilles which might be grotesque out of context become a common narrative process as recognized in other narrative works, in Chrétien's *Yvain* or in *Tristan and Iseult* for instance. In the *Roman d'Alexandre* the exotic, the fantastic and marvelous elements which would have related to the grotesque in the *Chanson de Roland* are too diffused and attached to too great a variety of characters and situations to form grotesque values comparable to those we have previously examined.

Turning to other Romance forms[26] we find that the sublime and poignant love story of Tristan and Iseult is 'romantic' only to the superficial reader of composite and abridged versions of the legend. In reality

---

[24] J. J. Salverda de Grave, ed., *Eneas, Roman du XIIe siècle* (Paris: CFMA, 1925).

[25] C. Constans, ed., 6 vols. (Paris: SATF, 1904–1912).

[26] Including lays, but excluding fabliaux, fourteenth- and fifteenth-century prose which we examine separately.

Tristan et Iseult[27] offers many grotesque episodes which increase the pathetic quality of this tragedy of love. Robert Bossuat writes: "Et le grand amour tyrannique, la folle passion née du philtre triomphera avec la mort des deux amants: 'Tristan murut pur sue amur, / E la bele Ysolt pur tendrur.' "[28] The grotesque of the story corresponds precisely to this *folle passion*. The lovers' passion is *folle*, a word which connotes and denotes the grotesque. Tristan and Iseult are the slaves of a supernatural power, the potion, and because of it they will be unto death condemned to live a life of sin and of fear. Because of the potion, pure love has been stained into several grotesque forms. In Beroul's version we meet a commonly grotesque figure of the middle ages, the dwarf; he is mean, evil, misshapen and possesses powers of necromancy.[29] In Beroul there are also many grotesque episodes: A band of lepers offer the grotesque parody of knights when their leader shouts to them: "Now, to your crutches!" Iseult, in another instance, this queen of love, is condemned to join the company of lepers, a grotesque punishment worse than fire.

We notice again in *Tristan et Iseult* that the grotesque, rather than functioning in relation to the novel as a whole, functions more frequently within certain episodes. The impact of the grotesque would seem therefore more localized in romance than in hagiography or epic.

Chrétien de Troyes does not deal with the fatal passion of Tristan and of Iseult; he deals with a more complex, ritualistic and difficult type of love, the triumph of which is the sublime of his romances. The grotesque will therefore be found in the characters which infringe upon the strict rules of the social Arthurian code, and also in the situations emerging from such infringements. The grotesque will also be found in the many 'ugly' obstacles to the courtly knight's achievements.[30]

In *Erec et Enide*[31] we also find a dwarf whose grotesque function is to insult Genièvre's maid and Erec. Erec himself, son of king Lac, assumes the grotesque role of *récréant* after his wedding to Enide; smitten with love he forgets his duties and his bride is reduced to inform him that "recreant vos apelent tuit" (l. 2551). This episode will have its sublime counterpart in the later *Joie de la Cort* episode. The rites of passage from the grotesque to the sublime are well marked in the episode during

[27] A. Ewert, ed., *The Romance of Tristan by Beroul*, 2 vols. (Oxford, 1939).
[28] Robert Bossuat, *Le Moyen Age*, p. 64.
[29] As expressed by Beroul in line 646: "Dehé aient tuit cil devin."
[30] The vilain *losangiers* of the troubadours is an example of this form of grotesque.
[31] Mario Roques, ed., *Erec et Enide* (Paris: CFMA, 1952).

which Erec must traverse an invisible wall of air before being able to defeat the giant Maboagrain.[32]

The romance of *Yvain*[33] perhaps offers the best picture of the interplay of the grotesque and the sublime in the Arthurian novel. Yvain is like Lancelot the perfect knight of the Round Table; he is a model of Arthurian sublime. However, his story involves multiple interventions of the grotesque. At the very start of the tale Calogrenant tells how he met a monstrous herdsman guarding some wild bulls. The *monstrous* shepherd and the *wild* bulls are grotesque prefigurations of the brutal attack of Esclados le Roux. Yvain, then, falls prey to the grotesque: in order to avoid Erec's lot, Yvain leaves his lady-love Laudine but fails to return at the appointed time. The grotesque scorn of Laudine replaces her precious love and Yvain, upon hearing of his lady's anger, loses all courteous and knightly appearance and behavior and lives like a wild man in the forest; he becomes a grotesque creature not unlike the monstrous shepherd or the wild bulls:

> Lors se li monte uns torbeillons
> el chief, si grant que il forsane;
> si se dessire et se depane
> et fuit par chans et par arees,
> et lessa ses genz esgarees
> qui se mervoillent ou puet estre:
> querant le vont destre et senestre
> par les ostex as chevaliers,
> et par haies et par vergiers.... (ll. 2806–14)

Then Yvain sinks to the depths of madness. He will gradually rediscover his senses and the sense of his true values after a series of expiatory acts. In *Yvain* we notice once more that the grotesque, rather than affecting the romance as a whole, the sublime of the romance, affects one episode. The grotesque is one step in the story and once the step is taken it loses much of its importance.

Since we touch the subject of madness, it seems appropriate to examine the *Folie Tristan*[34] before continuing with Chrétien. One of the first forms of the grotesque in the *Folie Tristan*[35] is the grotesque of words: *dolent, murnes, tristes, pensifs* (l. 2), *languir* (l. 10) and *murir* (ll. 6,

---

[32] Giants are signs of the grotesque which we have already met in this study.

[33] Mario Roques, ed., *Yvain* (Paris: CFMA, 1960).

[34] Joseph Bédier, ed., *Les Deux Poèmes de la Folie Tristan* (Paris, 1907).

[35] We refer here to the *Folie d'Oxford*.

7, 16) are all set up as opposite to *amur*, to *joie*. Like in the poetry of troubadours expressions such as *murir desiret* or *murir volt* signify the grotesque non-being of love. Another form of the grotesque is found under the word *fol*. To achieve his goal Tristan assumes a grotesque form; his *feintise* of *folie* is so successful that all the valets cry, "Veez le fol! Hu, hu, hu!" Grotesque also is the story of the *fol's* birth and infancy: "Ma mere fu une baleine . . ." (ll. 271, 273).[36] No passage stresses better the tension between the sublime and the grotesque than the answer of Iseult to Trantris:

> Isolt respunt: "Par certes, nun!
> Kar cil est beus e gentils hum,
> E tu es gros, hidus e laiz,
> Ke pur Trantris numer te faiz.
> Or te tol, ne hue sur mei;
> Ne pris mie tes gas ne tei."
> Li fols se turne a icest mot,
> Si se fet ben tenir pur sot.
> Il fert ces k'il trove en sa veie,
> Del deis desc'a l'us les cumveie,
> Puis lur escrie:" Foles genz,
> Tolez, issez puis de ceenz!
> Lassez m'a Ysolt consiler:
> Je la sui venu doneier."
> Li reis s'en rit, kar mult li plest;
> Ysolt ruvist e si se test. (ll. 367–82)

In this passage the oppositions between *beus*, *gentils* and *fols*, *gros*, *hidus* and *lais* evoke the discordant, almost absurd upside-down world in which the *fol* is not a fol, the ugly face is not really ugly and Trantris is in fact Tristan. Fortunately this grotesque state will not last, and order will be re-established when the mask will remove his mask, when Trantris will wash his face and become Tristan again (ll. 367–82): The grotesque disappears when *joie* is restored; the key words are now *joius* and *lez* (l. 997).

If we now return to Chrétien's works, we find in *Lancelot* several grotesque elements. First the traditional grotesque figure of the dwarf who offers the use of his shameful cart to the sublime Lancelot. This grotesque scene will be used by Chrétien to tie the threads of his romance. Lancelot, himself, is several times the victim of grotesque behavior: he

---

[36] See also l. 281.

almost falls from a window when he catches sight of Guenièvre below; he hugs and kisses the hair of Guenièvre after removing them from her comb; later he fights backwards and against himself. But in the end reason triumphs from the grotesque: "reisons anferme et lie son fol cuer, et son fol pansé . . ." (ll. 6846–47). Like in the case of the *Roman d'Alexandre*, in *Lancelot* the grotesque never seems to interest the whole story; rather it remains attached to specific episodes.

So the function of the grotesque in romances appears decidedly less predictable than in hagiography or epic. The grotesque and the sublime have much more tendency to walk their own way than to work one for the other.

Speaking of the lais of Marie de France,[37] Robert Bossuat says: "On a dit à juste titre que les lais de Marie de France peuvent être qualifiés de 'nouvelles courtoises'. Ce sont en effet de courts poèmes, de cent à mille vers, soigneusement rimés et consacrés à des récits d'amour dont les héros, Tristan, Lanval Iseut ou Guilliadon, parés de grâces tendres et d'aimables vertus, évoquent les seigneurs et les dames qui se plaisaient à les entendre."[38] It is true that one cannot understate Marie's courtoisie, and the charming *Lai du Chèvrefeuille* easily proves it. But it would also be to betray Marie's versatile talent not to recognize her extraordinary ability at handling the grotesque. In fact not all is *fin'amors* in the lays of Marie de France as we shall see.

Le *Lai des Deus Amanz* is basically a touching love story, but our poetess' originality appears in her use of a grotesque ending. We will recall that the only successful suitor of the daughter of the king of Neustria dies of heart failure seconds after his triumph and the girl follows him in the grave as she is overcome by grief. This story is a perfect example of performance of the grotesque under the form of irony. *Equitan* is one of the most violent pieces written by Marie de France; there the grotesque is of the family of Alfred Hitchcock films: Lord Equitan falls in love with the wife of one of his seneschals and she returns his love. But Equitan will marry her only if her husband is dead. So, she plots the latter's murder: she will bleed him while scalding him in boiling water. To cover the husband's suspicion Equitan accepts to be bled at the same time. Shortly before the execution of the plot Equitan is discovered in the arms of the wife, and in order to dispel the husband's

[37] A. Ewert and R. C. Johnston, eds. (Oxford, 1942); K. Warnke, ed., *Die Fabeln der Marie de France* (Halle, 1898).
[38] Robert Bossuat, *Le Moyen Age*, pp. 59–60.

suspicions Equitan jumps in a bath, the wrong one, and dies scalded by the boiling water destined to the husband! And to this first grotesque ironic episode, Marie adds a second one: the husband seizes his wife and plunges her into the boiling bath where she soon dies.

For the first time, perhaps, we can see the grotesque functioning by itself and for its own sake. If previously we have encountered the triumph of the sublime, in *Equitan* we have the triumph of the grotesque. *Bisclavret's* originality is that it mixes the fantastic and the grotesque: the Briton noblesman becomes a bisclavret, a garwarf or werewolf and he can't return to his human form unless he can change back into his clothes. His wife, unfaithful and terrified, helps another knight to wear her husband's clothes and she marries him. A year later the king having caught a werewolf keeps him at his court where the knight who married the unfaithful wife appears one day and the werewolf attacks him. Similarly when the unfaithful lady arrives, the werewolf bites her nose off. But, like in *Equitan*, Marie adds a second grotesque ironic ending: the werewolf gets his clothes back and becomes a knight, but he is banished along with the unfaithful wife and, worse (grotesque) punishment, their children are born *esnasees* (l. 314).[39] So Marie de France's use of the grotesque takes its originality in that it offers strong folkloric characteristics, the grotesque of many of Perrault's and Hoffman's tales.

Among other twelfth-century romances worth mentioning is the roman d'aventure of *Robert le Diable*[40] because of its similarities with hagiography in its use of the grotesque:[41] the duchess of Normandy gives birth to a child after having prayed to the devil. Naturally the child becomes an abominable tyrant who becomes renowned for his destructive talents and atrocities. But in the end the grotesque reverts into the sublime: the tyrant is converted into a faithful Christian, into a fierce enemy of the infidels. Renaud de Beaujeu's *Guinglain* presents an interesting use of the grotesque: a Welsh girl is transformed into a dragon and the hero must take the *fier baisier* from the dragon in order to rescue the maiden. The hero succeeds and the couple is eventually married. In that case the grotesque has its traditional function of increasing the suspense.

In considering some thirteenth-century romances for the sake of brevity we shall not analyze the manifestations of the grotesque in the

---

[39] See John Fox, *Middle Ages*, p. 171.
[40] E. Löseth, ed. (Paris: SATF, 1903).
[41] See also the *Miracle de Théophile*.

Mort d'Artu, though it presents its perverse features many times: Lancelot and Guinevere's adultery, anger, hatred and jealousy. In the long run it is the grotesque adulterous love which is the cause of the decadence and fall of the Arthurian world. There seems to be less reliance on the power of Providence and more power attributed to the *Roue de Fortune.*

Presenting original forms of the grotesque is the famed 'chantefable' of *Aucassin et Nicolete.*[42] Any reader will naturally be charmed by this "petit chef d'oeuvre,"[43] but an attentive reader will recognize in the story a wealth of grotesque elements. In fact *Aucassin et Nicolete* is replete with grotesque forms, parody, satire and perhaps others,[44] all under a pseudo-sublime disguise, the disguise of naïvety, of courtly love conventions and of an inverted logic which we recognized earlier in the *Folie Tristan.* Aucassin compares his love to a 'bunch of grapes' and to a soup; he declares preferring to go to hell rather than to heaven. In Torelore the king is in bed about to have a baby; a fierce battle is fought with rotten fruit and cheeses. Like in the *Folie Tristan* the world is upside down; it is a world reminding us of Bruegel and of Bosch. John Fox commenting on *Aucassin et Nicolete* writes: "In some respects all this may have been an oblique comment on the follies of the world, but above all it is innocent and amusing fun, and it would be doing it a disservice to try to discover any particular message."[45] Fox is really too cautious. The grotesque elements mentioned earlier are too obvious to be taken lightly. The problem is that the grotesque in *Aucassin et Nicolete* is more subtly presented in the style rather than in actual deeds; everything is scaled down: the grotesque here is the opposite of the grotesque of Raynouard or of Gulliver.

Because it would take us too far afield, we will not study the grotesque in the *Roman de la Rose,* though it is present almost everywhere in Jean de Meun's continuation. We must point out, however, that Jean de Meun's grotesque often assumes the form of folly, a theme which will continue to flourish in the later middle ages and the Renaissance. We could also point out the grotesque cynical views of the old woman or the praise of sexual intercourse by Genius in his mock sermon. We would find a grotesque similar *mutatis mutandis* to the grotesque of *Aucassin*

[42] M. Roques, ed. (Paris: CFMA, 1925; 1936). Also see John Fox, *The Middle Ages,* p. 207.

[43] Robert Bossuat, *Le Moyen Age,* p. 76.

[44] Grace Frank, *The Medieval French Drama* (Oxford: Clarendon Press, 1954), p. 238.

[45] Fox, *Middle Ages,* p. 208.

et Nicolete, a grotesque of parody and satire, but a grotesque chiefly of wit and style. But now we must turn to the fabliaux.

As early as the twelfth century with Jean Bodel, the fabliaux contributed their own genre of grotesque to literature. The fabliaux are grotesque in diverse ways, when they are naughty or mean,[46] in their depiction of treachery, debauchery or felony. Their key words include *engin, fol, vilain, desvez, convoiteus,* and *envieus*.[47] Naturally, the fabliau is a 'conte à rire,'[48] and the grotesque therefore will be functioning *quasi* for itself. In most cases we recognize that the grotesque is made up of basic simple and repeated formulae which are comic because of their repetition, of their essential incoherence or simplicity. That is the grotesque at the level of style. But there is another grotesque, more subtle, in the depiction of absurd situations, gestures or words as they clash with the privileged, ordered and providential Christian world. On the one hand we have a grotesque whose *raison d'être* is laughter and a grotesque of the absurd.

Of all the processes of the grotesque in the fabliaux, scatology and obscenity are perhaps their most common features.[49] Bodel's fabliau *Gombert et les deux Clercs* is replete with 'evocative' words, images, expressions or remarks for the author well knows that "la répétition du mot 'priapique' faite à dessein (dans le *Sohait desvez*) tend à un effet comique."[50] And Foulon adds: "L'auteur va jusqu'à une description détaillée. C'est la licence brutale du style et la violation des lois habituelles de la bienséance qui provoquent l'hilarité."[51] But obscenity is not the only form of the grotesque in the fabliaux. We will find also the grotesque of excess, of violence, of gestures and situations typical of the farce also. The key words in this context are *batre* or *ferir*. In *Du convoiteus et de l'envieus* the miser shouts: "Demande, ou ge te batrai tant / Que mielz ne fu asnes a pont" (ll. 66–67). Reminiscent of Raynouard au tinel is the scene in which Gombert is struck by the clerk:[52] "Cil le fiert du poing lez les costes / Grant cops du poing ..."

Next to the grotesque of physical violence we find a grotesque of phy-

---

[46] We would like to say *"grinçant"* like for some of Anouilh's plays.

[47] Charles Foulon, *L'Oeuvre de Jean Bodel* (Paris: Presses Universitaires de France), p. 78.

[48] Foulon, p. 78.

[49] See Bédier, *Les Fabliaux*, p. 285, note 8 and p. 286, note 1.

[50] Foulon, p. 77.

[51] *Ibid.*, p. 77.

[52] *Ibid.*, p. 80.

sical features. The villain of the *Vilain de Bailleul* is monstrously ugly, "maufez et de laide hure" (ll. 8–9). Next to ugliness the vices of lechery and gluttony serve well the grotesque. The same villain of Bailleul is such a glutton that he throws boiling soup down his throat, scorching himself into horrible grimaces and grotesque contortions.[53] Here the grotesque touches caricature which is also a land of the grotesque.

Without examining the hundred and fifty fabliaux which have come down to us we can safely say that they are another example of the fundamental duality of medieval thought and life,[54] of its acceptance of the coexistence of the high and of the low, of the noble and of the villain.[55]

One of the striking grotesque forms of the *Roman de Renart* is to be found in the different consequences of the fierce rivalry of Renart and Ysengrin "recalling a little that between Roland and Ganelon."[56] Renart copulates with Hersent (in front of the children!) and Ysengrin in his shame insults grotesquely his wife: "Haï! fait il, 'pute orde vivre, pute serpant, pute coleuvre, bien ai veüe toute l'euvre . . ." (ll. 6070–72). Like in the fabliaux the semantic level is frequently low, popular or vulgar: *foutre, pertuis, pet* are as frequent key words as *cul*. It is through these grotesque forms that the *Roman de Renart* may be said to be "a distorting mirror held up to all living society, a rich source of wit and laughter."[57] One main consequence of our survey is that in medieval narrative literature the grotesque, when it does not work for itself, works for the cause of comedy, laughter or wit rather than for the sublime.

Like in the fabliaux the grotesque in both the *Quinze Joyes de Mariage* and the *Cent nouvelles nouvelles*[58] is intended primarily to amuse and to serve the comedy of relations between men and women. The forms of the grotesque are therefore derived from society and more frequently from married life. They depict the grotesque of men and women's destructive relationships in marriage: the wife is selfish, extravagant while the husband is either violent or weak, in most cases grotesque. But the grotesque often goes deeper, when it reaches the point of the absurd, the absurd of an unhappy, gloomy, hypocritical, selfish and hostile world. This state is best illustrated by the repeated and decisive formula of the QJM: "Ainsi

[53] *Ibid.*, p. 81.
[54] John Fox, *Middle Ages*, p. 232.
[55] See P. Nykrog, *Les Fabliaux; étude d'histoire littéraire et de stylistique médiévale* (Copenhague, 1957), p. 235.
[56] John Fox, *Middle Ages*, p. 233.
[57] *Ibid.*, p. 236.
[58] Quoted below as CNN and QJM.

(the husband) use sa vie en paines, en douleurs et gemissements, ou il est et sera toujours, et finera miserablement ses jours."[59] In both the QJM and in the CNN the grotesque lies mostly in the lack of charity, of simple kindness or sympathy. The grotesque follows a conventional, even artificial pattern "to provide the reader with brittle and cynical amusement."[60]

In *Le Petit Jehan de Saintré*, a superior masterpiece of the fifteenth century, we find a remarkable use of the grotesque which grows more hideous up to the end, which is not unlike a Racinian dénouement. The figure of Damp Abbé is the very sign of the matured grotesque capable of trampling underfoot *courtoisie* in the shape of Belle Cousine. The play of feet of Belle Cousine and of Damp Abbé under the table is the mark of the grotesque death of *courtoisie* in the fifteenth century. The ironic grotesque of *Le Petit Jehan de Saintré's* ending is without a doubt what raises the story to the level of the first *roman de moeurs* in French literature.

But now we must conclude our essay by looking at two important aspects of the grotesque, first in the Medieval drama and then in Villon.

The Grotesque in Medieval Drama

The medieval drama offers such a variety of subjects, of characters and of situations that it is not surprising if it offers at the same time a great diversity of grotesque forms, chiefly when we pass from the liturgical drama to the farce.

The earliest form of drama is recognized by all as being the liturgical Easter or Christmas play or, at least, a play performed at important dates of the Church. And one early form of the grotesque in medieval drama is to be found in the so-called *Feast of Fools*[61] or *Asinaria fest*. Grace Frank writes: "Such revels, which originally may have been Christian adaptations of the pagan festivities of the Kalends, when great licence was permitted the lower classes, were widespread in France during the Christmas season and especially at the festivities of the subdeacons on 1 January. Though the observances varied in different churches, they usually included burlesqued services, censing with unseemingly objects, more or less rioutous behaviour, and in many places the presence of an

---

[59] QJM: 15th Joy. John Fox (*Middle Ages*) writes: "It is a sort of nuptial Huis Clos based on the premise 'l'enfer, c'est le mariage.'"

[60] Janet M. Ferrier, *French Prose Writers of the fourteenth and fifteenth Centuries* (Pergamon Press, 1966), p. 69.

[61] See Grace Frank, *The Medieval French Drama*, pp. 243–44.

ass. At Beauvais, Sens, Autun, and elsewhere a humorous Prose of the Ass was recited and at Beauvais there was mock braying by the participants. The Prose of the Ass began: 'Orientis partibus / Adventavit asinus,' and each stanza had as refrain some variant of 'Hez, Sire Asne, hez!' "[62] Although many critics[63] refuse to see any ribaldry in the role of the ass, this animal was a grotesque figure and an object of fun even when playing a serious part; the proof of it is that the Church soon forbade its presence in liturgical ceremonies.

The *Mystère d'Adam*[64] offers striking examples of the grotesque, in the presence of the ugly cunning devil and of his noisy demons for instance and of the mouth of Hell from which exudes clouds of smoke. Fox writes: "This early theatre was clearly not conceived primarily as entertainment, though one wonders what amount of horseplay accompanied the final demise of the Foolish Virgins in the *Sponsus*: 'Modo accipiant eas demones, et precipitentur in infernum.' The descent of Adam and Eve into hell was an even noisier and more fearsome occasion according to the extraordinarily detailed stage directions."[65]

In Jean Bodel's *Jeu de saint Nicolas* the grotesque, though not dominant, is found in the proper names, in the burlesque gestures and words of some of the characters. Grace Frank writes: "For example, his saint can call the thieves *fil a putain* when he orders them to restore the treasure, his angelic messenger embodies the Christian philosophy of the crusades, and his symbolic Preudom, despite great faith, humanly trembles before his goaler, exclaiming pitifully: 'Sire, con vo machue est grosse!' "[66] The thieves receive grotesque onomatopoeic names such as Cliquet, Pincedé, Rasoir; the old man is called Connart and the tavern servant-boy's name is Caignet (little cur)! Here the grotesque is a part of the dramatic liveliness of the play, of its effectiveness. Bodel has succeeded here in unifying the humorous and the serious, the grotesque and the sublime for the sake of the entertainment and its lesson.

With the development of passion plays, we meet the *Passion du Palatinus*, interesting by its use of the "hagiographic" grotesque. Fox writes: "The original aspects of this early passion play point all in the same direction, towards an earthy, matter-of-fact realism, marked by a touch of sadism and a little humour at times. The very nature of the

[62] *Ibid.*, pp. 41–42.
[63] *Ibid.*, p. 42 and Chambers, ii, 57, for instance.
[64] P. Studer, ed., *Le Mystère d'Adam* (Manchester, 1918).
[65] John Fox, *Middle Ages*, p. 246.
[66] Frank, *The Medieval French Drama*, p. 99.

enterprise cannot have favoured a more mystical approach, the whole point being to bring live before the eyes of the people the passion of Our Lord, and to present it in human terms that they could understand. Here, as in the miracle plays, something of the mentality of the age is revealed."[67] We note, for instance, the grotesque scenes depicting the torturers Cayn and Huitacelin or the executioners Haquin and Mosse. The episode of Harrowing of Hell is also mostly grotesque with a boastful Satan and a fearful Enfer throwing at each other picturesque curses. Here again we discover a grotesque which, while enhancing the sublime, mostly supports the play's dramatic qualities; it adds picturesque and enlivens the stage.

Also from the fourteenth century, the forty *Miracles de Notre Dame* present numerous elements of the grotesque, but like in hagiography they mostly serve sublime Christian motives. The grotesque figure of folly is presented in order to give the Virgin Mary the opportunity to warn against it or fight it. As a matter of fact the interplay between the grotesque folly of Satan and Notre Dame was represented over and over in the Medieval drama. In his excellent article Moshé Lazar studies the roles of these two "stereotyped characters" and writes: "In many ways, they resemble the masks of early comedy or of the 'commedia dell'arte' ".[68] Generally speaking Satan is a braggart, cunning 'miles gloriosus', but in the end 'maté' by the sublime Notre Dame. "Inevitably," writes Lazar, "because his defeat is prepared in advance by the scenario, he is the eternal *dummteufel* of the 'divine comedy' ". In all these plays, the intervention of the grotesque is most of the time at the service of the sublime,[69] but a new element has entered which was absent in hagiography, the contribution of the grotesque to the dramatic spectacle of the play. Moshé Lazar writes: "We must think in terms of didactic and spectacular theatre, of popular stage performances, in order to judge correctly these plays which use the simplest devices and the technique of the Grand Guignol to celebrate the victory of Good over Evil, of Notre Dame over Satan" (p. 14).

Now, when we come to comic dramatizations such as that of Luke XV.II.32, *Courtois d'Arras*,[70] we have to admit that the inherent comic-grotesque is still at the service of the sublime, at least for edification, but

---

[67] Fox, *Middle Ages*, p. 253.
[68] Moshé Lazar, "Satan et Nostre Dame."
[69] *Ibid.*
[70] E. Faral, ed. (CFMA, 1922).

no longer in the way the grotesque served the sublime in hagiography. *Courtois d'Arras*, in fact, has a grotesque which is not uncommon to its counterpart in *Aucassin et Nicolete*, a grotesque of parody, but a parody less witty and more realistic than in the chantefable. The naïve Courtois is a young boastful bumpkin with not a courtly bone in his body; he is quickly lured into drinking by two hussies, Pourette and Manchevaire, who steal his purse forcing him to leave his tunic and breeches to the innkeeper in payment for his debts. Again the grotesque character of the fol intervenes, but here the fol is in the characters' character rather than being a specific person. The innkeeper's servant cries out:

> Chaiens est li vins de Soisçons!
> Sor l'erbe verde et sor les jons
> on i boit a hanap d'argent;
> çaiens boivent tote la gent,
> chaiens boivent *et fol et sage*
> e se n'i laisse nus son gaje!
> Ne l'estuet fors conter la dete. . . . (ll. 103–09,
> italics mine)

Le *Garçon et l'Aveugle*, considered by some to be our earliest farce extant, offers a grotesque even more earthy than *Courtois d'Arras*. Even if playing tricks to a blind man was not particularly grotesque in the eyes of the medieval people, the often heartless and crude humor reaches the point of grotesque when it is played at the expenses of a crude, lecherous old man. In fact both characters "exchange obscene pleasantries about the joy of copulation."[71] Here the grotesque, if anything, serves the comic alone; in this traditional scenario of "vilain à vilain et demi," no sympathy is aroused and the grotesque plays a role quite similar to the one we meet in the fabliaux or in the *Roman de Renart*.

We have seen earlier many examples of dwarfs and fools or sots and the attraction for such grotesque figures did not diminish at the close of the middle ages. The sotties of the fourteenth and fifteenth centuries are proof that there was no lull in interest in the fool. "The sottie," writes Grace Frank, "was essentially a comedy played by 'fools' in their characteristic costume of cap with asses' ears, staff with bells and parti-coloured dress" (pp. 243–44). But unlike previous fools, the fools of the sotties are not necessarily grotesque with a certain sublime didactic purpose; most of the time they are grotesque for grotesque's sake, for the

---

[71] Frank, *The Medieval French Drama*, p. 221.

sake of action, or they are grotesque for the sake of satire. Grace Frank writes: "In their skits the *sots* deride all kinds of persons and ridicule social, political and ecclesiastical abuses, but as Thomas Sebillet said in the sixteenth century, their chief aim is dissolute laughter" (pp. 244-45). Though late, the *Recueil Trepperel*[72] offers magnificent examples of grotesque farcical characters and situations in the farce and the sottie.

Number 21 of the *Recueil Trepperel* is titled "Sermon nouveau d'ung fol changant divers propos"; it has a fol as simple character. But this sermon is not a sermon in the traditional sense of the word; it simply is a fool's monologue.[73] The grotesque is less in the character of the fol than in his obscene and scatological allusions and words and in the overall satire. *Cul, cornars, Bourguignon salé*, the proper name *Jennin*, the expression "vent de la chemise," are all grotesque in the sense that they are either nonsense or absurdity (ll. 10-35), obscenity (l. 45), stupidity (l. 197) or eroticism (l. 264). Another Trepperel play, number 24, is titled "Dialogue de beaucop veoir et joyeulx soudain." The theme of the farce is found over and over in the fabliaux: the lover is suddenly confronted by the husband's unexpected return, so he takes refuge in a 'grotesque' hiding place, grotesque because most of the time the place is totally inappropriate and absurd. The lover of our farce is hidden under the woman's bed where he will be found. This is a perfect example of the fundamental essence of the grotesque which appears whenever there is a total reversal of situation: the one on top falls to the bottom and vice versa. Grotesque also are the play's numerous onomatopoeiae: "hon, hon, hon; flou, flou, flou," for instance. Frequently the language is grotesque for its own sake. Beaucop says:

> Une fois entre tous
> Le mary de Bellot me vit
> Et je m'en vins fourrez dessoulz
> Ung grant filz de putain de lict. (ll. 349-51)

The grotesque word "putain" appears repeatedly in these farces, often representing desecration for desecration's sake. Beaucop never misses an opportunity to use the word; he says:

> Il y eut beau trippot
> Le filz de putain regnioit
> Dieu et sa mere de grant flot,
> Par le sang bieu qu'i me tueroit. (ll. 373-75)

[72] E. Droz et Lewicka, eds., *Le Recueil Trepperel* (Les Farces: Droz, 1961).
[73] Droz-Lewicka, p. 1.

Obscenities are the norm in such plays. The expression "faire la nicque ou la nucque" (l. 22) has obscene connotations, and the grotesque of "gecter de gros guillevardos" (l. 40) needs hardly to be explained.[74] Beaucop veoir's expression "J'en declique bien vingt reaulx" (l. 105) is a well-known sexual metaphor.

Nonsense, eroticism, obscenity or *gros mots*, however, are not the only form of grotesque found in the farce. There may also be a grotesque of cruelty, such as is found in Trepperel number 31 titled "Farce à trois personnages: le savetier, le sergent et la laitière." E. Droz writes: "Cette pièce, qui commence par deux scènes de marchandage assez amusantes, se termine par des injures et des horions" (p. 25). Indeed, the end of the play reaches cruelly grotesque proportions with the Savetier and the Laitière joining forces and tieing up the Sergent in a bag, beating him up and throwing him down a sewer.

Many other examples of farce could be given, including *Maistre Pathelin* whose originality is perhaps in the use of foreign tongues (ll. 863–68), and we would find other similar examples of the grotesque, but hardly any new ones. All farces seem to have in common a popular grotesque of characters and situations as well as a grotesque of words, and this grotesque is generally at the service of the plot, of comedy, not of satire for satire's sake, but, rather, satire for comedy's sake. In the farce we have an example of a totally free, so-to-speak liberated grotesque, a grotesque which is simply a part of a spectacle and of the interplay between the stage and spectators. The grotesque, in this case, is not the function of something, but something to function. And now we shall conclude, sort of arbitrality, but with the hope of having been fair to the most important aspects of the grotesque in medieval literature, with a study of the grotesque and Villon.

The Grotesque and Villon; Conclusion

Rather than trying to seek out grotesque forms in poetry, in the lyrics of Guillaume IX, for instance, we have chosen to end this essay by an examination of the grotesque in Villon, and that because Villon, in our opinion at least, is supremely a man of the middle ages, a man of transition too and chiefly a man-of-his-times, a poet, sensitive to the multiple grotesque aspects of his life and of life in the fifteenth century. For all these reasons a study of the grotesque in medieval French literature owed itself, we felt, to end with Villon's grotesque.

[74] *Ibid.*, note to line 40, p. 21.

A careful examiner of the historical context of any given period will, in most cases, be able to distinguish sharp oppositions in the reality of life of the period considered. In this respect the end of the middle ages is often offered as example to support such a statement.[75] Behind the superficial order, the formality of ceremonies, of feasts and turneys, the end of the middle ages was largely a period of disorder, not only because of the wars, but because of the erosion of most past social and religious values, because of the proliferation of money and of the decline of moral guidelines. If the *Petit Jehan de Paris* is a magnificent example of the regal excesses of the period, the *Petit Jehan de Saintré* is a better expression yet of the devaluation of all the values so far held sacred during the middle ages. Discussing Villon's times, Italo Siciliano writes:

> Il ne faut pas oublier que ce siècle c'est encore le moyen âge, sombre et grandiose, misérable et fastueux, parfois sublime, presque toujours excessif. Nous devons attendre la Renaissance, ou le classicisme, pour retrouver l'équilibre, la maîtrise, l'harmonie dans la conception et dans la pratique de la vie. Pour le moment, dans ce monde où la violence a troublé et presque détraqué les esprits et les moeurs, c'est l'excès dans toutes les manifestations: dans le crime aussi bien que dans les pratiques pieuses ou dans les réjouissances mondaines.[76]

The man of the fifteenth century, the common man, the peasant, the *petit bourgeois* even, this man we hear so little about but who composed the majority of the population, was, in Siciliano's words, "abruti par la terreur, vexé par ses maîtres, rançonné par les ennemis, massacré par tous, il était comme une pauvre bête traquée, rendue craintive et féroce par la souffrance, enfermée dans une forêt, autour de laquelle rôdaient la frayeur et la mort" (p. 6). Such was the ransom over years of worrying and of the evolution of man's society and therefore of his personality. In the time of Villon the grotesque forms of evil weigh heavily on the land and its people.[77] Now, considering this historical perspective, let us examine the poetical legacy of Villon.

Even a superficial review such as ours will no doubt reveal sublime and grotesque themes interplaying with each other, the seriousness and the irony of life, its smiles and its tears. In Villon both grotesque and sub-

[75] See for instance Huizinga, *The Waning of the Middle Ages*.

[76] Italo Siciliano, *François Villon et les thèmes poétiques du Moyen Age* (Armand Colin, 1934), p. 18.

[77] See Italo Siciliano, pp. 1–198 and his bibliographical references on the literature.

lime join each other to give its meaning to this original and ambiguous poetic adventure that is Villon's poetry. Although many more divisions could be elicited from Villon's rich work, we shall study the presence and nature of the grotesque in only four major areas: Villon the man and his fortune, death, women and love, and the language.

Who the real Villon is we will probably never know, but fortunately we know the poetic Villon of his imagination or of his dreams. From the first lines of the *Testament*[78] to the concluding *Ballade*, Villon paints a grotesque-sublime portrait of himself "Ne du tout fol ne du tout saige" (I, 3), a "povre Villon" (Ballade, 1. 1997) more often miserable and underfed or mistreated than satisfied or happy. He claims to have "maintes peines eues, / Lesquelles j'ay toutes recues / Soubz la main Thibault d'Aucigny. . . ." (I, 4-6), this bishop his enemy who has been so hard on him: "Peu m'a d'une petite miche / Et de froide eaue tout ung esté" (II, 13-14). Later on, in the *Testament* Villon comes back to the meanness of Thibault: "Qui tant d'eaue froide m'a fait boire, / En un bas, non pas en ung hault, / Menger d'angoisse mainte poire, / En-ferré. . . ." (LXXIII, 737-41). Villon is also this wretched creature "Povre de sens et de savoir, / Triste, failly, plus noir que meure, / Qui n'ay ne cens, rente n'avoir" (XXIII, 178-80), and also ". . . triste cueur, ventre affamé / Qui n'est rassasié au tiers. . . ." (XXV, 195, 6). Villon's picture would not be "grotesque" if he did not insist over and over on these traits, but he does, and so from pathetic or pitiful the features become so stressed and emphasized that they turn to the caricatural. Villon insists on his grotesque poverty: "Povreté, chagrine, doulente, / Tousjours, despiteuse et rebelle. . . ." (XXXIV, 269-70) or he says: "Povre je suis de ma jeunesse, / De povre et de peticte extrasse; / Mon pere n'eust oncq grant richesse, / Ne son ayeul nommé Orrace. . . ." (XXXV, 273-76). When Villon turns to his body, the portrait is even more grim, more grotesque. When he leaves his body "A nostre grant mere la terre" (LXXXVI, 842). Villon insists upon the skinniness of his flesh: "Les vers n'y trouveront grant gresse, / Trop lui a fait fain dure guerre" (LXXXVI, 843-44). If he is not dead yet, many grotesque signs of death are upon him: "Je congnois approucher ma seuf, / Je crache blanc comme coton / Jacoppins groz comme ung estuef" (LXXII, 729-31). Later he declares having the voice of an old man though he is still young (LXXII, 735-36) and he feels weak: "Je sens mon cueur qui s'affoiblist / Et plus je ne puis papïer" (LXXIX, 785-86).

[78] Jean Rychner et Albert Henry, eds., *Le Testament de Villon* (Droz, 1974).

This is one aspect of Villon, a wretched carcass abused by himself, by others and by Fortune.[79] In other words, Villon is the prefiguration of death itself which grotesqueness haunts the *Testament* and the *Ballades*.

To Marie "Dame du ciel, regente teriënne" (Ballade, 873), Villon opposes the grotesque forms of death, supreme enemy. Death has taken his love:

> Mort, j'appelle de ta rigueur,
> Qui m'as ma maistresse ravie
> Et n'es pas encore assouvye
> Se tu ne me tiens en langueur. (Lay, 978–81)

Pity overcomes the poet's heart in front of the grotesque of the decaying flesh: "Quant est des corps, ilz sont pourriz, / Aient esté seigneurs ou dames, / Souëf et tendrement nourriz / De cresme, froumentee ou riz, / Et les oz declinent en pouldre, / Ausquels ne chault d'esbat ne riz" (CLXIV, 1761–66). Villon is repugnant to the rotting of the body; he says: "Mieulx vault vivre soubz groz burau / Pouvre, qu'avoir esté seigneur / Et pourrir soubz riche tumbeau" (XXXVI, 286–88). Worse yet, Villon knows that, like all others, he will have to face death one day:

> Je congnois que pouvres et riches
> Sagez et folz, prestres et laiz,
> Nobles, villains, larges et chiches,
> Petiz et grans, et beaulx et laitz,
> Dames a rebrassés colletz,
> De quelconque condicïon,
> Portans atours et bourreletz,
> Mort saist sans exepcïon. (XXXIX, 305–12)

Death is not only grotesque in her putrefaction, but its symptoms are also grotesque in the unavoidable pain:

> Et meure Paris ou Elayne,
> Quicunques meurt meurt a douleur
> Telle qu'il pert vent et alaine,
> Son fiel se criesve sur son cueur,
> Puis sue Dieu scet quel sueur...." (XL, 313–17).

Obviously we don't have to quote here the famous *Ballade des Pendus* to find the obsessive power of death in Villon's poetry.

Old age is perhaps equal to death in Villon's mind; the grotesque of old age assumes as realistic and grotesque forms as death itself:

[79] See Italo Siciliano, pp. 307–11.

Car s'en jeunesse il fut plaisant,
Ores plus riens ne dit qui plaise
—Tousjours viel singe est desplaisant
Moue ne fait qui ne desplaise—;
S'il se taist affin qu'il complaise,
Il est tenu pour fol recreu;
S'il parle, on lui dist qu'il se taise
Et qu'en son prunier n'a pas creu. (XLIV, 429–36)

At times old age will bring the grotesque revenge to the poet:

Ung temps viendra qui fera dessechier,
Jaunir, flestrir vostre espanye fleur;
Je m'en risse, se tant peusse maschier.... (Ballade, 958–60)

Old age also deforms the body, makes it ugly and grotesque; that is, for Villon, "d'humaine beaulté l'yssue" (LV, 517). The complaint of the "belle" who was "heaulmière"[80] abounds in pathetic and grotesque descriptions of the erosion of beauty by time: "Les braz cours et les mains contraictes, / Des espaulles toutes bossues, / Mamelles, quoy? toutes retraictes, / Telles les hanches que les tectes, / Du sadinet, fy! Quant des cuisses, / Cuisses ne sont plus, mais cuissectes / Grivelees comme saulcisses!" (LV, 518–24).

If Villon has sung the sublime women of his life, Marie, his mother and the grotesquely sublime "povre femelettes," he has also sung the grotesque faces of love and of women.[81] To the woman who laughed of his love, Villon has grotesque harsh words:

Ceste ballade luy envoye,
Qui se termine tout par erre.
Qui luy portera? Que je voye ...
Ce sera Pernet de la Barre,
Pourveu, s'il rencontre en son erre
Ma damoiselle au nez tortu,
Il luy dira sans plus enquerre:
"Orde paillarde, dont viens tu?"

Why so much spite? "Car en amours mourut martir" (Ballade, 2001). Such is the answer of Villon.

The grotesque of death, of life, of love and of old age interplay breathlessly throughout the *Testament* and the *Ballades*, but the grotesque of

---

[80] Villon, *Testament, LI–LV*, ll. 485–524.
[81] See *Testament*, XC–XCIII and the *Double Ballade*, ll. 625–64.

language is another important manifestation of the grotesque in Villon's poetic work. The grotesque of Villon's language is surely the most constant and the most subtle form of the grotesque; in the very ambiguity of the terms, of the equivocations and of the multiple meanings lie the originality of Villon the poet.[82] Obscene allusions, puns and *langue verte* abound in Villon's poetry; whether he discusses the "jeu d'asne" (CXLVII, 1566) or tells his friend "Planter me fault autres complans / Et frapper en ung autre coing," Villon knows that he will be understood, at least by those who can read his code. Equivocation is perhaps Villon's best linguistic trick; some are obscene, such as "la dance vient de la pance!" (XXV, 200), and some operate at the syntactic level such as in the *Lais*: "Item, a maistre Ythier Marchant ... / Laisse mon branc d'acier tranchant, / Ou a maistre Jehan le Cornu, / Qui est en gaige detenu ..." (ll. 81–85). At the level of language the sense of caricature is also an important feature of the grotesque.[83] Demarolle[84] points out that Villon is a superb painter of grotesque characters and he quotes the caricatural figure of Cotard as an example: "Comme homme beu qui chancelle et trepigne / L'ay veu souvent, quart il s'alloit couchier, / Et une fois il se feist une bigne, / Bien m'en souvient, a l'estal d'ung bouchier. . . . Tousjours crioit: 'Haro, la gorge m'art!' " (Ballade, 1254–63). The diversity of tones is as great as the variety of themes. Demarolle writes: "La variété de la langue de Villon n'a rien de gratuit; le vocabulaire, le ton s'adaptent admirablement au sujet abordé; bien plus, le poète peut parler ou poitevin, sombrer dans l'obscénité ou jouer sur une équivoque, à travers tant de 'registres divers,' c'est toujours sa voix qu'on aime à reconnaître" (p. 17). Villon, in his complexity, offers us a large number of examples of the different levels of the grotesque which is so much of the human and poetic experience.

Although we arbitrarily end our study of the grotesque in medieval French literature here, and may be accused of formidable omissions, it seems appropriate to end this study with Villon for he offers the best synthesis of the different nature, aspects, uses and meanings of the grotesque as we met them in our survey of literature from the eleventh to the fifteenth century. We found a grotesque at the service of the sublime and a grotesque which functioned for the sake of irony, of parody, of cari-

---

[82] Pierre Demarolle, *L'Esprit de Villon* (Paris: Nizet, 1968); *Villon, Testament ambigu* (Librairie Larousse, 1973).

[83] See Fernand Desonay, *L'Art de la Caricature dans le Testament de Villon.*

[84] Pierre Demarolle, *L'Esprit de Villon*, p. 68; pp. 69–71.

cature and, at times, for the sake of ambiguity itself. In the last analysis we may say to have reached the top of the mountain of the grotesque, but it remains to be conquered over and over, again and again. This essay has revealed the grotesque as a multiple-faced function of literature, always changing from genre to genre, from text to text, from paragraph to paragraph. What then is the grotesque? Certainly not a thing to be defined; it is an aesthetic experience to be grasped in motion, in the *mouvant* of life and literature. We hope that our study was quick enough to have enabled us to catch some valid glimpses of this fugitive but so important factor of literature.

Dante: Comedy and Conversion

Howard H. Schless
Columbia University

Behind all studies of comedy, but especially behind studies of medieval comedy, there rises the awesome majesty of *The Comedy, La Commedia,* of Dante.[1] Those who write on comedy have been inclined to look at the genre in such a way that *The Comedy* obstructs their view as little as possible and, when it does, they refer to *The Divine Comedy*, with the stress on *Divine*, a stress that seems somehow to remove the work— through beatification and Assumption—quite beyond all previous or pertinent discourse.

In many ways, one sympathizes. The poem has a sublimity, a massiveness, a didacticism and a power so formidable that the boldest non-*dantesco* critic might well be excused for recalling the fate of other well-meaning Uzzahs who dared put forth a hand and touch the ark. Yet, no matter how understandable such trepidation might be, *The Comedy* must be fully considered in any discussion of the genre. But how can one discuss comedy when one may well feel, on the one hand, oppressed by the torments of Hell, or, on the other, forced to elevation by the weighty theology of Heaven? Whether we feel that it will be crushed by the density of evil or left behind by the rapture of an "o altitudo," comedy seems almost destined to be an obscenity when one enters the actual verses of the poem.

Dante, we know, clearly saw his work as a comedy, and his reasons help us approach the topic. In the dedicatory letter to Can Grande della Scala, Dante explains his title:

[1] *The Comedy* is, as I shall shortly emphasize, Dante's title. This is no *humilitas* topos but rather an elevation on the word *comedy*. As Auerbach points out, Dante, in the poem itself, speaks of his work "by a new term of his own coining as 'the sacred poem,' *il poema sacro* or *lo sacrato poema* or simply as 'the vision.'" Eric Auerbach, *Dante: Poet of the Secular World*, trans. Ralph Mannheim (Chicago: University of Chicago, 1961), p. 92. Auerbach's references are to Par. xxv, 1; xxiii, 62; xvii, 128. The word "divine" was added by an unknown editor in 1555.

The title of the book is "Here beginneth the Comedy of Dante Alighieri, a Florentine by birth, but not by character." And for the comprehension of this it must be understood that the word "comedy" is derived from κωμη, *village,* and ωδή which meaneth *song*; hence comedy is, as it were, a *village song.*[2]

After briefly contrasting comedy with (Senecan) tragedy, he states:

> Comedy, indeed, beginneth with some adverse circumstances, but its theme hath a happy termination, as doth appear in the comedies of Terence. . . . Likewise [Comedy and Tragedy] differ in their style of language, for Tragedy is lofty and sublime, Comedy, mild and humble. . . .

Then, having cited Horace's *Ars Poetica,* 93–95, he looks specifically at his own poem:

> From this it is evident why the present work is called a comedy. For if we consider the theme, in its beginning it is horrible and foul, because it is Hell; in its ending, fortunate, desirable and joyful, because it is Paradise; and if we consider the style of the language, the style is careless and humble [remissus et humilis], because it is the vulgar tongue, in which even housewives converse.

For Dante, therefore, comedy is the movement from disaccord to accord, from the discordant shrieks of individual sinners in Hell to the harmonic expression of the choirs of Heaven.

The *entire* work, it must be emphasized, is to be seen as a comedy. Dante is quite explicit when he concludes, three paragraphs later, "For if the title of the book is: Here beginneth the Comedy, etc., as above, the title of this [third] part will be: Here beginneth the Third Canticle of the Comedy of Dante, which is called Paradise." By implication, we may posit the line: Here beginneth the First Canticle of the Comedy of Dante, which is called the Inferno.

In what way can we consider the Inferno comedic? In the whole work (which is what Dante had been discussing), it serves of course as the "horrible and foul" point of departure of a vector which ends in the "desirable and joyful." But in the essential movement of comedy from discord to accord, in what way does that initial point, the discord, manifest the comic? Are we in fact so obscene as first appears if we consider the Inferno an example, indeed a masterly example, of the genre of comedy

[2] I am here using the standard translation of Charles S. Latham (*Dante's Eleven Letters*) conveniently given in the still useful work by Charles A. Dinsmore, *Aids to the Study of Dante* (Houghton Mifflin, 1903), pp. 262–86; esp. 269–71.

136

in the Middle Ages, if we consider it a canticle that is for Dante as much a part of *The Comedy* as any other?

Though they may be obvious to many, two sets of distinctions must be set forth and discussed at the start. First, we must distinguish between risible comedy (i.e., that which is intentionally comic or unintentionally comical) and high comedy (which, for purposes of this essay, is that which, in attaining comedic harmony, instructs).[3] Secondly, we must keep in mind Eliot's distinction between belief and assent, which seems to me to be essential to any inquiry.[4] Professor Freccero has ably summarized this:

> Eliot suggested that we distinguish the philosophical "belief" necessary for the writing of the poem from the poetic "assent" necessary for an understanding of it. While we are reading the poem, we give momentary assent to the poet's belief in the same way we give momentary assent to the reality of the journey. The broader question of belief or disbelief simply does not rise in a strictly "literary appreciation."[5]

This idea, which Eliot refined and expanded, is essential since any discussion of comedy in the Inferno depends on our poetic assent to Dante's beliefs.

Let us return to our first set of distinctions. Both forms of comedy— risible comedy and high comedy—would seem to work on the same general assumption; that is to say, the genre of comedy (like the genre of epic) depends on an accepted social context, or norm, for its success. This norm, in a literary work, is the ethic or pattern of behavior that author and audience decide is acceptable; the distance beyond this norm constitutes the degree of contrast, the discord, that comedy seeks to reduce in order to achieve harmony or accord. But we must constantly remind ourselves that the distance from the norm may be measured in at least two directions, for though we are most often struck by the gap

[3] We are close, of course, to Baudelaire's distinction between laughter and joy, a distinction that, for *The Comedy*, fails only at the critical moment, that is, when we must move from one plane of understanding to another. The 1855 essay "On the Essence of Laughter," as pertinent as ever, states: "Joy is a unity. Laughter is the expression of a double, or contradictory, feeling; and that is why a convulsion occurs." I am here using the translation of Jonathan Mayne, *The Mirror of Art*, 1955, reprinted in the excellent essay collection *Comedy: Meaning and Form*, ed. Robert W. Corrigan (Scranton [Pa.]: Chandler, 1965), p. 457.

[4] T. S. Eliot, *Selected Essays, 1917–1932* (New York: Harcourt Brace, 1932), pp. 199–237; esp. pp. 218ff.

[5] *Dante: A Collection of Critical Essays*, ed. John Freccero (Englewood Cliffs: Prentice-Hall, 1965), "Introduction," p. 2.

between the Seems and the Is (taking the latter to be the operative norm), there is also the gap between the Is and the Ought-to-be. It is in this framework that I wish to enlarge somewhat upon the distinctions between the two types of comedy: risible or corrective, and utopic or instructive.

In the first, a negative condition is brought up to an accepted norm; in the second, a positive depiction extends the norm to new bounds. Both, so to speak, end in accord or harmony, though these may prove to be of quite different tone since the one kind of accord may come from a sense of fear or shame (There but for the grace of God go I/we), while the other may come from a sense of conviction or common longing (If only I/We could attain such a state). Using a metaphor that is perhaps too unrefined, let us imagine a vector going from area A to area B to area C. Here, B is the norm, that area of agreement where the reader accepts in his own fashion what the author promulgates as his criteria. The course of risible or corrective comedy is to pass through the area of A until it achieves the norm; in the process, the world of area A is progressively rejected or corrected, while the ethical or societal norm of B is progressively accepted. In utopic or instructive comedy, on the other hand, there is a comparison of the societal norm of B with the area C, a logical or idealized extension of what B sought to deal with in practice. To cite (for example) Molière or More as instances of the two sorts of comedy would not be incorrect but it would not fully explain the complexity that *The Comedy* presents. While it is true that in the Inferno and the Paradiso Dante is using the two patterns of comparison, he does so (as we shall see) with a brilliant development that makes them a part of the didactic plan of the entire work and extends our idea of the comedic beyond anything previously encountered.

So again we confront our initial question: what is there that is comic about the persons or the situations that one finds in Hell? When we move to the specifics of the poem, how are we, for example, to approach a Paolo and Francesca, the two lovers who are whirled eternally by the winds of lust for so brief an embrace? Or again, how do we respond, and how are we meant to respond, to the daring of a Ulysses? Or, what makes Dante's treatment of Fra Alberigo no more "obscene" than our suggestion that the reader of Dante's poem, *The Comedy*, must never lose the essential idea of comedy.

Admittedly, this idea of comedy is a difficult one to sustain since we, as readers, sympathize deeply for those sinners whose humanity Dante so feelingly depicts. To sustain the idea of comedy, the reader must first admit the justice of the judgment rendered against the sinners, for not until then can he possibly view the sinner as the object of comedy. Every reader is torn—as Dante wished him to be and as Dante himself must have been—now by a sense of sympathy, now by a sense of justice; and since we are loathe to doubt our sympathies, we question the justice, its lack of forgiveness and mercy for what appear to be single moments of understandable error. Dante, however, was certainly not being frivolous; the tensions, anxieties and doubts that we feel, we feel through him and because he wishes us to feel them. The path to their resolution has (as so often) been pointed to by Auerbach:

> Thus Dante undertook to portray the human beings that appear in the *Comedy* in the time and place of their perfect actuality, or in modern terms in the time and place of their ultimate self-realization, where their essence is fulfilled and made manifest forever.[6]

Paolo and Francesca are not put eternally in Hell for that one impassioned embrace, that particular lapse of morality. What is important for them and for all those found in Dante's poem is not the particular act *in se* but rather the single act as representative of their lives. In it, they "represent the sum of themselves. . . . they . . . disclose in a single act the character and the fate that had filled out their lives."[7] In order for comedy to function, we must have the sense that the justice which has placed the various sinners in Hell at least balances our sense of sympathy for them. And Dante counterpoises superbly the two forces: our human and emotional side which can identify with these tragic failures; our spiritual and intellectual side which can regard them as ludicrously obstinate.

We can perhaps begin to see the emergence of a comic pattern. Joseph Mazzeo has inadvertently given us a start in his extraordinarily perceptive essay on "Dante's Three Communities." After discussing how Dante has shaped his Hell as "a moral category," he states:

> All of the damned chose something less than the infinite and they get in return the finite eternalized. In other words, they are stuck with themselves for all time, confined to the circle of self by a final definition which compels them to repeat their sins and perpetuate their identities forever.[8]

[6] Auerbach, *Dante*, p. 90.
[7] *Ibid.*, p. 91.
[8] Joseph A. Mazzeo, "Dante's Three Communities: Mediation and Order" in *The World of Dante*, ed. S. B. Chandler and J. A. Molinaro (Toronto: University of Toronto Press, 1966), pp. 71–72.

This pattern of repetition is the very essence of Hell's operation; it is a pattern which in the realm of risible comedy is immediately recognizable: the repetitious, jack-in-the-box response that Bergson saw as a primary example of "something mechanical encrusted upon the living."[9] While we are obviously not in the realm of Bergson's risible comedy, we are faced with the same pattern in the high comedy of Dante's *Comedy*, with the sinners re-acting ludicrously throughout eternity their myopic mischoice, like some village ignoramus continually opting for the glittering bauble. Deeper investigation of Dante's use of this pattern reveals certain intriguing aspects of both the poem and the genre that are not otherwise so apparent.

In contrasting the pattern of repetition in risible comedy and in Dante, the word "living" ("something mechanical encrusted upon the living") stands out immediately. Understandably, writers concerned with risible comedy try to insist that "the comic does not exist outside the pale of what is strictly human";[10] as always, however, *The Comedy* presents us with a far more complex situation. While in the most limited sense of the word there is only one "living" character in the work (namely Dante himself), such precision is more of a technicality than an actuality. Years ago, in writing about the "Transfiguration of Beatrice," Etienne Gilson remarked that there was in fact not one dead person in the whole poem, that they were all "vivants," living beings who responded vitally.[11] For Dante, those in the Inferno were vital people, people who endlessly act out their self-elected punishment. They were real for him and they are very real for us by virtue of the very pattern of repetition which they undergo. Now, in risible comedy, such a pattern often creates a target character whom we view at a distance and almost as a caricature. In Dante, however, our alliance with the target characters is very close, for they are persons (mostly historical) who do not come from some

[9] Henri Bergson, "Laughter," trans. Fred Rothwell in *Comedy*, ed. Wylie Sypher (New York: Doubleday, 1956), pp. 61–190.

[10] *Ibid.*, p. 62. See also, among many others, Baudelaire, who concludes Section V with: "The comic can only be absolute in relation to fallen humanity, and it is in this way that I am understanding it." (*Comedy*, ed. Corrigan, p. 458.)

[11] Etienne Gilson, *Dante et la Philosophie* (Paris: Vrin, 1939), p. 72. "Si le poème sacré vit encore, c'est que son créateur ne l'a peuplé que de vivants. Lui-même, d'abord, par une décision unique que jamais aucun poète n'avait osé prendre ni n'a jamais reprise. Tous les autres ensuite, car non seulement tous les personnages qui s'y meuvent ont vécu dans l'histoire ou dans la légende, mais ils y vivent plus intensement que jamais, dans leur essence propre telle que la manifeste enfin l'inflexible loi de la justice divine."

parodied world "out there"; they come as fellow humans, representatives of our common humanity, from the world as we know it, from the very world which gives us the norm of social behavior that we referred to earlier. In brief, we are being whipsawed between the conventions of risible comedy and the new uses to which Dante's high comedy puts those conventions: the very world that should supply us with the norm needed to judge the targets of comedy has supplied us instead with the target characters.

We are, then, in a situation that pulls us both ways. We associate ourselves with the sinners through pathos, through common humanity, through familiarity with their temptations, and even through a kind of *Schadenfreude*. But with at least equal force, we seek not only to *dis*sociate ourselves because they are spiritually sinners who are being so endlessly punished (indeed, these reasons often inspire sympathy and even indignation), but as well we wish to dissociate ourselves from the endless and absurd and futile commission of sins that make the sinners mere automata, no matter how understandable the reasons for their actions might be for us. We sense, through the pattern of repetition, that they are quite rightly the targets of comedy, and we therefore wish not to align ourselves with the objects of this comedy. We can overcome our sympathies and dissociate ourselves only if we recognize that the whole comic relationship must be shifted up one entire step when we read Dante; in other words, where conventional risible comedy sets an accepted social norm in order to look down and judge the aberrants from that norm, Dante's high comedy assumes an eternal universal norm in order to look down and judge those of this world who found their ultimate self-realization in the finite. Once we make this quantum shift, once we begin to accept a God's-eye view (the only view that allows for Dante's beliefs), then the foolishness, even the oafishness, of the sinners' choice, as well as their absurdity in wishing to reassert that choice eternally (like the idiot always choosing the bauble), turns the actions depicted in the Inferno into comedy *sub specie aeternatatis*. But the shift is not without its consequences. Our sympathies and our humanity now become all too understandable; Dante has evoked them with unremitting purpose. In the Inferno, after all, sins are depicted not as immediately repulsive and frightening to the ordinary person; rather they are presented to the reader as a choice still to be made by him, attractive to the degree that we accept the standards of this finite world, and derisible to the degree that we assume an eternal norm. Once we have chosen rightly, once we begin to assume that higher norm, we can look down onto the absurdity, the comic absurdity, of this world with its (and our) human follies endlessly repeating, like some small bug endlessly gathering, or endlessly climbing up some glass bowl. In *The Comedy*, we may not laugh, but, like Chaucer's Troilus, we are able to look down upon "this litel spot of erthe"and smile.

Dante, then, has accomplished a major part of his pedagogic task when he maneuvers the reader into the position of seeing the ludicrousness of sin; he has forced the reader out of his understandable but finite norm and towards a higher ethic, one that derives from the super-human, the super-natural. Seen this way, the poem is the pedagogy; the very pattern of comedy serves to educate, to lead forth, the reader. Dante is attempting to gradually mold assent into belief, to have a change in degree become a change in kind, in short, to have us acknowledge as a general thesis what we have already accepted as the basis of his high comedy. It is a process that can be seen, vastly reduced, in risible comedy's ethnic joke where, in "getting" the joke—be it anti-Polish, anti-black, anti-Semitic, or whatever—we are accepting, for the length of the joke at least, the morality that it entails. Somewhat analogously, the reader who accepts the high comedy of the Inferno accepts also personal, philosophical consequences that are as enduring as they are difficult. Thus, we may stretch our human sympathy extraordinarily in order to be on the side of those who see the absurdity of the sinners; but Dante does not stop there. He seems to want to push us on to ever more difficult testing, and he does so perhaps most dramatically in what we, according to our human nature, see as his gratuitous insensitivity towards Fra Alberigo. Human nature and universal justice here seem in a stark confrontation which to a degree we have been prepared for by our continued acceptance of the norms of Dante's high comedy, norms of such universal magnitude that sinners seem to dwindle into obstinate ants by what becomes virtually a ludicrous comparison.

In fact, the decision on whether to align ourselves with fallible man or with divine justice is an agonizing one in that we can no longer retain our unmodified anonymity of "reader" but are directly engaged as the *individual* reader by Dante. The difference can perhaps be demonstrated by looking again at risible and at high comedy. In risible comedy, where the center and norm are primarily societal, we align ourselves relatively easily with the group and condemn with laughter those who vary from approved social patterns.[12] In *The Comedy*, however, the center is not primarily society but the Self, the individual reader who must undergo the spiritual growing pains that allow him to establish a distance between himself and his sinful world. For the individual reader following a step behind Dante, each one of those steps is painful as it is salvific; but being salvific, the journey constitutes the very essence of high comedy: a move from eternal discord to eternal accord. *The Comedy*, then, has as its primary object the reader and not the reader's society in that he is confronted with painful decisions about it. The new order that crystallizes around the hero in most social comedy[13] here centers on the "new" universe of the "new man," properly the individual reader of *The Comedy*. This regeneration and salvation of the self (and not of society) begets the universal accord at the end of the poem, but to achieve it fully the individual reader will have had to reject his societal and even human standards for God's standards. At that point the reader may well appear absurd to the ordinary (discordant, unregenerated, "old") man if only because he has achieved ultimate accord. Actually, he can now see the two extremes of comedy: at one end, that which he fled, the low comedy of man repeating endlessly and willfully his particular ethical or theological pratfalls; at the other end, that which he seeks, the high comedy of accord and delight.

In the movement from low to high comedy, the laughter and ridicule of risible comedy give way to joy and comprehension, just as the triumph of youth over age gives way to the triumph of the New Man over the Old, and just as Eros[14] gives way to Amor. The fundamental patterns of comedy remain though we have shifted the relationship up one whole stage, that is, from the accepted social world looking at the discordant individual or type, to the accepted individual looking at the sinful representatives of the discordant social world. *The Comedy* works across the whole range of the comedic genre, never really leaving it but rather using its more familiar forms to achieve astonishing ends. Yet, in considering

[12] Bergson underlines the necessity of *"social* significance," as do most writers on the genre (Bergson, *loc. cit.*, p. 65).

[13] Northrop Frye, *Anatomy of Criticism* (Princeton: Princeton University Press, 1957), p. 163.

[14] *Ibid.*, p. 181: "The presiding genius of comedy is Eros, and Eros has to adapt himself to the moral facts of society." For Dante, Amor is the final statement: "l'amor che move il sole e l'altre stelle" (the Love [i.e., God] that moves the sun and the other stars, Par. xxxiii, 145.)

[15] *Ibid.*, p. 185.

the genre, even so insightful a critic as Northrop Frye seems to elevate Dante out of a discussion that is otherwise highly evocative:

> In the fifth [phase of comedy, society] is part of a settled order which has been there from the beginning, an order which takes on an increasingly religious cast and seems to be drawing away from human experience altogether. At this point the undisplaced *commedia*, the vision of Dante's *Paradiso*, moves out of our circle of *mythoi* into the apocalyptic or abstract mythical world above it. At this point we realize that the crudest of Plautine comedy-formulas has much the same *structure* as the central Christian myth itself, with its divine son appeasing the wrath of a father and redeeming what is at once a society and a bride.[15]

But only if the critic has rigorously and arbitrarily limited the genre can he assert that "at this point, the undisplaced *commedia*, the vision of Dante's *Paradiso*, moves out of our circle of *mythoi* into the apocalyptic." Restrictions of this kind mean that our understanding of the genre of comedy will be crippled from the start, for they ask us to exclude, at one end, the depths of discord in which comedy can begin, and, at the other, the heights of accord in which it can end. Thus limited, the study of the genre will, not surprizingly, concentrate on social and risible comedy; but in so doing it will be in danger of ignoring the universal and instructive possibilities that certain writers, Dante not the least among them, seek to achieve through the genre.

Even putting aside the general movement from discord to accord, comedy (in its larger sense) is the natural genre for conveying certain major statements of religion. The almost breath-taking disproportion that exists between the grandeur of God's plan and the inadequacy of the human agent who wittingly or unwittingly makes manifest that plan is a prime example of one of comedy's most enduring formulae, that of disparity or incongruity—the dwarf and the giant's robe. In the realm of religious literature, this radical difference can be set forth in two ways: either the writer can show how self-proclaimed giants are in the end proven to be dwarfs, or he can show how self-proclaimed dwarfs are in the end proven to be giants. In the first instance, we have the Dantean sinner whose "ultimate self-realization" proves ludicrously inadequate to eternal fulfillment; in the second instance, we have, typically, Biblical figures such as Joseph or Noah in certain medieval dramas,[16] or Jonah in

---

16 See V. A. Kolve, *The Play Called Corpus Christi*, Edward Arnold, 1966; also Rosemary Woolf, *The English Mystery Plays* (Berkeley: University of California Press, 1972); also Howard Schless, "The Comic Element in the Wakefield *Noah*,"

Patience, figures of almost desperate ordinariness. The historical figure in Dante and the Biblical figure in *Patience* must be seen against the background in which they are set, for they demand, in a sense, opposite emphases the understanding of which may give us further insight into this realm of comedy.

Let us look at the latter first. In *Patience*, where the central figure is archetypal and from the meta-history of the Bible, the author attains comic disparity by imbuing Jonah with actual-ness, by localizing time and place, and by reducing to the quotidian. Jonah's common, almost peasant, sense, makes strikingly real for us a character of comic vitality who yet avoids, even in the woodbine scene, the ridiculous. We are, at the same time, aware that the God of this poem is not a wordless presence perceived through metaphor, but rather he is the patient Father, dignified, waiting for the almost child-like Jonah to understand both His words and His deeds. This translation of the Biblical material from meta-history to very human history underlines the comic disparity that exists between the extraordinariness of the events that take place in the poem and the ordinariness of Jonah, the prophet-in-spite-of-himself.

Poems such as *Patience* attain a disparity by creating a sense of time-ness. Dante's poem, with its bold and innovative use of actual historical figures, achieves its disparity by creating for those figures a context of timelessness. Yet this disparity seems to us today as somehow dulled, and for a reason that is as evident as it is ironic. For the modern reader, the contrast of historical figure to timeless background has lost much of the sharp and shocking effect that it first had. With the passage of time, Brunetto Latini, Paolo and Francesca, Ugolino and all the other "living beings" that people the poem, have become for us mere names, bereft of all the emotion they once evoked, anaesthetized in footnotes. Having lost, over the intervening years, their time-ness, their urgency, they have increasingly taken on the coloration of the timeless background into which Dante had set them, with the result that the original disparity, both in degree and in immediacy, no longer strikes us. It may not be too unjust to attempt to recreate some sense of that disparity by the admittedly imprecise substitution of more recent "living beings." If we were to find at the appropriate levels of an "updated" *Comedy* names such as W. H. Auden, or the Duke of Windsor, or Pope Pius, or Lyndon Johnson, or J. Paul Getty, the sudden conversion of the specific person into the representational figure, and of the particular event into universal in *Studies in Medieval Literature*, ed. MacEdward Leach (Philadelphia: University of Pennsylvania Press, 1961).

history, might suggest, however ineptly, the degree of disparity of the original *Comedy*. In effect, we would be poetically asserting on the one hand that these are men who thought they had found "their ultimate self-realization," and on the other that they are men whose very particularity, whose very familiarity, causes them to be all the more swiftly and devastatingly reduced to absurdity when they are set against an eternal schema. To show the eternal foolishness of some particular sin is one thing; but to use (for example) your local politician, by name and specific event, as its everlasting embodiment, is to create an incongruity that is quite another thing.

If we look at Dante's use of historical figures and his setting for them, we can see that he was, in effect, reversing the approach of allegory, the major mode of poetry of the Middle Ages. Dante depicted realistically a particular person of history and set him in a totally allegorical setting. Obviously we cannot go into the complex subject of allegory in any depth, if only because there often seem to be as many varieties of allegory as there are allegorists; still, a comparison of Dante with a fine allegorist such as Langland will allow us to see some of the poetic implications of his comedy. Langland (and other allegorists) are able to deal with an abstract characteristic by making a person of (i.e., personifying) that characteristic and then speaking about it in human words and phrases. Langland's genius in this can be seen in his brilliant tour-de-force on the seven deadly sins, where he moves from simple one-for-one equivalence virtually devoid of any ambiance, through ever more realistic settings, to the point where we find Gluttony in the brawling, stinking, noisy tavern finally getting so drunk that he pukes into someone's lap—"coughed up a caudle" says Langland—and, after a snoring sleep, goes staggering home with a monumental hangover and a firm resolve to head for church next time. He is a personification, a "majuscule" (to use Gilson's derisory term), but the whole passage is so close to realistic writing by virtue of the background into which he is set that, given a local habitation and a name—the Boar's Head Tavern and Sir John Falstaff—he would virtually be a *symbol* of gluttony. Langland, then, is an excellent example of those who moved allegory from the internal to the external world in his vital depiction of the events of his poem. The background and setting of these events is no longer the realm of conflicting abstractions but rather it is the actual daily life of the England of his day. He has surrounded his personifications with (to use Gilson's phrase for Dante's innovation) "living beings."

Dante's technique to a great extent reverses Langland's pattern. Dante takes a living being, one who is for the poet representative of a particular vice or virtue, and puts him into a totally allegorical background. Paolo and Francesca are in a realm that is lust, not simply by assertion but by the radiation of descriptive setting. The historically real Paolo and Francesca come to represent, symbolize, their vice not by being set into the actual, daily life of Italy, but by existing in an abstract realm informed by that characteristic they embody. As Langland's abstract personification Gluttony fulfills all gluttony and triumphs poetically by its realistic background, so Dante's very real historical persons embody, represent, symbolize, a characteristic and triumph over their particularity by the background of timeless abstraction into which they are set. Langland and Dante seem to come from opposite directions and yet to meet at some meridian of comedic genius. The disparity that they achieve between figure and background creates an artistic incongruity that the reader can only resolve by understanding fully the complex nature of what is being depicted.

Dante the pilgrim is of course the most pervasive example of Dante the poet's technique, for Dante the pilgrim has as his background the entire poem, from Inferno to final vision, and therefore his "setting' 'is that of human salvation, from the discord of original sin to the harmony of regeneration. Or perhaps it is better to say that he and his journey represent the change in degree that becomes a change in kind, in the very nature of being, becoming increasingly purified until, at the end, disparity is resolved in the absolute, and discord or doubt no longer exist. The symbol (Dante) and his setting (the pure Empyrean) become consonant and in accord. In terms of our discussion of comedy, the final vision and the final verse—L'amor che move il sole e l'altre stelle—come like the punch line of some universal joke, incapable of being topped, an ultimate assertion of unity not only between Dante and his vision but also between Dante and his ideal reader at this moment when poetic assent gives way to Christian belief. Through antipathy and through longing, comedy has led to spiritual regeneration.

If the language of the foregoing paragraph seems assertive, it is responding to the declarative nature of the poem itself. Only when we contrast *The Comedy* with the *visio* literature of the time do we see how bold Dante was from a theological point of view. He did not claim that he saw Hell, Purgatory and Heaven in a dream; he wrote the whole of *The Comedy* without evasion or equivocation. Now, how, for example, could

Dante mount through the crystalline spheres of the universe unless he had—that is to say, poetically assumed for himself—divine sanction which purified his earthly being to the point where he was capable of that final ecstatic vision?

When we turn for contrast to outstanding examples of *visio* literature of the more traditional sort—works such as *Piers* or *Pearl*—we find an interesting difference in tone and direction. Here, in *Piers* or *Pearl*, the poem is set out as a dream not as actuality, and the journey tends much more to come from the inner space of vision than the external space of the universe. Here, the movement is circular, a return to this world emphasized by the wakening of the dreamer or the repetition of the opening line. Here the poem, for all its brilliance, its pathos, its easier availability and its humanity, fails to achieve that level of certain accord that is *The Comedy's* unique and most challenging assumption. *Pearl* and even *Piers* exhibit each a spiritual way of life that we should seek to imitate in this world if we are to hope for grace and salvation. *The Comedy*, for all its historicity, is not so much concerned with this world as the next. The journey is in itself an indication of grace, and the final vision a mark of salvation. Dante takes a straight line from sin to salvation, from this region of spiritual death to the region of spiritual life. Wylie Sypher in discussing "Ancient Rites of Comedy," makes the extraordinarily penetrating observation that "Comedy is essentially a Carrying Away of Death, a triumph over mortality by some absurd faith in rebirth, restoration and salvation."[17] Here he is not speaking of Dante's poem but rather of what would seem at first to be its opposite, the Saturnalian aspect of comedy.

The pertinence of Sypher's seemingly impertinent remark is a good example of the importance of *The Comedy* in any study of the genre, and of the importance of the genre in any study of *The Comedy*. In the first case, Dante's work has too often been passed by with all but silent awe, elevated out of sight, and finally rejected, perhaps because it is one of those special works which demand that the individual reader immediately and directly experience the work. Yet the liberation of comedy from its present limits of social correction or human folly depends upon our willingness to see the comedic transformation that takes place in works that look not only to the discordant folly of this world but to the harmony of the next, that develop, in short, the attractive power of

[17] Sypher's essay, generally titled "The Meanings of Comedy," is appended to *Comedy*, ed. Sypher; the reference here is to p. 220.

comedy. In the second case, the importance of the genre in any study of *The Comedy* has, it is hoped, been looked to (however cursorily) in the present essay. In the Inferno, patterns of repetition become a ludicrous recidivism, comic disproportion is seen as the "great man" diminished to a pathetic bug *sub specie aeternatatis*, Bergson's "reciprocal interference of series"[18] adumbrates the cosmic irony,[19] and one could go on listing from conventional studies of the genre, a whole series of devices the application of which illuminate our understanding of *The Comedy*. Probably none is so important, however, as the "shifting up" of the reader, that movement whereby he detaches himself from the pathetic sinners and aligns himself with a higher eternal view that makes clear the sinners' petty absurdity. And one is reminded, as Sypher reminds us in another context, of Kierkegaard's remark: "The religious individual has as such made the discovery of the comical in largest measure."[20]

[18] Bergson, *loc. cit.*, p. 123.

[19] The term is perceptively investigated by D. C. Meucke in *Irony*, Methuen *Critical Idiom Series* (London, 1971).

[20] Sypher is discussing "The Guises of the Comic Hero" in his appended essay in *Comedy*, ed. Sypher, p. 234.

Comic Modalities in the *Decameron*

Marga Cottino-Jones
University of California

In its compositional structure, the *Decameron* fits a traditional definition of comedy—one which Boccaccio could have found, most notably,
in Dante. For example, the latter wrote to Can Grande della Scala that:

> comedia vero inchoat asperitatem alicuius rei, sed eius materia prospere
> terminatur . . . in modo loquendi . . . comedia vero remisse et humiliter;

and more precisely still:

> si ad materiam respiciamus, a principio horribilis et fetida est . . . in fine
> prospera, desiderabilis et grata . . .; ad modum loquendi, remissus est modus
> et humilis, quia locutio vulgaris in qua et muliercule comunicant—*Epistola*
> xiii, 10.

The *Decameron* corresponds to this twofold formula on both counts. As
to the development of its *materia,* one can trace a movement in overall
human terms from a negative, sordid beginning to a positive, dignified
end. The work opens with a view of an unhappy, chaotic, and corrupted
world. This view is projected through an account of the Black Plague
which ravaged the author's city in 1348, and is carried forth through the
novelle of the First Day as well. The first of these presents the apotheosis
of "il piggiore uomo . . . che mai nascesse" (I, 1, 15),[1] Ser Ciappelletto,
and those which follow also deal with sinners and their sins. The *novelle*
of the next nine days—ninety stories portraying all manner of relations
between individuals and social groups—gradually suggest more balanced
forms of life. The Tenth Day crowns the work with a set of *novelle*
which rise progressively towards a perfected form of behavior, nobler
forms of conduct, until, in the last, is presented the character of Griselda
as a paragon of perfected womanhood. As to *modus loquendi,* the cor-

---

[1] All quotations from the *Decameron* in the text are from the V. Branca edition
(Firenze: Le Monnier, 1965).

respondence is no less neat. Boccaccio declares his novelle "non solamente in fiorentin volgare e in prosa scritte . . . sono e senza titolo, ma ancora in istilo *umilissimo* e *rimesso*" (IV, Intro., 3, emphasis mine), echoing Dante in his very choice of adjectives. Furthermore, Boccaccio has dedicated his work to "women in love" and thus it must be written, just as for Dante's *muliercule*, in the vernacular: ". . . perciò che nè ad Atene, nè a Bologna, o a Parigi alcuna di voi non va a studiare, più distesamente parlar vi si conviene che a quegli che hanno negli studi gl'ingegni assottigliati" (Concl. dell'autore, 21). Therefore, both by its general structure and by its author's direct avowal, the *Decameron* hews to an important Trecento view of comedy.

On the other hand, these basic features do not result in any single, unvarying comic tone, since the shifting narrative perspective offered by the different narrators make for a highly complex comic atmosphere. It is necessary to speak of narrators in the plural inasmuch as we are faced with (1) a first person Narrator (henceforth designated with a capital N) who comes forth in the Preface, in the Introduction to the Fourth Day, and in the general Conclusion, to stress the "written" quality of the work for which he is consciously responsible; and (2) ten other narrators, the party of storytellers, who "orally" recount the stories to each other and discuss them, thereby participating as characters in the fictional "frame" of the work, that is, in the narration that flows around the novelle. The juxtaposition and interplay of these narrative voices give the work ironic dimensions which complicate and enrich its comedy. A few examples should suffice to illustrate how the narrative strata are built up. In his Preface, the Narrator dedicates the present written version of the novelle, together with the account of the events occurring in the frame, to women in love, (who are) in need of consolation and distraction, with the express intention of providing them with "diletto . . . e utile consiglio" (Preface, 14). The intent of the ten storytellers in orally narrating to each other the one hundred novelle is somewhat different. They appear at the end of the Introduction to the First Day and represent a group of well-born young women and gallants who decide to flee the plague-ridden city, with its social chaos and moral decay, and retire to the country in order to recreate a balanced, civil society. They base their decision on the fundamental organic need for life and health, coupled with the more particularly human craving for happiness and order (see Intro., 93ff). It is in answer to this latter need that they choose to occupy themselves with an exchange of stories: their *novellare* will be a social art whereby "dicendo

uno, a tutta la compagnia che ascolta [porgerà] diletto" (Intro., 111).
Mutual pleasure and delight (*diletto*), however, is their only explicit
goal, which contrasts with the narrator's broader purpose to give "utile
consiglio" as well as "diletto." Thus, from the very outset, two levels of
consciousness and intentionality are juxtaposed. They are held in tandem
throughout the work by the constant superposition of the written form
over the oral, as well as by the recurrent entry of the Narrator's voice
over the storytellers'. Subtler to perceive, but analogous in effect, is the
superposition or infringement of the Narrator's audience or "narratees"[2]
on his storytellers' narratees. That is, Boccaccio's "women in love" come
to overlay momentarily the "onesta brigata"—each storyteller's immediate listeners. This brief touch or interfacing of narrative voices through
narratees is palpable in the addresses which open almost all the novelle.[3]
Each storyteller before commencing his or her novella proper addresses
his or her narratees. The more frequent formulae of address are "carissime donne" (eleven times), "piacevoli donne" (nine times), "valorose
donne" (eight times), and "amorose donne" (seven times).[4] Yet the
brigata counts three men along with its seven women, and therefore requires an ambigeneric address. One can only conclude that the Narrator's narratees, Boccaccio's women in love, are the women addressed.
And indeed, the Narrator's "dilicate donne innamorate" are echoed
verbatim as the "dilicate donne" addressed in the central and last days (V,
2 and X, 2). These addresses to an exclusively feminine audience represent ambiguous points of flux between the narrative strata: periodically,

[2] On narratees, see especially G. Prince's articles: "On Readers and Listeners in
Narrative," *Neophilologus*, 55 (1971), 117–22, and "Introduction à l'étude du nar-
rataire," *Poétique*, 14 (1973), 178–96.

[3] The only exceptions are II, 5 and 8; III, 4–7 and 9; IV, 1; V, 5; and VII, 1
and 6.

[4] In the whole "belle donne" (II, 2, 10; VI, 2; VII, 8; VIII, 2), "giovani donne"
(I, 9; IV, 3; VI, 1, 6; X, 4) and "graziose donne" (I, 2; III, 10; IV, 5; VIII, 6, 10)
occur five times; "bellissime donne" (III, 1; V, 7; IX, 3) and "vezzose donne" (V,
3; VI, 10; IX, 1) three times; "amabili donne" (V, 8; IX, 9), "care compagne" (I,
8; IV, 7), "dilettose donne" (V, 1; VIII, 5), "dilicate donne" (V, 2; X, 2), "leggiadre
donne" (VI, 9; IX, 10), twice; and "amorose compagne" (I, 3), "bellissime giovani"
(IV, 10), "care giovani" (I, 6), "carissime donne mie" (VII, 2), "donne mie belle"
(I, 5), "gentilissime donne" (IX, 5), "graziosissime donne" (II, 4), "innamorate
giovani" (V, 10), "laudevoli donne" (IX, 6), "magnifiche donne" (X, 8), "man-
suete mie donne" (X, 10), "morbide donne" (X, 5), "nobili donne" (X, 3),
"nobilissime donne" (VII, 5), "onorabili donne" (X, 1), "reverende donne" (VII,
9), "savissime donne" (IX, 8), "pietose donne" (IV, 9), "raguardevoli donne"
(X, 7), "reverende donne" (VII, 9), "splendide donne" (X, 6), "vaghe giovani"
(VI, 8), and "valorose giovani" (I, 10), only once.

fleeting by, they open the inner narration of the *brigata* by directly engaging the larger audience of the Author-Narrator.

Now, beside these two omnipresent levels of intent, others may be added temporarily, often to play against them for humorous or ironic effect. While collectively the storytellers are seeking only their mutual amusement of *diletto*, they attribute other specific values to their individual *novelle*. The Seventh Day novella of Emilia is a case in point. Dioneo, the prime advocate of *diletto* (cf. I, 4, 1; V, 10, 4; et passim), has suavely reasserted the pleasure principle to induce the troup's young ladies to tell about women's tricks under his Kingship: "Non per dovere con le opere mai alcuna cosa sconscia seguire, ma per *dare diletto* a voi e ad altrui" (VI, Concl., emphasis mine). Emilia, who first speaks to his theme, points up instead the *utile* in her novella, slyly echoing the Narrator's second aim: "ingegnerommi, carissime donne, di dir cosa che vi possa esser *utile* nell'avvenire" (VII, 1, 3, emphasis mine). Yet neither the useful example nor the *santa e buona orazione* she provides light the way to moral betterment. The "prayer" is an ingenious tissue of *double-entendre*, strongly sexual and scatological, extemporized by a woman to alert her lover to her husband's presence. Thus Emilia's feigned homilectic adds a third layer of intent which ironically undercuts the Narrator's primary goal of usefulness, reaffirms the *brigata*'s commitment to *diletto*, and, by the interplay, complicates and enriches the comic mood of the entire work.

We may now look more closely at the comic modalities in the novelle themselves to discover a few of their general features.[5] By way of preliminary, let us call to mind the main formal characteristics of the Decameronian novella.[6] Most of the novelle, like other short stories of similar form, are built around a compact narrative nucleus, that includes an initial situation (most of the time unbalanced), a central action or actions intended to transform the initial situation, and a final condition

---

[5] I should point out that this discussion at no point pretends to be exhaustive. However, clarifying as it does parts of a very complex narrative system, it is a first step in what will be a more involved process.

[6] On the "analyse du récit," see especially R. Barthes, "Introduction à l'analyse structurale des récits," *Communications*, 8 (1966), 1–27; C. Brémond, "La logique des possibles narratifs," *Communications*, 8 (1966), 60–76 and *Logique du récit* (Paris: Seuil, 1973); A. J. Greimas, *Semantique structurale: recherche de méthode* (Paris: Larousse, 1966); R. Scholes, *Structuralism in Literature* (New Haven & London: Yale University Press, 1974); C. Segre, *Le strutture e il tempo* (Torino: Einaudi, 1974); T. Todorov, *Poétique de la prose* (Paris: Seuil, 1971).

introducing a new balanced outcome.[7] This transformational process occurs through temporality and causality. The situations and actions of the novelle are related to characters who tend to fall into three major categories: (1) agents, (2) objects, and (3) latives or helpers. They interact among themselves in time and space through the modalities of (1) emotion (love-hate), (2) understanding (intelligence-stupidity), (3) communication (communicativeness-secrecy) and (4) power (authority-impotence), and function within the fictional conventions of reality or fantasy. What differentiates a given novella form from others is the author's handling of characters and situations according to his own cultural formation and to the historical and social milieu which condition his experiences. In the *Decameron*, for instance, we find that the characters tend to fall into the two categories of agents and objects, with the agents endowed of a large sphere of influence over their surroundings, while the third category of latives or helpers is practically non-existent. This observation already discloses the presence of a simplified and manageable social milieu, where the individual can successfully confront his environment, and eventually control his own existence.

The most common modalities of interaction among the Decameronian characters are those of emotion, understanding, and communication, with strongest stress given to love, intelligence, and communicativeness. The modality of authority occurs only in the so-called tragic novelle, where an unresolved conflict breaks out between the individual and an official form of authority, with the resulting downfall of the individual. The relevance of the modalities of love, intelligence, and communicativeness in the narrative system of the Decameronian novella reveal a preference for a well-rounded human being, sensitive to a range of emotions, and capable of expressing them intelligently, so as to overcome selfishness and create a well-balanced social environment where the individual functions within a group of kindred spirits. Often, in order to achieve this goal, the intelligent individual uses his verbal gifts to transform reality into make-believe in such a way that even the less intelligent, over-emotional, or self-centered beings who constitute an obstacle to his goal will be able to accept the *status quo*, and harmoniously contribute to the final positive outcome of the situation. This is the case, for instance, of the woman protagonist of III, 3, who successfully accom-

[7] On the three-event groupings of any basic narrative, see especially C. Brémond, "La logique des possibles narratifs," p. 60, and G. Prince, *A Grammar of Stories: An Introduction* (The Hague, Paris: Mouton, 1973), especially Ch. I, "The Minimal Story," 16–37.

plishes her amatorial goals through the persuasive speeches she addresses to her gullible confessor; or of madonna Filippa who through her vigorous eloquence succeeds not only in rescuing herself from a death sentence—the penalty required by law against adultery—but also in persuading the population and law officials of Prato to change that unfair law (VI, 7); or still of the wise *scolare*, who passionately exercises his verbal fluency to chastise the beautiful widow who had so scornfully ridiculed his love for her (VIII, 7).

Time and space dimensions also provide specifics for identifying certain characteristics of the Decameronian narrative world: as for time, most novelle take place in the contemporary fourteenth century with some set in the thirteenth and a very few at an earlier time; the space dimension generally coincides with geographical boundaries of the world known by fourteenth-century businessmen, with a preference for France, England, and North Africa among foreign locales, and for central (especially Tuscan) and southern Italian settings. In this way, both its temporal and its spatial dimensions point to a single significant feature of the Decameronian novella, that is, its close connection with the historical and social milieu in which it was produced and to which it was directed. The characters strengthen even more this characteristic, inasmuch as most of them are either actual historical figures, well-known personally or through their fame to the author and his narrators, or realistic portraits of everyday people, interacting in a mid-fourteenth-century European, and especially Italian, society.[8]

Turning to the specifically comic aspects in the novelle of the *Decameron*, we may start by suggesting the types of comic novelle that are most frequently found in the collection. (1) A large group of comic novelle fall into what can be called "situational comedy" in which the psychological intuition of the main characters is essential, and the interaction among characters is worked out through the modalities of intelligence and communication, and the central conflict is overcome through

---

[8] Fundamental historical presentations of fourteenth-century and Renaissance society are to be found in M. B. Becker, *Florence in Transition* (Baltimore: The Johns Hopkins Press, 1968); G. A. Brucker, *Florentine Politics and Society, 1343–1378* (Princeton: Princeton University Press, 1962), *Renaissance Florence*, (New York: Wiley, 1969), and *The Society of Renaissance Florence. A Documentary Study* (New York: Harper Torchbooks, 1971); D. Hay, *The Italian Renaissance and its Historical Background* (Cambridge: Cambridge University Press, 1961); G. Luzzato, *Storia economica d'Italia: Il Medioevo* (Firenze: Sansoni, 1963); and A. Sapori, *Studi di storia economica medievale, secoli XIII–XIV–XV*, 3 ediz. (Firenze: Sansoni, 1955).

the characters' successful handling of reality: most novelle of the Third and Seventh Days belong to this group. (2) Another group of novelle better typifies an alternative form of comedy, the "comic of language," where the central conflict is resolved, rather than by action among characters, by the appropriate use of certain words, the "motti," which through their verbal immediacy force upon the audience a pleasant message of moral or social interest. Here the intellectual dimension is essential together with the ability to respond verbally to certain outside stimuli: many novelle of the First Day and all novelle of the Sixth Day belong to this group. (3) A third group illustrates the "comic of character" where a farcical mood develops out of a particularly "debased" character[9] incapable of understanding his environment and bound to become the ideal victim of some clever rogues: this type of comedy is characteristic of the so-called *beffa* novelle, especially those of the Eighth Day (the novelle of Calandrino, VIII, 3 and 6; and IX, 3 are prime examples). It also appears in some novelle of the Third Day where we encounter such peculiar characters as the confessor (III, 3), Frate Puccio (III, 4), and Alibech (III, 10). In these novelle, because of the wider implications derived from the cultural background of the protagonists, the social dimension is essential. These types have been set up with external criteria, since, at this juncture, I am attempting only an external classification of the multiform comic of the *Decameron*. One should bear in mind, therefore, that the psychological dimension so typical of the first group may also appear in the comic novelle of language or of character. Similarly, the social dimension may also be present in comic novelle of situation or language. Nor need the intellectual dimension be absent from the comic novelle of situation or character.

I wish to pursue the analysis of these three main types of comic novelle, by examining a representative of each: (1) the novella of the *fantasima* (VII, 1) as a comedy of situation; (2) the novella of Chichibio (VI, 4) as a comedy of language; and (3) the novella of maestro Simone (VIII, 9) as a comedy of character.

The novella of the *fantasima* belongs to the Seventh Day, given over at Dioneo's request to the "tricks played by wives on their husbands, either for love's sake or for their own safety" (VI, Concl.). In its

[9] I am borrowing this term from the discussion of comic characters provided by Paul G. Ruggiers in his essay "A Vocabulary for Chaucerian Comedy: A Preliminary Sketch," *Medieval Studies in Honor of Lillian Herlands Hormstein*, ed. J. B. Bessinger, Jr. and R. R. Raymo (New York: NYU Press, 1976), pp. 193–225; 216–17.

structure, each of the novelle moves through four basic steps: (1) an initial situation which generally presents or projects a rendez-vous between a woman and her lover; (2) an intrusion, usually by the husband, which advances the situation to the danger point; (3) the woman's reaction—and here we find the play on reality vs. make-believe—which serves to neutralize the potential danger; and (4) a final positive and harmonious situation. The third narrative step occupies the central interest of the action of these stories, emphasizing the interplay among the characters through the dynamic juxtaposition of reality and pretence.

In the first novella of the Seventh Day, the action takes place "in un luogo molto bello . . . in Camerata," that is, in the Tuscan countryside near Florence; the action, however, is triggered by the presence of the two main male characters, the lover and the husband, who move from the city to the country in order to enjoy the woman's embraces. Monna Tessa, the woman protagonist, contrives a special device as a rendez-vous signal for her lover. The signal consists of the skull of an ass atop a pole in the vineyard beside her house; when the jawbone points towards Florence, the city, it signifies that her husband is away and her lover may come to her; when, on the other hand, it points to the *contado* village of Fiesole, her husband's presence is indicated and her lover must stay away. The action moves from an initial situation in which monna Tessa is expecting her lover (jawbone pointing towards Florence) to a second moment of intrusion caused by her husband's unexpected arrival from Florence, which produces the dangerous possibility of an encounter between husband and unsuspecting lover. Monna Tessa's reaction to the whole affair proceeds in two steps: first she takes partial care of her lover by sending the maid out into the garden to set a sumptuous supper under the tree where the two had intended to dine, so that at least he will have a good dinner. In so doing, however, she forgets to have the skull's snout turned toward Fiesole so as to warn her lover of her husband's presence. When the unsuspecting lover knocks at her door and the situation becomes decidedly critical, monna Tessa succeeds in neutralizing the danger by the witty invention of the *fantasima* or ghost, which she introduces into the nocturnal scene in order to take advantage of her husband's superstitiously religious penchant, and thus transforms reality into fantasy: " 'ohimè,' " she says, " 'Gianni mio, or non sai tu quello ch'egli è la fantasima, della quale io ho avuta a queste notti la maggior paura che mai s'avesse . . .' " (VII, 1, 79). Gianni's reply reveals his flaw, bigotry and superstition, of which his clever wife is ready to take advantage:

Va, donna, non aver paura se ciò è, ché io dissi dianzi il *Te lucis* e la
'ntemerata e tante altre buone orazioni ... e anche segnai il letto di canto in
canto al nome del Padre e del Figlio e dello Spirito Santo, che temere non
ci bisogna ... (VII, 1, p. 20).

The conflict between reality and make-believe is already noticeable in
these last two speeches, especially in the woman's, which is based on a
ghost story—pure make-believe—and is accepted as reality by her husband, who mixes superstition with religion in practices such as making
the sign of the cross—clearly a religious act[10]—all around the bed, an
object which hardly conveys a religious connotation. Such a combination
of superstitious and even openly sexual signals, which in the husband's
speech and actions occurs unconsciously and naïvely, demonstrates his
stupidity, while on the other hand it is consciously manipulated by monna
Tessa in her prayer-incantation:

Fantasima, fantasima che di notte vai, a coda ritta ci venisti, a coda ritta te
n'andrai: va nell'orto, a piè del pesco grosso troverai unto bisunto e cento
cacherelli della gallina mia: pon bocca al fiasco e vatti via, e non far male
né a me né a Gianni mio. (VII, 1, p. 781)

The ghost-like image of the *fantasima* is here comically materialized
through the sexual implication of the *coda ritta*, twice repeated as to hint
at the conceivable disappointment on either side, the woman's and the
lover's. Furthermore, the entire performance asked from the ghost con-
flictingly stresses in a comic crescendo a physical quality hardly possessed
by ghosts. This develops through the actions requested from it: first of
moving to a normal, everyday natural environment—*l'orto* and *il pesco
grosso*—and then through the references of consuming food—*unto
bisunto*—and the partially scatological *cento cacherelli della gallina mia*,
and finally through the drinking connotation of *pon bocca al fiasco*. The
process of materialization is further stressed in the husband's physical
participation in the prayer: " 'Sputa, Gianni' e Gianni sputò." The
comic of the situation acquires an ironic innuendo when one realizes the
pun on bigotry and superstition here clearly hinted at by the details in
dealing with a supposedly spiritual matter.[11] Furthermore, it is interesting

[10] On such incantations, see especially G. Bonomo, *Scongiuri del popolo siciliano*
(Palermo: Palumbo, 1953); T. Casini, "Scongiuro e poesia," *Archivio delle Tra-
dizioni Popolari*, 5 (1886), 560–68; and M. P. Giardini, *Tradizioni popolari nel
Decameron* (Firenze: Olschki, 1965).

[11] On the rôle of spitting in incantations, see Giardini, *op. cit.*, 26–28, and P.
Pajello, "Lo sputo e la saliva nelle tradizioni popolari antiche e moderne," *Archivio
delle Tradizioni Popolari*, 6 (1887), 250–54.

to note that oral metaphors are used contrastingly for the actions respectively of the lover and of the husband: the lover's characteristic conviviality and festivity are stressed by the expression "pon bocca al fiasco,"
which can be visualized in an "out vs. in" motion of imbibing the flask's
contents for the purpose of enjoying a good meal, while the husband's
gesture of spitting has the opposite, "in vs. out" movement, stressing his
superstitious and short-sighted character by expelling, an act with asocial
connotations. At the end of the novella part of the incantation is explained: *unto bisunto* = *due capponi* and *cento cacherelli della gallina
mia* = *l'uova*; the *orto* and *pesco*, then, provide the background for the
lover's understanding of the situation, as well as for his enjoyment, if not
of the pleasures of sex, at least of those of food and drink. In Emilia's
concluding remarks a few conjectures are offered as to how the various
events of the story might have actually taken place, and the natural elements of the vineyard and the ass' skull are brought back into the
discussion.

The comic modalities of this novella seem therefore to point at a specific comic situation confronting the three main characters, which is
eventually resolved by the psychological insight the woman possesses of
her husband's flaws. This insight is especially visible in her actions in the
third narrative moment of the novella, where she succeeds in restoring a
well-balanced situation by transforming reality into make-believe, playing upon her husband's superstition. Such a clear realization and ensuing
exploitation of the husband's flaws on the part of the woman—the character with whom the author manifestly sympathizes—uncovers in the
narrative texture an intention of satirizing ignorance and superstition.
Consequently the novella reveals also a social dimension developing out
of the interplay between these two characters, the wife and the husband.
Furthermore the perspicacity shown by the woman and her ability to
adapt an actual situation to a metaphorical rendition in her prayer-
incantation, implies intelligence and creative awareness, qualities shared
also by her lover in his instant understanding of her incantation and
planning. Thus also the intellectual dimension is here present by in-
ference, in the characters of the woman and her lover. A fun-loving, com-
municative, merry form of existential plight seems to permeate the whole
novella, and is especially visible in the last lines: "e poi dell'altre volte,
ritrovandosi con la donna, molto di questa incantazione rise con essolei"
(VII, 1, 30). Thus the modalities of emotion (love), of understanding
(intelligence), and of communication (communicativeness through in-

cantation) are all present here and actively functional in the development of the action: love as the instigator of the action; intelligence as the factor responsible for a positive solution; and revelation through incantation as the direct means to reach the solution. The comic develops out of the conflicting situation created by the woman's momentary flaw (forgetfulness) and the husband's basic flaws (bigotry and superstition): the woman, through intelligence eliminates her own flaw, taking advantage of her husband's, and successfully communicates with her lover on the level of reality, while keeping her husband constantly on the level of make-believe. The *double-entendre* of the incantation introduces an ironic connotation that is stressed later, at the end of the novella, as previously noticed, by the juxtaposition of the Narrator's voice over Emilia's, the storyteller of this novella. The whole closing passage is in fact a teasing invalidation of two of the pivotal events of the novella as related by Emilia: the first invalidates the woman's responsibility towards her lover implying the presence of a third party, "un lavoratore," who "per la vigna passando" had inadvertently changed the position of the ass' skull, so that "Federigo, credendo esser chiamato, v'era venuto" (VII, 1, 31–32); the second changes and simplifies accordingly the texture of the incantation: "Fantasima, fantasima, vatti con Dio, che la testa dell'asin non vols'io, ma altri fu, che tristo il faccia Iddio, e io son qui con Gianni mio" (32). In both cases the changes introduced weaken the modalities of understanding and communication, degrading the potential of creativity and ingenuity of the characters, and reduce the narration to a simplistic chronicle of everyday events.[12] This chronicle trend is stressed also by the introduction of a witness well-known to the narrative voice who is speaking: "una mia vicina, la quale è una donna molto vecchia" (33), and at this point one cannot help thinking of the "Conclusione dell'autore" where the Narrator uses the same terms "una mia vicina" to testify to his writing ability. This witness personally relates her experience naming a specific historically traceable figure as the victim of such a trick on the part of his wife: "uno che si chiamò Gianni di Nello, che stava in porta San Piero, non meno sofficente lavaceci che fosse Gianni

---

[12] Professor Branca's note on the historical authenticity of Giovanni di Nello tends to strengthen the chronicle quality of this last paragraph: "Un Giovanni di Nello, speziale, era nel 1342 consigliere del Comune, nel 1345 console della propria arte; il 15 agosto 1347 fu sepolto proprio in Santa Maria Novella dove a sue spese si era fatto costruire una cappella; ai domenicani di quel convento aveva destinato alcuni lasciti. Abitava però nel popolo di San Donato de' Vecchietti e non in quello di S. Pier Maggiore, cui appartenne la famiglia del B" (VII, 1, p. 782, note 3).

Lotterighi" (33–34). All these details create a different narrative tone that ironically contrasts with the previous one of the novella as a whole, and clearly hints at a different narrative voice. This is further stressed by the last paragraph in the passage where the address appears to "donne mie care," the Narrator's usual form of address to his narratees, and followed here by an ironic play on the "utile" of both prayer-incantations that the women are supposed to learn and use for their own unspecified good: "elle hanno grandissima virtù a cosí fatte cose, come per esperienza avrete udito: apparatele a potravvi ancor giovare" (34). Thus, the use of a different narrative voice in the last passage of this comic novella deepens its ironic mood, by offering conflicting interpretations that, while intensifying on one side the social dimension of the text, raise doubts on the other about the internal modalities of the characters.

The second example that I have chosen, the Fourth novella of the Sixth Day, will help in defining the "comedy of language" in the *Decameron*. In the Sixth Day, among the topics stressed, the art of speaking or of *novellare* and the power of the "word" stand out. The former topic is already visible in the first novella of the Day, when one of the *cavalieri* of Madonna Oretta's company decides to make use of the *novellare* during their outing in the country: " 'Madonna Oretta,' " says the *cavaliere*, " 'quando voi vogliate, io vi porterò gran parte della via che ad andare abbiamo a cavallo con una delle belle novelle del mondo.' " The *novellare*, here figuratively rendered in equestrian terms, is seen as the best means to entertain the group and provides therefore another tie between the form of entertainment used by the *brigata* in the country and that used by the protagonists of the novella in the same type of environment. Similar instances can be seen in other stories of this same Day: one of the most valuable qualities of Giotto's character (VI, 5), for example, is the fact that he is a "bellissimo *favellatore*," while Michele Scalza (VI, 6) owes his popularity in Florence to the fact that he knows "le più belle novelle ... per la qual cosa i giovani fiorentini avevan molto caro, quando in brigata si trovavano, di poter aver lui." In the novella of Madonna Filippa (VI, 7), the importance of "saper ben parlare ... dove la necessità il richiede" is especially stressed, and Dioneo himself, the individualist of the *brigata*, also mentions the importance of the art of storytelling in his introduction to the concluding novella of this Day: " 'Nè vi dovrà esser grave, perchè io, *per ben dire la novella compiuta*, alquanto in parlar mi distenda.' " And Frate Cipolla, the protagonist of Dioneo's novella (VI,

10), is the perfect example of this mastery of the art of words, present throughout the Sixth Day.

Besides advocating the art of speaking and the *novellare*, this Sixth Day also places a very strong emphasis on the power of the *word*, both as a narrative activator—that is, as the *motto* or punch-line essential to the dramatic action of nearly every novella of the Day—and also as an important stylistic device which plays a vital part in the portrayal of the open-minded and witty citizens of Florence, whatever their social class or group. In fact, the protagonists of the novelle of this Day come from a wide range of social classes: there are noblemen, such as Geri Spina (VI, 2), Currado Gianfigliazzi (VI, 4), and Guido Cavalcanti (VI, 9); professional people or artists like messer Forese and maestro Giotto (VI, 5); commoners, like Cisti (VI, 2), Michele Scalza (VI, 6), and Fresco da Celatico (VI, 8); and witty ladies, such as madonna Oretta (VI, 1), Nonna de' Pulci (VI, 3), and the incomparable madonna Filippa (VI, 7), an early champion of women's rights.

Structurally, each novella of this day develops through three basic steps: (1) an initial situation that shows a potential difficulty for the individual, involving a confrontation with society or with a conflicting external reality (Cisti's relationship with the representatives of the Florentine upper class; Chichibio's encounter with Brunetta and his subsequent confrontation with his master: Giotto and Forese's sudden encounter with bad weather; madonna Filippa's confrontation first with her husband and then with the whole society of Prato; Guido Cavalcanti's encounter with messer Betto's *brigata*; Frate Cipolla's sudden discovery of the exchange of relics); (2) a reversal of the initial situation, accomplished by the same individual who was the victim of the previous confrontation, through cleverness and witty handling of the verbal instruments at his disposition (Chichibio's incredible *motto*; Cisti's ability in inviting messer Spina and the ambassadors, and his ingenious expression to punish the servant's gluttony; Giotto and Forese's quick exchange of witty remarks; madonna Filippa's artful defense of her rights; Cavalcanti's elegant reply and disappearance; and frate Cipolla's brilliant tale to the credulous *Certaldesi*); and finally (3) a total reintegration into society of the clever and verbally capable individual, with a final vision of comic harmony. The comic rhythm of the novelle of the Sixth Day develops out of a basic process by which the human object of the initial opposition transforms himself into the agent of the counteraction which

163

(often through a witty *motto*) brings him into a condition of accepted supremacy, allowing for a final reunion of individual and society.

The novella of Chichibio moves through the three-step pattern common to other novelle of the Sixth Day—confrontation, reversal of the initial situation, and finally positive integration into society—with the first moment, that of the confrontation, providing the longest segment of the narrative action. As a result of this special handling of the narrative, the dramatic conflict between the two main characters, the servant and the master, is predominant, and produces the suspense which is intensified, as in the novella of Cisti (VI, 2), by the wide difference in the social status of the protagonists.

The nobility and magnificence of Currado—and through him, of the Florentine way of life—are again present in this novella:

> sempre della nostra città è stato nobile cittadino, liberale e magnifico, e vita cavalleresca tenendo, continuamente in cani e in uccelli s'é dilettato . . . (VI, 4).

The festivity and warmth of this noble environment are particularly stressed by the rich, almost Flemish, setting of the kitchen, and by the scene of the preparation and actualization of the banquet. The linguistic texture of this novella is particularly interesting, as it carefully underlines the lively movement of the narrative action. All through this novella, in fact, specific word arrangements produce an uneven and broken rhythm reminiscent of a hopping movement, which works very effectively to underscore the central narrative motif of the story, a crane with only one leg. This hopping rhythm is produced partially by very short words, often oxytones, which intensify the springy sound connotation of the language —words such as *mai più, gru, avrì, in fe', piè, colà, ho ho,* etc. The same rhythmical pattern is also conveyed by the syntax based upon short clauses that contain fast-moving, finite verbal forms. These definite, clear verb forms create a rapidity of linguistic as well as of emotional tone, which stresses the quarrel between Chichibio and his master over the leg of the crane: " 'Signor mio, le gru non hanno se non una coscia e una gamba,' " says Chichibio; and Currado, "turbato disse: 'Come diavol non hanno che una coscia e una gamba? non vid'io mai più gru che questa?' " And Chichibio replies: "Egli è, messer, com'io vi dico; e quando vi piaccia, io il vi farò veder ne' vivi' " (VI, 4, 10–12). At times the brevity and rapidity of the clauses impart a sing-song cadence to the language of this novella, particularly to Chichibio's speech, which echoes the cadence of the Venetian dialect: " 'Voi non l'avri da mi, donna Brunetta, voi non l'avrì da mi' " (8). Besides its rhythm, the linguistic texture of this novella is also very revealing for the use of other grammatical devices, such as the gerund, which seems to emphasize the endless quality of the argument about the crane's leg. We find three such verbal constructions in connection with the character of Brunetta, who is the cause of the missing leg and thus of the argument between servant and master: "*sentendo* l'odor della gru ... *veggendola* ... *essendo* un poco turbata" (7-9). Two gerundive constructions occur in relation to the crane, the object of the dispute: "*essendo* già presso che cotta," and "*Essendo* ... messa la gru senza coscia." Finally, four gerunds occur at the most important points of the action, stressing Chichibio's fear and the seeming impossibility of his plight: "*veggendo* che ancora durava l'ira di Currado ... non *sappiendo* come ... non *potendo* ... non *sappiendo* egli stesso donde si venisse..." (15-18).

It is particularly in relation to the character of Chichibio and his involvement with the *gru* that the rhythm of this novella becomes most lively. The two words that correspond respectively to the agent and to the object of the narrative action—*Chichibio* and *gru*—with their harsh and broken sound, intensify the special hopping sound that is a linguistic constant of the novella. It is Chichibio, the *vinizian bugiardo*, the *nuovo bergolo*, who cannot resist his lady Brunetta's threat (" 'tu non avrai mai da me cosa che ti piaccia' "), and dutifully sacrifices one of the crane's legs for her, with the result of having to lie to Currado and face his anger. Thus the narrative moves from action (Chichibio's removal of the crane's leg for Brunetta) to *motto* (" 'le gru non hanno se non una coscia e una gamba' "), which covers up the action with a lie. This lie then provokes a counteraction (movement into the country to see live cranes and make them run on two legs), which in turn motivates Chichibio's final *motto* (" 'Messer sì, ma voi non gridaste *ho ho* a quella di iersera' ") which converts the atmosphere of the story to a totally festive and convivial mood.

A Currado piacque tanto questa risposta, che tutta la sua ira si convertì in festa e riso ... Così adunque con la sua pronta e sollazzevol risposta Chichibio cessò la mala ventura e pacificossi col suo signore. (19-20)

Thus *action* and *word* alternate in this novella, with a final predominance of the *word* in the re-creation of a jovial and pleasant form of life.

The social dimension then is present also in this novella, particularly in connection with the character of Currado, who represents the higher level of the Florentine society, still capable of appreciating a good show of wit even from a servant. Eventually Chichibio's brilliant and unexpected remark displays an intellectual ability that works towards his final reintegration into his own milieu and produces acceptance of his own individual characteristics even by his master. We find many comic modalities here, but handled differently than in the novella previously discussed: the modality of emotion is here too the initiator of the action, inasmuch as it is Chichibio's love for Brunetta and his inability to refuse her the leg of the crane that start the conflict between himself and his master: love is only hinted however in the very beginning of the novella through the character of Brunetta, and does not appear again in the text afterwards. Intelligence flashes in very suddenly at the conclusion of the novella, without being visible anywhere before. The modality of communication works negatively through secrecy, rather than positively through communicativeness, inasmuch as Chichibio, out of fear, keeps the truth away from Currado, thus intensifying the lack of communication; only at the end, through Chichibio's clever answer, that reveals a partial truth, communication and understanding are restored. In this story, the modality of power is also present, in the authority that Currado exercises over Chichibio and that works narratively in the build-up of the atmosphere of terror that precedes and contrastingly strengthens the final comic relief provided by Chichibio's wise remark. Chichibio then as a character is motivated by love and fear, lack of communication, and momentary intelligence. Currado's character develops through authority and eventually through understanding. It is the momentaneous flash of intelligence at the end that brings together the two main protagonists of this novella and creates a comic outcome.[13]

Finally, as an example of a "comedy of character," I have chosen the story of maestro Simone and the incredible trick played on him by the two clever painters and masterful trick-players, Bruno and Buffalmacco (VIII, 9).

The main topic of the Eighth Day is the *beffa*, as it is for the Seventh Day, but this time with representatives from both sexes as *actants*. A certain structural pattern repeats itself, with some variations, in most of the Day's novelle, including the last one. There is usually a first stage, in which the intention of the *beffa* takes shape, and then is put into effect in

[13] These are amplifications to a previous discussion of this novella in my book *Anatomy of Boccaccio's Style* (Napoli: Cymba, 1968), pp. 83–96.

the second stage to be finally accomplished in a third stage in which the outcome of the *beffa* is also presented.

In the ninth novella of this Day, Bruno and Buffalmacco, by creating an incredible story about a magic society of which they are members, bring maestro Simone, a doctor from Bologna, constantly qualified as "pecora," "animale," etc., to accept a ride on a devilish animal—actually it is Buffalmacco masked as such—with a resulting head-down fall into a heap of excrement. The doctor is constantly qualified by terms such as "pecoraggine" or "qualitativa mellonaggine da Legnaia"[14] (VIII, 9, 15), "la cui scienza non si stendeva forse più oltre che il medicare i fanciulli dal lattime" (31), a typical "lavaceci" (52), "medico" able only to treat "orina d'asino" (70), and ready to "cavalcar la capra delle maggiori sciocchezze del mondo' (73), etc. These degrading qualifications, connected extensively with a rustic background ("mio padre . . . stesse *in contado*," 50) are further stressed by indicial elements such as the doctor's residence ("prese casa nella via la quale noi oggi chiamiamo la *Via del Cocomero*," 6) and by the proliferation of images that the "Cocomero" suggestion creates: "qualitativa *mellonaggine*" (15), "*zucca* mia da sale" (22), "voi apparaste . . . l'abbicci . . . in sul *mellone*" (64), "*pinca* mia da seme" (74), etc. Furthermore, animal images are also connected with maestro Simone, beginning with his favorite painting made by Bruno in his *loggetta* representing "la battaglia dei topi e delle gatte" (34) and ending eventually with his fearful ride on "una bestia nera e cornuta." These degrading and animalesque qualities characterizing the unfit doctor, prepare for and explain the *beffa* played on him by Bruno and Buffalmacco. The *beffa* here tends to point out the difference between typically Florentine wit, embodied in the professionals of the *pennello*, and the unsuited foreign-trained doctor. Bruno's paintings for the "medico . . . pecora" indeed hint at his intention of poking fun at him even on this level:

> Bruno . . . gli aveva dipinto nella sala sua la quaresima e uno *agnusdei* all'entrar della camera e sopra l'uscio della via un orinale . . . e in una sua loggetta . . . la battaglia dei topi e delle gatte, la quale troppo bella cosa pareva al medico. . . . (34)

[14] These degrading qualifications, as Professor Branca suggests in his commentary (VIII, 9, p. 973, note 7), play constantly on maestro Simone's ignorance and stupidity, as well as on his lack of information about Florentine toponymy: "Legnaia" here, for instance, refers to a small place in the Florentine countryside well-known for its muskmelons. Maestro Simone's unawareness of this simple information intensifies his comic misunderstanding of the whole situation.

The presence of the "quaresima," suggesting fasting, is in fact rather perplexing in the dining room of such a food-lover as maestro Simone, who offers "le più belle cene e i più belli desinari del mondo" (61) and the representation of the Annunciation in the bedroom of such a woman-lover, worthy of having "per donna la contessa di Civillari" (73) is equally puzzling. And the *orinale* introduces by its functional yet unesthetic quality the actual profession of maestro Simone, whom Bruno and Buffalmacco consider the epitome of a "medico che s'intenda d'*orina d'asino*." The picture of the battle between mice and cats may very well imply the actual game that Bruno is playing at the expense of "maestro Scipa," "più che femina pauroso" (94). Bruno's creative ability is even more striking in his verbal descriptions, such as the "andare in corso"[15] scene:

> ... è maravigliosa cosa a vedere i capoletti intorno alla sala dove mangiamo
> e le tavole messe alla reale e la quantità de' nobili e belli servidori, così
> femine come maschi, al piacer di ciascuno che è di tal compagnia, e i bacini,
> gli urciuoli, i fiaschi e le coppe e l'altro vasellamento d'oro e d'argento ...
> e oltre a questo le molte e varie vivande ... i dolci suoni d'infiniti istrumenti,
> e i canti pieni di melodia ... né vi potrei dire quanta sia la cera che vi
> s'arde ... ne quanti sieno i confetti che vi si consumano e come siano
> preziosi i vini che vi si beono ... egli non ve n'è niuno sì cattivo che non vi
> paresse uno imperadore, sì siamo di cari vestimenti e di belle cose ornati ...
> (20–23)

The power of verbal depiction here conveys a conviviality befitting the highest form of social life, specifically associated with Florence: Michele Scotto's followers, in fact, "piacendo lor la città e i costumi degli uomini, ci si disposero a voler sempre stare, e preserci di grandi e di strette amistà con alcuni, senza guardare che essi fossero, più gentili che non gentili, o più ricchi che poveri, solamente che uomini fossero conformi a' lor costumi" (18–19). Bruno and Buffalmacco thus represent the Florentine élite of witty professionals, equally capable of engaging successfully in their professions and of exercising their wits in the pursuit of conviviality and fun. They are thus in net contrast with the gullible and unfit majority of outsiders, incapable of intelligently exercising their professions

---

[15] I have discussed these terms "andare in corso" as representing a typical nocturnal reunion of the so-called "società di Diana," that is a magic society of pagan and medieval times, in my article "Magic and Superstition in Boccaccio's *Decameron*," *Italian Quarterly Special Issue: Boccaccio Reconsidered*, 18, no. 72 (1975), 5–32; 22–25.

or of recognizing in others or enjoying themselves the pleasure of wit. The word-pictures that Bruno makes of both the worlds of fantasy and reality sharpen the contrast between these two groups; furthermore, Bruno and Buffalmacco project for themselves as mates "la reina di Francia e . . . quella d'Inghilterra" (27), that is, characters who even in a joking context maintain a well-defined social connotation, while, on the other hand, maestro Simone's promised lover is described in such a way as to create an ambiguous aura of undefinable social reality. The first paragraph of the description, for instance, works on a relatively clear referential level that stresses social power and popularity: "'ella è una troppo gran donna, e poche cose ha per lo mondo nelle quali ella non abbia alcuna giurisdizione . . .'" (74). The second paragraph, however ("'i Frati minori a suon di nacchere le rendon tributo'"), introduces verbal signs which work on two different levels: one that continues the referential level of power and popularity expressed in the first paragraph, with the specific introduction of one of the groups influenced by the woman, the "Frati minori"; while the modality "a suon di nacchere" introduces a sudden, unexpected sequence that contains the referential level of excremental innuendo which, combined with the former level, creates the above-mentioned semantic ambiguity. The following long paragraph moves from one referential level to the other, thus producing an atmosphere of comic suspense intensified by the conflict between the trend of depicting the "contessa di Civillari" as a normal woman engaged in rather obvious actions ("'quando ella va dattorno, ella si fa ben sentire, benchè ella stea il più rinchiusa. . . . ella vi passò innanzi all'uscio una notte che andava ad Arno a lavarsi i piedi e per pigliare un poco d'aria,'" 75) and the metaphorical one that plays heavily on the excremental connotation of which maestro Simone, however, is unaware. The metaphorical trend includes the description of the contessa's "sergenti" who "tutti a dimostrazion della maggioranza di lei portano la verga e il piombino" (typical tools of the *nettacessi*) and the suggestive names such as "Tamagnin della porta, don Meta, Manico di Scopa, lo Squacchera," down to the all-too-clear scatological comparison of the lady to the "gran donna . . . da Cacavincigli." The actualization of the *beffa* thus moves from the initial moment of verbal description to the dynamic moment of action, which climaxes in maestro Simone's actual head-first fall into one of the "fosse, nelle quali i lavoratori di que' campi facevan votare la contessa a Civillari per ingrassare i campi loro" (98). The action therefore brings out the real essence of the "contessa a Civillari" and physically drags the *lattime* doctor out of his world of fantasy into the reality of stinking excrement. The results of the *beffa* for maestro Simone are a malodorous and unhealthy bath in ordure, followed by his wife's recriminations and the loss of his most precious dream—that of becoming a member of the *andare in corso* brigade. His social condition, however, does not change, nor is he alienated from his supposed friends: "se da indi addietro onorati gli avea, molto più gli onorò e careggiò con conviti e altre cose da indi innanzi" (112). What is strongly reaffirmed at the end of the novella is the lesson that the *beffa* purposely tried to convey to an unworthy professional man: "Così adunque, come udito avete, senno s'insegna a chi tanto non n'apparò a Bologna" (*ivi*).

This last novella then conveys its comic mood especially through the "debased" character of maestro Simone whose professional ineptitude and blundering inexperience are constantly commented upon through the degrading tricks played on him by Bruno and Buffalmacco. This "beffa" situation creates the prevalent social dimension of the novella, which is intensified by the irony developing out of the satire against the medical profession as personified in maestro Simone. The intellectual dimension is also clearly visible in the actions of Bruno and Buffalmacco, the intelligent and playfully aware characters who succeed in transforming the whole novella into a make-believe play at maestro Simone's expense. We find all comic modalities in this novella also, but they are constantly worked out on the level of make-believe: the modality of emotion, for instance, is revealed through the playful presentation of make-believe lovers, such as the queens of France and England for Bruno and Buffalmacco, and the countess of Civillari, or better the "grand donna . . . da Cacavincigli" for maestro Simone; the same holds true for the modality of communication, whereby communicativeness between the two tricksters and their victim is always kept on the level of make-believe for the fun of the former. The modality of understanding, then, is present in its two opposites, total awareness and playful intelligence in Bruno and Buffalmacco, and total unawareness and gullibility in maestro Simone. The comic mood of this novella develops, therefore, out of the character of maestro Simone, who is constantly functioning on the level of make-believe and through the modalities of gullibility and false communication.

Within its stated limits, this essay focused on the interplay of the narrative strata and comic modalities to analyze a few of the prime sources of Decameronian comedy. In conclusion, the narrative world of the

Decameron seems to offer ample material for the formulation of a theory of the comic—beginning from point of view and narrative personae, and working through characters, situations, space and time dimensions—based on the comic modalities of its narrative system.

Chaucer and Comedy

Thomas J. Garbáty
The University of Michigan

Geoffrey Chaucer is our "owene maister deere" of English comedy, and he has been identified with this genre of literature as completely as he has mastered it. But England's greatest medieval author has also been faulted, as we know, for not taking the world seriously enough, and this view unfortunately clouds the understanding of many today, especially those who watch the stage or see the movies but never read a book. Hot coulters, bare bottoms, and swyved wives—Chaucer represents the teller of dirty tales, the agent of bawdy comedy. Ah, Geoffrey, forgive us these trespasses!

In principio, let there be clarity: Chaucer's view of the world is quite serious enough; it just happens never to be a tragic one, for to describe such a world with its final despair was alien to his temperament. If we look at the whole corpus of his work, we see his tragic poems all interrupted, unfinished, or transfigured into celestial comedy.

It would be interesting to know whether Chaucer wrote with a comic theory of his own. It appears so, but only implied in opposition to his well-known Boethian definition of tragedy that occurs in the Prologue to *The Monk's Tale*:

> Tragedie is to seyn a certeyn storie
> As olde bookes maken us memorie,
> Of hym that stood in greet prosperitee,
> And is yfallen out of heigh degree
> Into myserie, and endeth wrecchedly.[1] (*CT*, VII, 1973-77)

The Knight interrupts the Monk's endless list of fallen men, and protests:

> I seye for me, it is a greet disease,
> Whereas men han been in greet welthe and ese,

---

[1] All references to Chaucer's works are from the edition by F. N. Robinson, *The Works of Geoffrey Chaucer*, 2d edition (Cambridge, Mass., 1957).

To heeren of hire sodeyn fal, allas!
And the contrarie is joye and greet solas,
As whan a man hath been in povre estaat,
And clymbeth up and wexeth fortunat,
And there abideth in prosperitee. (*CT*, VII, 2771–77)

This view coincides with that of Lydgate in his *Troy Book* (2.847): "A comedie hath in his gynnyng ... a maner compleynyng, And afterward endeth in gladnes," wherewith we should point out that a Lydgate statement on literary theory usually originated with Chaucer anyway, as a Wordsworth comment often did with Coleridge.

Of course in a theological and medieval sense, any punishment of evil, any justice, or final bliss in heaven constituted comedy, divine according to Dante. As has been ably shown, under these liberal conditions all of Chaucer's finished works can be defined as comedy.[2]

But it would be meager fare for our modern, mundane world, if we were left with this. Nor are we. Surely Chaucer has known the "smiler with the knife" and enough of "sorrow" to describe it well:

> For whoso seeth me first on morwe
> May seyn he hath met with sorwe,
> For y am sorwe, and sorwe ys y. (*BD*, 595–97)

The images of the Temple of Mars in the *Knight's Tale*: the burned town, the corpse murdered in the bush with cut throat, the pig chewing up the baby in the cradle reflect war time experiences he could not have gained from books. But never does he indulge himself, or us, by settling in on the dark side of life, whether with his Pardoner, his Black Knight, or his Troilus. *In extremis*, as with Troilus, he may pull in heavenly bliss for a deathbed conversion into comedy, but generally, he provided us with laughter closer to home. Indeed, Chaucer ends up laughing at himself as a representative of witless Mankind, and that is a kind of funny comedy which is neither Boethian, nor Dantean, but Chaucerian, the complete embodiment of Meredith's Comic Spirit: "Men's future upon earth does not attract it; their honesty and shapeliness in the present does...."[3]

Yet Chaucer was also the great master craftsman of this genre. He was

[2] Cf. Helen Storm Corsa, *Chaucer, Poet of Mirth and Morality* (Notre Dame, 1964).

[3] George Meredith, "Essay: On the Idea of Comedy and of the Uses of the Comic Spirit," in *The Works of George Meredith*, Memorial Edition (New York, 1968), XXIII, 46–47.

its student, as well as its teacher. He drew from the greatest traditions of the past, and he initiated some of the most penetrating concepts of the future.

Basically, Chaucer reworked tradition as he used it. His debt to the French fabliaux has been adequately discussed elsewhere. These comedies of situation, stories of intricate sexual jokes involving coincidences, contrivances, and manipulations seem to have been preferred by romance audiences in the Middle Ages, with Boccaccio their best-known advocate. But nowhere is fabliau skill of precision, punning, parody, and punch line demonstrated with such virtuoso technique as in Chaucer's *Miller's Tale*. Humor of situation was ever one of the poet's strengths.

Nor did he neglect the tradition of character type. Chaucer's famous wandering Wife of Bath, and his equally peripatetic Pandarus were both well-known confidants and intermediaries in the Roman comedies. But there they were stereotypes, and Alisoun is seen again as such in Juan Ruiz's Trotaconventos, and the later famous Celestina. After Chaucer, Pandarus went into a well-known, and dramatic, decline. Both characters received their humanity with Chaucer, which had not been given them before, nor since. But more of that anon. We must not sentimentalize Chaucer, for our poet belongs in other aspects of his multifaceted comic genius to the tradition of the eighteenth century. A gently satiric outlook on life was surely part of Chaucer's nature, and irony its method of expression. His General Prologue to the *Canterbury Tales* is written in heroic couplets, but it does not ever portray the waspish mind of Pope; it bares the soul of contemporary society without succumbing to the misanthropy of Swift. Control and balance are the disciplines of Chaucer's comedy, whose bounds his interpretors may transgress, but the poet never does.

The tradition of ironic and satiric verse was not invented by Chaucer (nor even by Petronius), but the English poet undoubtedly fathered this form of humor in Britain, and it is today one of the hallmarks of the national temper. But Chaucer also leaves his own earnest age behind when he discovered his genius for parody of literary styles, combined with burlesque of social conventions. We must leap the centuries to rediscover the mock heroic, and even here Chaucer goes Pope one better, comedy on top of comedy. *The Rape of the Lock* mocks an epic situation, but the contestants are still only poor mortals, eighteenth-century gallants. Chaucer's heroes are, after all, chickens, for the *Nun's Priest's Tale*, perhaps his comic *chef d'oeuvre* (in spite of Dr. Johnson who felt that

"The tale of The Cock seems hardly worth revival" [by Dryden in his Fables]), is a double hit, a compound burlesque, of beast fable as well as classical epic. And, finally, we must leap over to the twentieth century to find for him in Max Beerbohm a worthy match in parody.

To place Chaucer in a continuing tradition, however, skews the perspective on his art. Chaucer is the master of every form of comedy, and as such he even has a personal signature on all his creative endeavors, a private joke that runs from youth to age throughout the totality of his works. This is the dumbstruck and frightened "Geffrey" of the *House of Fame*, the dim-witted poetaster pilgrim called "Chaucer" in the *Canterbury Tales*; it is the narrator in all his works. No one in English literature has achieved such a lifetime of personal but shared comedy. Only a supreme artist could have accomplished this feat, only a wise and secure man could have afforded it, only a humble man would have ventured it.

But this brief descriptive survey of Chaucer's comedy should not mislead anyone into misunderstanding the poet's motives. As royal servant to three kings, Edward III, Richard II, and Henry IV, and occasional poet to the royal family, Chaucer could not afford to be openly didactic, nor did he ever judge. But he teaches as he delights; his "sentence" is often implied as clearly as his "solaas" is explicit.

The most striking aspects of Chaucer's comic genius are undoubtedly seen in his fabliaux, his comedies of situation. "Sentence" seems to go begging here (or perhaps we lack the *caritas* to notice it), but we have "solaas" enough. The *Miller's Tale*, if not also the tales of the Reeve, the Shipman, and the Merchant, is surely known to everyone who has ever heard the name of Chaucer. These are the tales, after all, which have made our poet among the populace such a jolly good fellow, that nobody can deny. But in what specifically lies their brilliance? At their best, of course, they are feats of controlled verbal and coincidental pyrotechnics. Standard motifs of folklore and literature: the *senex amans*, the ill-matched marriage, the shrewd lover, appear again and again. The jealous and/or niggardly husbands are cuckolded by crafty clerks, by sly monks, or by boisterous students. There are no heroes and no villains. Nanny Morality has taken a day off and left the children to their own devices. The beautifully contrived and directed turbulence that ensues is at times awesome to watch. Indeed, we find ourselves rooting for the action rather than the actors. In the *Miller's Tale*, Chaucer combines two plots: that of the old story of Noah's Flood, often staged by the miracle plays, and the folkloric tale of the misdirected kiss. The old carpenter hangs in a tub from the ceiling, awaiting the deluge while the clerk is "swyving" the wife underneath. A second precious lover, armed with a coulter to avenge a previous slight, approaches the window and is met by the bare bottom and fart of the clerk. The hot coulter is rammed, the clerk cries "water" in anguish, the old carpenter thinks the flood is at hand and cuts the rope. The rest is hullabaloo. It is as simple as that, and yet I know of no one who has equalled Chaucer in this technique.

Not all of the fabliaux, of course, reach this supreme achievement of situational comedy. The Reeve's tale is more episodic, less genial in the "justice" executed by the two students on husband, wife, and daughter for an attempted trickery, than the Miller's tale. But in all this the tale fits the Reeve's thin, rusty, choleric personality. The Shipman's story is based on an old folklore anecdote called "the lover's gift regained" as here, where a wife receives money from a "loving" monk who in turn had borrowed it from her husband. She requites her lover in bed, and he later tells the husband that the loan had been repaid to the wife. When questioned, she admits getting the money and spending it, having thought that it had been given outright, in friendship. But she would repay her husband: "Fro day to day, and if so be I faille, / I am youre wyf; score it upon my taille" (*CT*, VII, 415–16), and the poem ends, "Thus endeth now my tale, and God us send / Taillynge ynough unto our lyves ende" (*CT*, VII, 433–34). Tale, tail, and tally, Chaucer's triple puns are part of the dextrous humor in these harmless stories. Not quite so harmless or kindly, however, is the comedy in the *Merchant's Tale* with its famous pear tree episode. The picture of a lecherous May using the back of her blind old husband January as a ladder to join her lover in a pear tree is bitter humor, even though the pit may laugh loudly when "sodeynly anon this Damyan / Gan pullen up the smok, and in he throng" (*CT*, IV, 2352–53). To some it is always funny, I suppose, when they don't wear pants, even in the southern parts of Lumbardye.

However, if this is the only aspect of Chaucer that makes some people think him jolly, then indeed they do deny him. True, the fabliaux are filled with nuances of speech, vignettes of every day medieval life, allegros of parody, and deft character sketches which defy description but demand personal acquaintance. They are elegant and polished pieces in spite of their earthy content, but they don't pretend to probe much below their surface. If we critics do so, we tend to find what is perhaps not meant to be.

When Chaucer himself gets interested in a character, however, he achieves unqualified greatness. And this is what obviously happened with Alisoun, the Wife of Bath. Geoffrey liked her so much that he had her appear in and out of the *Canterbury Tales*. Aside from her description in the General Prologue, her long introductory dramatic monologue, and her tale, she is mentioned by the Clerk in the *envoi* to his tale and by Justinus, a character *in* the *Merchant's Tale*! The apparent paradox of this last appearance, reality entering into fiction, is easily resolved when we remember that Alisoun was the *primum mobile* of many thoughts, of the sequence of tales called the "Marriage Group," and of the Clerk's sarcastic outburst. Why then could she not also enter into the Merchant's imaginative process? Indeed, Chaucer mentions her again in his later poem, the *Envoy to Bukton*, à propos the latter's ensuing marriage.

Alisoun is definitely the grande dame of the pilgrimage, and probably also of Chaucer's literary life. She is his great creation, whom he dearly loved, along with Criseyde, though the Wife of Bath is a comic character, where Criseyde is not. But why is the Wife of Bath so intriguing? Because she openly talks about sex, her urges, and the trials and tribulations she caused her first three husbands? I think not. Not for this did Chaucer admire her. Rather, I suspect, it was because she, like himself, understood well enough the seriousness of life, that she had suffered anguish and heartache and personal misfortunes, as he may have done, but in spite of this, her outlook on life was not a tragic one, her optimism was unassailable, as she pilgrimaged forth with the rest, ready for an adventure, good or bad, with a sixth husband. No man can create but what is in himself; both the light and the dark are part of him. In the Wife of Bath Chaucer reflected the great sympathy he had for mankind and mirrored the strength of his own comic view of existence.

She did not, of course, jump out of his head like Athena out of the mind of Jupiter. Her forebears were ancient, evil and benign witches, spinners, matchmakers who knew the remedies of love and hustled for others when they could no longer go it alone. The Grimm fairy tales are full of them, and they have spun and woven the fates of men from the beginning. They are not lovable women because their motives and machinations remain a mystery to us. But Alisoun makes herself understood, even beyond her intent. Her rambling, naively blithe confession of how it was she who laid her husbands low: "As help me God, I laughe whan I thynke / How pitously a-nyght I made hem swynke!" (*CT*, III, 201–02), of her prowess in carping, her vanity, and greed could easily be passed off as being no more than a clever exposition of the medieval antifeminist tradition, did not her romantic tale, which yearns for youth and beauty and *gentilesse*, give her character a roundness and her personality a psychological depth of which before we had received only hints: "But, Lord Crist! whan that it remembreth me / Upon my yowthe, and on my jolitee / It tikleth me aboute myn herte roote. . . . / But age, allas! that al wole envenyme, / Hath me biraft my beautee and my pith" (*CT*, III, 469–71, 474–75). The Wife of Bath's Prologue was one, I suspect, that Chaucer was loath to finish.

Alisoun's male counterpart is Pandarus in the *Troilus and Criseyde*. They have the same ancestors and lineage, except that Pandarus is unsuccessful in love and thus his emotional life is a vicarious one. Here too a sadness lurks in the background, and his bustling efforts on behalf of hie niece and friend have become suspect through the action of time. But Chaucer's Pandarus is not yet tainted. He moves the action with zest and joy in the hunt. He huffs, and puffs, and sweats through the streets of Troy; he carries letters, stuffs them down the breast of the unwilling receiver, organizes a series of complex rendezvous worthy the efforts of our best P.R. men, which involve scores of people and feigned motives, in order to attain a brief secret meeting, and finally tears the shirt off the fainting lover and "into bed hym caste." Admittedly, his values are surface ones compared to those of Troilus. Pandarus would hold with the lower birds in the *Parlement of Foules* rather than with the courtly eagles. But it must be remembered that Pandarus never knew love, whereas Troilus had tasted it to the full. Pandarus therefore never got over his concern about the basic need for sex; a starved man can not wait for gourmet food. However, these considerations could lead us into an area that is not necessarily comic and there is no need to pursue them here. I have mentioned them, and Alisoun's complexity, only in passing, to show that Chaucer produces a comedy that is human and compassionate, truly humane.

But "Awak!" It is not always human. Among the greatest comic figures that Chaucer produced, the Wife of Bath and Pandarus, we must not forget his birds! Perhaps the most astonishingly delightful of all of Chaucer's comic characters is the enormous golden "Egle" that appears at the end of Book I of the *House of Fame* and is the main actor in Book II. The eagle is at first a fearsome animal as he swoops down to pick up Geoffrey in his claws. Diverse thoughts, of Dante, of the rape of Ganymede, even of the terrible bird Roc in the Arabian Nights pass through

our mind, and possibly Chaucer's as he is swooped up, and the poet fears
that he perhaps might join other dead notables among the stars: " 'O
God!' thoughte I, 'that madest kynde, / Shal I noon other weyes dye? /
Wher Joves wol me stellyfye?' " (*HF*, 584–86). But as it turns out, the
eagle is a kindly, if authoritative teacher, who shows his hapless burden
the world from the skies, initiates him into the mystery of the law of
sound, as they behold beneath them fields and plains, valleys and forests,
and ships sailing in the sea. The Egle would even have shown Chaucer
the stars close up, had not the poet demurred, pleading his age and
danger to his eyesight. The avian guide will lead Chaucer to the House
of Fame, to hear tidings of love, but the more he talks, the less the poet
dares to answer. In fact, this preceptorial eagle is enthused with his
ability and the opportunity to teach a student of little mind, as Geoffrey
appears to be. Like any good teacher who wishes to establish rapport, he
has addressed the poet by his first name, and he even asks for "student
feedback," delighting already in his assured success:

> Telle me this now feythfully,
> Have y not preved thus symply,
> Withoute any subtilite
> Of speche, or gret prolixite
> Of termes of philosophie,
> Of figures of poetrie,
> Or colours of rethorike?
> Pardee, hit oughte the to lyke!
> For hard langage and hard matere
> Ys encombrous for to here
> Attones; wost thou not wel this?"
> And y answered and seyde, "Yis."
>   "A ha!" quod he, "lo, so I can
> Lewedly to a lewed man
> Speke, and shewe hym swyche skiles
> That he may shake hem be the biles,
> So palpable they shulden be." (*HF*, II, 853–69)

If I might enter into this discussion with a personal remark, I would
say that for me Chaucer's Egle represents one of the high points of his
comedy, truly funny for many complex reasons, of which the most important probably are the lovable pedantry of the bird and the author's
identification with his own persona; the "lewed man" in the eagle's claws
is "Geffrey." Also, in spite of the eagle's obvious enthusiasm for his own

wisdom, he is a powerful teacher, an enormously learned, and eccentric bird of a man. It seems only natural to identify him with an individual we know through legend, perhaps a great professor. As a Chaucerian, impressed, admittedly, only by hearsay, the Egle has always seemed to me like a huge, flying George Lyman Kittredge, and how apt (or ironic?) that he should be teaching Chaucer.

Eagles also appear in the *Parlement of Foules*, although there they are of lesser interest than their "lower class" counterparts. Notwithstanding that there is much doubt of the exact meaning of this poem, with its debates on love and common profit, there is no question that it is one of the finest small jewels in Chaucer's collection of gems. The poet's sympathy here clearly lies with the rabble in their impatience with the courtly love ritual of the noble birds of prey, the stultifying debate of the "tercels" who woo a shy "formel" lady eagle. They too have their humor, but it is the cuckoo, the goose, the duck, and turtledove who really get this show on the road. The representatives of water, seed, and worm fowls have their say in no uncertain terms:

> The goos, the cokkow, and the doke also
> So cryede, "Kek kek! kokkow! quek quek!" hye
> That thourgh myne eres the noyse wente tho.
> The goos seyde, "Al this nys not worth a flye! (*PF*, 498–501)

The goose's advice is simple: If she won't love him, let him love another, to which the sparrow hawk replies with open contempt, "Lo, here a parfit resoun of a goos!" The duck reacts scornfully to the turtledove's romantic idea of everlasting love: " 'Wel bourded,' quod the doke 'by mye hat!' " What a silly idea! "Ye quek!" There are more stars in heaven than a pair. But this remark angers the falcon: "Now fy cherl! . . . Out of the donghill cam that word ful right!" reminding us that we are very much part of a class society. But there is so much of earnest absurdity shown by the members of this parliament or congress of birds, all of which leads to no resolution, that to look for underlying symbols or meaning here is to take the edge off the comedy. It is enough to have the duck swear by his hat (which he would not do if he did not wear one) and to envision this bird with a headdress taken from the Ellesmere MS illustrations. Perhaps a Flemish beaver hat might stand him well, since he supposedly represents the merchant class. However, we must never forget that he is but a duck.

Nor must we forget that Chauntecleer is but a cock! For the mock-heroic beast fable of the *Nun's Priest's Tale* is the most delightful marriage story of them all, and wifely Pertelote's long helpful speech from VII, 2907–68 (after her mate has awakened from an ominous dream of death by a hound-like beast) runs a very human gamut of rhetorically noble outrage at her caitiff, coward of a husband, to wise counsel on humors and dreams, and finally to the truly basic, solicitous advice to "taak som laxatyf." Earnest thoughts, which surely have overextended the knowledge of Pertelote as no situation ever had before, she who was used to listen meekly to the endless crowings of her noble lord and master. To all of which her husband patronizingly answers, smiling condescendingly through his beak: "Madame, . . . graunt mercy of youre loore." And then we are launched into fine rhetoric, great speeches, which never seem to stop, the upshot of which are ". . . I seye forthermoor, / That I ne telle of laxatyves no stoor. . . ." Truly, Chauntecleer is a magnificent cock, in his own eyes certainly like to Ozymandias, king of kings, of the barnyard, and equally unstable of perch.

The Beast Fable of the continent, with its Reynard and Ysengrim and various fowls, was, like the fabliaux, not too well known in England. Here, as everywhere, Chaucer took the roots of material from foreign soil, fertilized the ground with new genius, and let the plant flower. Chauntecleer is literature's greatest rooster. He is as long-winded as the Egle, but he is less lovable, for he lacks the Egle's ingenuous enthusiasm for teaching and concern for his student. Chauntecleer, we remember, is so superior to all, that he will indulge himself in a private joke, with no one around to understand it, except (perhaps) himself:

> For al so siker as *In principio*
> *Mulier est hominis confusio,*
> Madame, the sentence of this Latyn is,
> 'Womman is mannes joye and al his blis.' (*CT*, VII, 3163–66)

Indeed, such pride goeth before a fall. But, although much of the rooster's glory is but a sham, though he is at times so infuriating that one would love to call him a pompous ass if he were not a bird (and indeed such a one would by his very inflated nature hate the undignified thought of laxatives), still, his wit wins out, and all is well in the end. Chaucer's birds follow a definite line of comedy. They are all very talkative (as birds seem to be on an early summer morning), and they pontificate to various degrees. Thus their comedy is a verbal one, and as characters they are not so dimensionally drawn, so deeply probed as Chaucer's human creations. The birds are caricatures; were they more they would be humans masquerading in feathers, and that, of course, is not the point of the game.

Language in general was Chaucer's most effective comic tool. Where his humor appeals to our intellectual sense it is always in the ironic statement, the understated conclusion in many portraits of the General Prologue, the implication in the accumulation of irrelevant material, and the quick-running, highly realistic dialogue of the pilgrims. We recognize many of his portraits in Langland's *Piers Plowman* where this "earnest contemporary of Chaucer's" has included stereotypes and broad comedy of similar individuals: friars, physicians, pardoners. But where Langland cuts with a broadsword, Chaucer pierces with a foil. His Friar is an individual; his name is Huberd. Such a worthy man as he should have no truck with lepers and other unwholesome beings. And the Prioresse, a most elegant and truly charming woman! We learn all about her table manners, her dress, her love of dogs, her physical beauty, her jewelry. Forty-five lines of description but not a word of her spiritual qualities or duty. She did sing the divine service well, but then so might have the Wife of Bath or "hende" Nicholas. Everywhere in the General Prologue Chaucer challenges our values, the standards we go by, of getting and spending and laying waste our powers. But he does not judge us, or his pilgrims. Indeed, he defends them, in the guise of his little-witted alter ego, the pilgrim Chaucer. At one point, we remember (*CT*, I, 183–88), he explains that he had conversed with the Monk, and in this conversation had agreed fully with the Monk's worldly principles. Nor did he do so ironically then, for at the present moment he is telling us, the reader, about this little talk, and even justifies himself to us as to the reason why "I seyde his opinion was good." How, after all, should the world be served! It is here, in the General Prologue, that our enjoyment of Chaucer's comedy becomes an exciting game which involves our own sharpness of mind and appreciation for the most delicate shades of irony. This is intellectual humor. Few of the pilgrims are exempt from the poet's finger. It points at high and low, at religious as well as secular: The Sergeant at Lawe, "Nowher so bisy a man as he ther nas / And yet he semed bisier than he was" (*CT*, I, 321–22); the Merchant, "This worthy man ful wel his wit bisette: / Ther wiste no wight that he was in dette. . . ." (*CT*, I, 279–80); the Cook, "But greet harm was it, as it thoughte me, / That on his shyne a mormal hadde he. / For blank-manger, that made he with the beste" (*CT*, I, 385–87). For most, the trip to Canterbury was indeed a necessary one.

Again, language unifies the various tales into a human comedy of pilgrims. The so-called "links" among the tales, the argumentative chains of cause and effect among the narrators, provide the living magic; for the Miller wishes to "quite" the Knight, and in doing so insults the Reeve, whose tale enthuses the drunken Cook—three tales and a fragment thereby tied into unity. The Wife of Bath's brilliant monologue, interrupted by the nervous Pardoner and commented on ironically by the Friar, who provokes the Summoner, leads into a series of six tales. Everywhere there is movement, medieval England on the highway, but the road that is travelled seems never very distant from our own. For if we have not met these people, then our friends have, and indeed some of them are our friends. Worse luck, at times we even see ourselves! This acquaintance with Chaucer's pilgrims, then as today, stems from familiarity with the little touches and gestures of our fallible humanity, as when the Wife of Bath forgets for a moment the point of what she was saying (*CT*, III, 585–86), or the Friar in the *Summoner's Tale* shows his arrogant familiarity with the house he visits: "And fro the bench he droof awey the cat" (*CT*, III, 1775). As Dryden said, here indeed is God's plenty, and it is brought about through the word.

But when the word mocks the word, when language makes fun of language, then indeed our sense of humor is cerebrally challenged. And such it is with Chaucer's amazing gift of parody. In this most literate form of comedy, Chaucer was the great innovator in English letters. Here was virgin territory, a new world, and only an independent, uninhibited mind would have had the urge to leave the old world of literary convention, and embark out.

For Chaucer, this old world consisted in the main of the traditional French themes of *amour courtois*, *service d'amour*, and romance literature. Machaut and Deschamps schooled him in the early days; the *Roman de la Rose* was at his bedside. Thus it was this type of standard noble fare which proved to be grist for Chaucer's satiric mill. Parody and mockery of courtly love themes appear throughout the *Canterbury Tales* and, in fact, form part of the last poem he presented at court, one of his wittiest verbal games, employing double and even triple entendres, the *Complaint to his Purse*.

One can imagine that Chaucer could hardly wait to finish the *Knight's Tale*, so that he could "quite" it with the Miller's. In the latter we find his most pervasive imitation, on a lower and absurd level, of the courtly *descriptio* and painstaking ritual of the game of love previously played by Arcite, Palamon, and Emily. The Miller's wife, Alisoun, is described in eye, brow, mouth, hue, and song, but she is dark rather than fair, and her body is not like to a goddess, but rather a weasel. The parallels to the portrait of Emily are exact in form, but on a lower, animal scale. "Wynsynge she was, as is a joly colt," and class difference is made explicit in the conclusion: "She was a prymerole, a piggesnye, / For any lord to leggen in his bedde, / Or yet for any good yeman to wedde" (*CT*, I, 3263, 3267–70). Though her first lover, Nicholas, is a handy man, her second, Absolon, woos only by word and mouth. He sings a love song, "Lemman, thy grace, and sweete bryd, thyn oore!", chews licorice, and puts a sweet-smelling herb under his tongue to change the odor of his breath. Like a courtly lover, he will languish and pass a sleepless night, but to endure this vigil he must first take an afternoon nap. We have burlesque here and parody, for Absolon addresses his beloved weasel in the words of the Song of Solomon, explaining that she makes him "swete" for love of her. Unfortunately, as we know, his oral tactics backfire, and "His hoote love was coold and al yqueynt!" (On his home court Chaucer's word play is indeed hard to beat.)

Since we find a similar mockery of convention in the *Merchant's Tale*— the secret message, *complaint d'amour*, the rather quick "mercy" of May and illicit assignation in the bower of love (a pear tree), and even a parody of the French Aube in the *Reeve's Tale*: "Fare weel, Malyne, sweete wight! / The day is come, I may no lenger byde. . . ." (*CT*, I, 4236–37)—it seems clear that one of the main themes of Chaucer's fabliaux is the burlesque of romance tradition and that the joke is always at the expense of the middle and lower class.

This is perhaps best seen in Chaucer's two most brilliant tours de force, *Sir Thopas* and the *Nun's Priest's Tale*. The first is a parody of the endless Middle English tail rhyme romances. A continuous repetition of the rhyme scheme *aab, aab* over a long period of time tends to engender a range of reactions, from sleep to irritation. But it does not ever inspire delight. And yet *Sir Thopas* is a thoroughly delightful piece. Chaucer takes a bourgeois Flemish "knight" who swears by ale and bread, a "doghty swayn" described in feminine terms, white of face, red of lips, and with a "semely nose." He loves an elf queen he has never seen, rides through a forest: "Therinne is many a wilde best, / Ye, bothe bukke and hare," (*CT*, VII, 755–56) on a war horse that "gooth an ambil in the way." Nothing is sacred in this piece, neither romance style, nor action, nor hero. In the romances, the tail rhyme line, for instance, does have a specific narrative function as transition, or as strong concluding statement. The stanzas should build up to these lines and to the last important line especially:

> Sir Thopas was a doghty swayn
> Whit was his face as payndemayn
> His lippes rede as rose;
> His rode is lyk scarlet in grayn,
> And I yow telle in good certayn,
> He hadde a semely nose. (*CT*, VII, 724–29)

The letdown can be heard. The "semely nose" is not only burlesque of noble heroic description, but also parody of the romance stanza, and this double effect is seen throughout a work which is of major importance in English literary history. The poem is a fun house of delight for medievalists, but we are not all too unhappy when the Host puts a stop to it, though we must disagree with his opinion that the pilgrim Chaucer's "drasty rymyng is nat worth a toord."

From a misplaced middle-class burgher in a fairy world of romance, we descend further into the henyard of the *Nun's Priest's Tale*. This simple story of a rooster's dream of death, his abduction by a fox, and his subsequent rescue is the core of an extremely intricate, fascinating, and intriguing web of Chaucer's highest art, especially since many of the poet's major literary and philosophic themes are here tossed about in rapid sequence and apparent wild abandon. The narrative moves from the lowest style of barnyard communication: "Out! harrow! and weyl away! / Ha! Ha! the fox!"—and after him ran Colle the dog, and Malkin with a distaff in her hand—to the highest style of noble rhetoric and lament after Chauntecleer had closed his eyes to the fox who did him "by the gargat hente." "O destinee, that mayst nat been eschewed. . . . O Venus, that art goddesse of plesaunce. . . . O Gaufred, deere maister soverayn . . .

> O woful hennes, right so criden ye
> As when that Nero brende the citee
> Of Rome cryden senatoures wyves
> For that hir husbondes losten alle hir lyves. (*CT*, VII, 3369–72)

Earthshaking is the tragedy of Chauntecleer's fall. He is classed with the great heroes of all time and his enemy the fox with the greatest of biblical, classical, and romance villains:

> O false mordrour, lurkynge in thy den!
> O new Scariot, newe Genylon,
> False dissymulour, o Greek Synon,
> That broghtest Troye al outrely to sorwe!
> O Chauntecleer, acursed be that morwe
> That thou into that yerd flaugh fro the bemes! (*CT*, VII, 3226–31)

His Fall is sung in Boethian terms, and it is blamed on the advice of woman in true anti-feminist, or anti-hen, fashion. The glorious romance fury of the cock's outraged sovereign mistress ends with homely advice against constipation. A topsy-turvy world, a spectacular literary production where almost every line turns a new corner, brings new lore divertingly into play, about dreams, references to the medieval Bestiary, saints' legends, and the ways of Fortune. Indeed, this is Big Game. Its true splendor is surely wasted on the newcomer to Chaucer although, unfortunately, the tale is often found on the high school reading list. It is a work that can be enjoyed to the fullest extent only by those who are familiar with the poet, his major themes, and their medieval background. A comic masterpiece like the *Nun's Priest's Tale* occurs but once in English literature. It merits a prepared reader.

When we view this literary wealth of a lifetime, it is hard to imagine that its creator was a man taken to task continually for his ignorance, his dullness, his little wit. Wherever he went or flew, he was treated with impatience by the Black Knight, lectured to by an Egle, yanked out of bed and shoved hither and yon by the Noble Roman Africanus, condemned to talk about endlessly faithful women by the God of Love, and finally told to shut up by the Host of the Tabard Inn. And there is no question about the identity of this hapless individual. His name was "Geffrey" in the *House of Fame*, and "Chaucer" in the Tales. He is a poet, and round of form. This is how Chaucer saw himself and developed himself as the "persona" in most of his works, throughout the vast adventure of his life.

He was himself his own greatest comic figure, and the delight he took in having himself appear again and again, in the most ludicrous of situations, is patent. We can only conjecture on why he took such pleasure in this unusual device, a figure which paradoxically seemed to increase in naiveté as Chaucer grew older, and undoubtedly wiser. There are many theories; the subject has been a central debate of our times. Let me say here only that it represents a kind of comedy that issues from the poet's heart. Chaucer's own pose was not an intellectually planned device. In some ways it was traditional, having been used in French literature and in English by Langland and the author of *Pearl*. But Chaucer's persona had a specific name, the poet's, and his own profession. As I have mentioned above, the use of this kind of narrator is revealing. *Ad hominem* humor was alien to Chaucer, though Pynchebeke was a living lawyer, Roger of Ware a cook, and Harry Bailey host of the real Tabard. All of these, however, were portrayed as experts in their work; none was derided as being dim or dull. Chaucer had enough confidence in his name and reputation to be able to point the finger at himself. Rather would he do it so that others would not. But to reason this way is to insert a calculating quality into his humor. It is not there, although Chaucer could not have survived three kings in the English civil service, had he not been capable of diplomacy. His persona may indeed have been a shield, at Court or in affairs, but the symbol it bore represented Geoffrey Chaucer's main characteristic: he was wise to himself, and to his world, and thus he could be no man's fool.

Our mention of the Sergeant at Law at whose writing none could "pynche" (*CT*, I, 326) brings to mind that we should say a few words about Chaucer's lost humor. Much of the poet's comedy was topical of course. We need new Manlys with their Rickerts to come up with more historical identifications. No doubt there are such. Also, a full understanding of Chaucer's pervasive and complex punning will have to await the "zodiak" or other terminal word of the *Middle English Dictionary*. At present we find many puns where we should not, but overlook, I am sure, even more. Again, the recent stress on the oral presentation of Chaucer's works—but only by himself, I would suppose,—must lead us to study cadences and rhythmic patterns of his verse. Perhaps the joke lay in the telling, though possibly Chaucer was as dull a reciter of his own verse as some of our modern poets today.

In the process of rediscovering Chaucer's lost humor, two caveats should be observed. First, we cannot trust any of his specific descriptive references to be merely ornamental; an underlying narrative reason may always be lurking in the bush. Second, we must be careful never to stop looking until we are sure to have reached the basic level of a term. In describing the Reeve in the General Prologue, for instance, Chaucer writes (or reads aloud to his audience):

> Of Northfolk was this Reve of which I telle,
> Biside a toun men clepen Baldeswelle. (*CT*, I, 619–20)

The reference to Norfolk and Baldeswell is meaningless to us today except as it specifies the home of the Reeve, and thus adds to a sense of realism. But it cannot serve as a joke. And yet it did probably provoke chuckles in Chaucer's listeners, for we know today that the provinces sent many immigrants to London at this very time, and most of them came from Norfolk, specifically even from Baldeswell. Their dialect was just on the fringe of comprehension, and their manners quite uncitified. Baldeswell is a topical joke, rediscovered, but, in finding it, the spectre of countless undiscovered others rises before us.

Again, the ugly, disfiguring disease of the Summoner, of whose "visage children were aferd" has been identified in the past as "alopecia," a medieval form of "leprosy," and there the matter was allowed to stand for decades. It added something to the portrait of this cunning and lecherous church warden of social morality: it made him even uglier than he was. But as has been noted, Chaucer rarely wastes words purely for descriptive reasons. When we look a little further and see that in the Middle Ages "leprosy" was a venereal disease, and thus more often than not confused with syphilis, the joke of the Summoner's disease broadens indeed. The face of this corrupt member of the Church's "vice-squad" betrays him to the world. All these are indeed only stones in Chaucer's grand mosaic, but they prove that the reconstruction of this mosaic is incomplete, that much can still be done by scholars, historical or critical, to add to their own enjoyment, and all our benefit.

For Chaucer repays a lifetime of study with a lifetime of ever-increasing pleasure in his works. And it is more than that. Chaucer provides for many that very thing which Matthew Arnold felt he lacked, an essential quality in his work "which gives to our spirits what they can rest upon." This is so because Chaucer's comedy is not of the intellect alone, and here Meredith's thought is incomplete when he writes that comedy laughs through the mind, that it is really the "humour of the mind." But when the critic adds that "the test of true Comedy is that it shall awaken thoughtful laughter,"[4] we would agree, for thoughtfulness is characterized by a searching, a depth of feeling. We respond emotionally to Chaucer's comedy of life, do we not? The Wife of Bath or Pandarus do not affect us on an intellectual plane alone, nor can we react to the com-

---

[4] Meredith, p. 46.

plex implications of Chaucer's own portrait throughout his works only on this level. In spite of the poet's frequently discussed relativism of view, and his refusal ever to give a specific judgment, Chaucer does have a consistent overall sense of life, one of attained optimism fostered by a genial and tranquil spirit, which we are taught again and again when we study what he tells us. This sense is not only, as a later author explains, that

> All the world's a stage
> And all the men and women merely players.
> They have their exits and their entrances. . . .
>   (*As You Like It*, II.vii.139–41)

although it may have seemed so to the writer, for, no doubt, he knew his craft well. But life is not really play acting, with each of us set in our predestined comic or tragic parts. Some more useful information about the world would seem preferable, even if the news were bad. I can, for instance, accept the Chaucerian statement that

> This world nys but a thorghfare ful of wo
> And we been pilgrymes, passynge to and fro (*CT*, I, 2847–49)

for I know that the man who has recognized this "lytel erthe" for what it is, can, in spite of such knowledge, continually look past the sorrow at the world's joy, take cheer in the pilgrimage, hold the "heye weye" and sustain us as well along the road.

Those of us who have devoted our lives to the lessons of this great teacher of comedy, dissimilar as we may at times appear to be, have been united by his spirit into a unique fellowship, with Chaucer himself as our prime mover and friend. Like the Host,

> He served us with vitaille at the beste;
> Strong was the wyn, and wel to drynke us leste.

On the pilgrimage, I admit, I have "rested upon" him and drunk with him often, and he has lightened my mood. Truly, I cannot imagine for any of us a more happy vocation than the continuing opportunity to pass this sustaining pleasure on to others.

Indeed, all things considered, and with all due humility, I think we Chaucerians are a fortunate lot.

Italian Renaissance Comedy

Louise George Clubb
University of California

Italian Renaissance comedy, a phrase to open a debate about genre. It could be argued that the comic novella or Folengo's mock heroics or the smiling narrative cosmos of the *Orlando Furioso* are no less comedy than the *commedia* which preempted the name at the first performance of Ariosto's *La Cassaria* in 1508 and was still flourishing when Della Porta died in 1615. Even if limited by Frye's "radical of presentation," Cinquecento comedy in a liberal definition comprehends many theatrical kinds, including *farse*, moral and otherwise, various secular outgrowths of rhymed *sacre rappresentazioni*, Ruzante's peasant plays and the improvisations of the professional *comici*. Distinct from all of these is the vernacular five-act drama with intrigue plot employing characters and situations developed from Attic New Comedy and from the Boccaccian novella tradition, regulated by unity of time and place according to principles of generalized realism, representing a contemporary urban middle class as festival entertainment for an élite audience. So run the rough specifications of the model that emerged early and determined an enormous production in the sixteenth century alone, from the definitive examples set in Ferrara, Florence, Urbino and Rome by Ariosto, Machiavelli and Bibbiena, through comedies of Piccolomini, D'Ambra, Firenzuola, Grazzini, Cecchi, Caro, Aretino, Gelli, Pino, Razzi, Bargagli, Oddi, Calderari, Parabosco, Loredano the elder, Borghini and Della Porta.[1] The genre was published as well as performed, discussed by

[1] These are the general boundaries of *commedia erudita* not disputed by recent Italian scholarship, for significant examples of which, see Mario Baratto, *La Commedia del Cinquecento* (Vicenza: Neri Pozza, 1975); Nino Borsellino, *Rozzi e Intronati. Esperienze e forme di teatro dal Decameron al Candelaio* (Roma: Bulzoni, 1974); Nino Borsellino and Roberto Mercuri, *Il Teatro del Cinquecento* (Bari: Laterza, 1973), pp. 10-72; Ettore Paratore, "Nuove prospettive sull'influsso del teatro classico nel '500," *Il Teatro classico nel '500* (Roma: Accademia Nazionale dei Lincei, 1971), pp. 9-95; Gianfranco Folena, ed., *Lingua e struttura del*

theoreticians, and soon illustrated by its own classics. Modern taste on the whole confirms the opinion entrenched by 1554, when Girolamo Ruscelli edited a collection of "elect" comedies already long in print: Bibbiena's *La Calandra* (or *Calandria*), Machiavelli's *La Mandragola*, *Gli Ingannati* of disputed authorship, Piccolominis *L'Amor costante* and *L'Alessandro*.[2]

Treatises on drama and prologues to comedies of the time bear witness to continuing agreement about tradition and the status of the new classics. Bernardo Pino, spokesman for the serious *commedia* admired later in the sixteenth century, addresses his *Breve considerazione intorno al componimento de la comedia de' nostri tempi* to Sforza Oddi, with whose *L'Erofilomachia, overo Il Duello d'amore, et d'amicizia*, it was published six years after its composition:[3] predictably, Pino refers with

teatro italiano del Rinascimento. Machiavelli. Ruzzante. Aretino. Guarini. Commedi dell'Arte (Padova: Liviana, 1970); Giulio Ferroni, *"Mutazione" e "riscontro" nel teatro di Machiavelli, e altri saggi sulla commedia del Cinquecento* (Roma: Bulzoni, 1972); Aulo Greco, *L'Istituzione del teatro comico nel Rinascimento* (Napoli: Liguori, 1976). Discussions in English include Marvin T. Herrick, *Italian Comedy in the Renaissance* (Urbana: University of Illinois Press, 1960); Douglas Radcliff-Umstead, *The Birth of Modern Comedy in Renaissance Italy* (Chicago: University of Chicago Press, 1969); Beatrice Corrigan, "Italian Renaissance Comedy and Its Critics: A Survey of Recent Studies," *Renaissance Drama*, New Series V (Evanston: Northwestern University Press, 1972), 191–211; Franco Fido, "Reflections on Comedy by Some Italian Renaissance Playwrights," *Medieval Epic to the "Epic Theater" of Brecht*, ed. Rosario P. Armato and John M. Spalek, *University of Southern California Studies in Comparative Literature*, I (Los Angeles, 1968), 85–95; Louise George Clubb, *Italian Plays (1500–1700) in the Folger Library* (Firenze: Olschki, 1968), Introduction *passim*; Leo Salingar, "Shakespeare and Italian Comedy," *Shakespeare and the Traditions of Comedy* (Cambridge: Cambridge University Press, 1974), pp. 175–242. For neo-Latin predecessors, see Antonio Staüble, *La Commedia umanistica del Quattrocento* (Firenze: Sede dell'Istituto Palazzo Strozzi, 1968). For the *commedia dell'arte*, the still indispensable Kathleen M. Lea, *Italian Popular Comedy: A Study in the Commedia dell'Arte, 1560–1620, with Special Reference to the English Stage*, 2 vols. (Oxford: Oxford University Press, 1934), and more recently, Roberto Tessari, *La Commedia dell'Arte nel Seicento. "Industria" e "Arte giocosa" della civiltà barocca* (Firenze: Olschki, 1969). In addition to editions of works of individual authors, there are collections by Ireneo Sanesi, ed., *Comedy del Cinquecento*, 2 vols. (Bari: Laterza, 1912), rpt. a cura di Maria Luisa Doglio (1975); Nino Borsellino, ed., *Commedie del Cinquecento*, 2 vols. (Milano: Feltrinelli, 1962–1967); Aldo Borlenghi, ed., *Commedie del Cinquecento* (Milano: Rizzoli, 1959), 2 vols.; and the collection included in *Il Teatro italiano*, announced by Einaudi Editore under the general editorship of Guido Davico Bonino, *Teatro del Cinquecento*, 4 vols. (2 voll, 4 tomi).

[2] *Delle comedie elette novamente raccolte insieme, con le correttioni, et annotationi di Girolamo Ruscelli* (Venetia: Plinio Pietrasanta, 1554).

[3] (Venetia: Gio. Battista Sessa, e fratelli, 1578), rpt. in Bernard Weinberg, ed., *Trattati di poetica e retorica del Cinquecento*, II (Bari: Laterza, 1970), 629–49.

admiration to Oddi, as to Plautus and Terence, but with pointed discrimination he also names Piccolomini's comedies as models and pays homage to Bibbiena. He forbears to observe, however, that *La Calandria* was composed on moral grounds very different from those he was urging for the genre in his own time.

The *comici dell'arte* exhibited a kindred taste in choosing plays to borrow. The actor-manager Fabrizio de' Fornaris was given the comedy he published in 1585 under the title *Angelica* by "a most accomplished Neapolitan gentleman,"[4] probably the author himself, Giovanni Battista Della Porta, whose *L'Olimpia* is clearly the original version. In an "Amoroso contrasto sopra la comedia," one of the "Contrasti scenici" culled from her repertory of scenes for improvisation and published posthumously, the foremost actress of the century, Isabella Andreini, speaks authoritatively of Aristotle's *Poetics* and of peripety and recognition in comedy, and recommends imitating Plautus, Terence, Piccolomini, Trissino, Calderari, Pino and Aristophanes.[5] What the literary dramatists and the professional actors agreed on as the model of the genre is the subject of this essay.

For the High Renaissance, genre was not solely a hypothetical instrument of analysis; it was a fact of art and a prescription. The *commedia* determined by this view is called *erudita* because it was deliberately developed from a learned tradition after centuries of hiatus, *regolare* because linked with nascent theory in search of rules for literary and dramatic criticism, *letteraria* because written with attention to classical and Trecento linguistic precepts or in polemic against them, *classica* for these reasons and because it was cultivated by an avant garde to whom neo-classicism was still an innovation.

Theorizing through their prologues in the spirit of *serio ludere* that so often governed humanists in the first half of the Cinquecento, play-

---

[4] *Angelica, comedia* (Parigi: Abel L'Angelier, 1585), Dedication, "gl'anni adietro mi fu da un gentil-homo Napolitano virtuosissimo spirto, donata questa comedia. . . ."

[5] *Fragmenti di alcune scritture della Signora Isabella Andreini Comica Gelosa, et Academica Intenta. Raccolti da Francesco Andreini Comico Geloso detto il Capitano Spavento, a dati in luce da Flamminio Scala Comico* (Venetia: Gio. Battista Combi, 1620), p. 60; in the preface Isabella's husband, Francesco, states that the volume contains his compositions also, but does not say which they are. Aristophanic airs were put on early and late: by Alessandro Vellutello, Preface to Agostino Ricchi's *I Tre tiranni* (Vinegia: Barnardino de Vitali, 1533), and by Melchiore Zoppio, *Il Diogene accusato* (Venetia: Gasparo Bindoni, 1958). Perhaps Machiavelli's lost *Le Maschere* was more genuine.

wrights could apologize slily with Ariosto for the inevitable inferiority of modern vernacular comedy to its Greek and Latin prototypes (prose *Cassaria*, Prologue),[6] explain with Donato Giannotti that one could improve on a Plautine plot to make a comedy both new and old (*Il Vecchio amoroso*, 1533–36, Prologue),[7] or boast with Francesco D'Ambra of not having written a "comedia grave" with sententious speeches like one of Terence (*I Bernardi*, 1547, Prologue);[8] the differences in the attitudes struck in these prologues and the forty years separating the first from the last obscure neither the kinship of the comedies they introduce nor the fact that the three *commediografi* were at one in identifying the context of their genre. They saw themselves as heirs and, above all, as competitors of Menander, Plautus and Terence.

Scholarly attention has often singled out the departures from the generic norm and the challenges to it presented by individual comedies. Probably the most original achievement in Italian comedy, however, was the collective one of setting that norm. It took a considerable time to do, more than three decades merely to cast the first mould, and the emergence of a definitive shape did not end the experimentation with genre. If the construction of a generic model in the early Cinquecento is interesting, moreover, so is the re-affirmation and testing which simultaneously occupied comic dramatists after the 1540's. The form of the *commedia* was continually tried for flexibility and balance, its limits prodded, its capacity for meaning stretched. An unremitting concern for genre is attested by what remained constant, from that most representative, often performed and prophetic of *commedie*, *La Calandria* of 1513, to the atypical *jeu d'esprit*, *Il Candelaio*, Giordano Bruno's *anti-commedia* of 1584. Even the changes that bear the comedies of Oddi, Borghini and Della Porta far away from *Calandria* and *Mandragola* are motivated by curiosity about the genre and vigilance about its fundamental principles.

First among these was the principle of *contaminatio*. Defending his *Andria* from the critics who objected to contamination of one plot with another ("disputant contaminari non decere fabulas," *Andria*, Prologue),[9] Terence had owned to mixing the two Menandrine comedies,

---

[6] *Commedie e satire di Lodovico Ariosto*, ed. Giovanni Tortoli (Firenze: Barbéra, Bianchi, 1856). Further references to Ariosto are to this edition.

[7] Borsellino, *Commedie*, I. Further references to Giannotti are to this edition.

[8] Borlenghi, *Commedie*, 2.

[9] *Terence*, with trans. by John Sargeaunt, I, Loeb Classical Library (1912; rpt. Cambridge, Mass. and London: Harvard University Press and William Heinemann, 1959).

Perinthia and *Andria*. What Terence defended, Ariosto boasted of, pointing out his mixture of Terence's *Eunuchus* with Plautus' *Captivi* (prose *Suppositi*, Prologue). What had been simply a convenient practice of the ancients determined a formal goal of generations of Italian *commediografi*: fusion of increasingly numerous and disparate sources, displaying of composition and its exaggerated emphasis on story in contrast with the Terentian comedy he admired (*Essais* II, 10).

Corollary to the principle of contamination was that of complication, proceeding from an early preoccupation with structure and plot which would be re-enforced by the later vogue of Aristotle's *Poetics*. The standard of form demanded not only unity of action, aided by the strictures on time and place that were supposed to guarantee the tension of crisis to the plot, but multiple intrigues as well. The specific flaw in his Plautine source, *Mercator*, that Giannotti aimed to remedy in *Vecchio amoroso* was that "it was very simply woven" (Prologue).[10]

Even in the first three decades of experimentation, exceptions to the principle of complication were rare and not persuasive. After the first *La Cortigiana* of 1525, Aretino set about building intrigue structures; the plots of his *La Talanta* and *L'Ipocrito* even over-compensate for an initial lack of complexity. *L'Anconitana* (1534–35?) shows Ruzante's willingness to sacrifice his best gifts on the altar of structural principle. *La Mandragola*, numbered among the "comedie elette" that Ruscelli edited as monuments in the history of the genre, was not admired for its structure. Although he praises Machiavelli's language and even his disposition of scenes, and excuses the simple plot as a consequence of his wanting to make all the action arise from Messer Nicia's stupidity, Ruscelli nevertheless recommends against imitation, for "from the first act through the fourth and often midway through the fifth, Comedy should proceed by ever-increasing upheavals, differences, intrigues," whereas in *Mandragola*, "the fourth and the beginning of the fifth acts, in which usually occurs the greatest complication, proceed quietly from good to better; which certainly, as far as plot is concerned, is something to be avoided in a Comedy."[11]

---

[10] "che molto semplicemente fusse tessuto . . . ."

[11] *Delle comedie elette*, "Annotationi," 182–83, "la Comedia dal primo atto fino al quarto, et ancor molte volte sino al principio o mezo del quinto, ha da andar sempre crescendo in disturbi, in difficoltà, in intrighi. . . ." "La onde il quarto e il principio del quinto, ne' quali suole essere la maggiore intentione de gl'intrichi, procedono tutti quietamente, e di bene in meglio; che per certo in quanto al soggetto è cosa da fuggirsi in una Comedia."

If form was the primary aspect under which Italian comedy was seen as a re-emerging genre, content also required an ideal formulation. A spacious one with excellent credentials was at hand in the phrase that Aelius Donatus had attributed to Cicero and applied to the comedies of Terence: "comoediam esse Cicero ait imitationem vitae, speculum consuetudinis, imaginem veritatis."[12] This was translated into early Cinquecento comedy as realistic, that is, verisimilar imitation of contemporary middle-class life. However stylized the human relationships or overcharged with coincidence the *commedia* seems to an audience familiar with nineteenth-century drama and twentieth-century films, Renaissance playwrights' pride in their truth to reality is caught in Giovanni Battista Gelli's boast that his clever contemporaries were not to be taken in by the unbelievable stuff of saints' lives,[13] standard fare in medieval *rappresentazioni* combining religious and local folk legend in modes at brief remove from pageant and ritual. Modern *commedia* seemed closer to real life because it reduced the strain on the spectators' credulity. The physical and temporal confines of the action dispensed the audience from having to imagine more than that the events of one day in one city could be reflected in a few hours on one piazza. At the same time new demands were made. Ruscelli was not alone in emphasizing that the function of modern audiences was to see.[14] As spectators, observing rather than participating, they were invited to engage in an unaccustomed exercise of conscious detachment from the immediate reality of life in the street outside of the palace in which they were gathered for the performance, a reality reproduced inside by canvas, paint, wood and costumed friends or familiars. This aping of quotidian reality seems to have been exhilarating in itself; the act of counterfeiting was drawn often to the spectators' attention in prologues. Reality was treated as an object and the act of assuming a position apart from it, so as to compare its substance with its theatrical reflection, was a stimulating game.

The fictional time in the *commedia* was the present, the place a specific Italian city, and although the scenery was often general, an ideal model of Cinquecento urban architecture, re-usable for a comedy set in another

[12] *Aeli Donati quod fertur Commentum Terenti*, ed. P. Wessner, I (Leipzig: Teubner, 1902), 22.

[13] *La Sporta*, 1543, Prologue (Firenze: Bernardo Giunta, 1550), "le genti sono diventate tanto astute che Santa Anfrosina non istarebbe più cinque anni frate, che quei padri non si fossero accorti s'ella fossi maschio, o femina: ne Santo Alessio dieci anni sotto una scala senza essere di suo padre e da sua madre riconosciuto."

[14] "Annotationi," 170–71.

city (and therefore conducive to jesting in the prologue about the evanescence and arbitrariness of the theatrical illusion), it was the realism of the scene in perspective that was valued. Giorgio Vasari's praise of Baldessare Peruzzi's scene for *Calandria* does not dwell on its resemblance to any particular quarter of Rome, where the action is supposed to take place, but makes much of the success of the *trompe l'oeil*; it was the more original, adds Vasari, in that in Baldessare's day comedy had been out of use for a very long time and *feste* or *rappresentazioni* were undertaken instead.[15]

The characters of the street scene, at doorways, in alleys, windows, loggias and church porches are for the most part burghers, whether the setting is courtly Ferrara, papal Rome or nominally bourgeois Florence, and with them their economic dependents, those to whom they are employers, relatives, clients or gulls. Their concerns are domestic, turning on money and love and the conflict of generations, parents against children in the manner of New Comedy, old husbands against young wives and lovers in the Decameronian style.

Denouement may work in two ways: to conceal and to reveal. The plots lifted from novellas about cuckolds and *mal maritate* accommodate adultery and the deceits accompanying it, potentially anti-social actions which are kept secret when the order disturbed at the beginning is restored at the end. *La Mandragola* is entirely comedy of concealment: the revelation made to the audience is not fully shared with the society of the fiction, which remains split into the deceived (Messer Nicia) and the deceivers (everyone else). Plots from New Comedy, with its inheritance from romance, on the other hand, are resolved by marriages and new beginnings, correction of old errors, forgiveness of past deceits, recognitions and re-identifications of kin. Both sorts of denouement would persist in the late Cinquecento. *Il Candelaio* is essentially a comedy of concealment: the old order is not overthrown by the demonstration that its only realities are sex, violence, deceit and words. But comedy of concealment, if hardy, lost some ground as the century unfolded. The spirit of carnival gave way to the celebration of social order. The conclusion of the *commedia* became increasingly a tour de force of denouement culminating in a revelation, or series of revelations, sweeping all complexities into a neat design of marriages, family reunion, economic recovery and neighborhood pacification, extending in some late plays even to munici-

---

[15] *Delle vite de' piu eccellenti pittori scultori et architettori*, 3 (Fiorenza: Giunti, 1568), 141.

pal concord. The comic Oedipus situation which Frye descries behind New Comedy underlies the triumph of the younger generation in comedy of revelation; the re-integration achieved at the end is one that continues the old order but that, by shifting power to those who are next in line to become parents, makes the society new.

Both concealment and revelation are the ends of Bibbiena's *Calandria*. This play has so often been cited as containing what Baratto calls the "dramaturgical matrix" of Cinquecento comedy that any other example of generic principle in practice would be less hackneyed. But no other example is so apt. The early date, the unique comprehensiveness and the waxing prestige of *Calandria* throughout the sixteenth century give it a primacy in the genre that must still be acknowledged as it was by Ruscelli.[16]

Bibbiena's *contaminatio* merges two sources, Boccaccio and Plautus, but more than two plots. Several *novelle* of the *Decameron* are fused in the dramatic action involving Calandro, the feebleminded cuckold in love with the transvestite lover of his wife, and Fulvia, the *malmaritata* who employs a fake magician to further her love affair and is enabled by luck to conceal her adultery from Calandro and to regain the domestic upper hand by discovering his. Simultaneously, other *novelle* and Plautine sources in addition to *Menaechmi* are tapped for the plot of Santilla and Lidio, twins from the Greek city of Modon, whom fortune reunites in Rome. The mistakes inadvertently provoked by her disguise as a boy, for the sake of safety, and his as a girl, for the sake of love, are compounded by the deliberate deceits practiced for fun and for gain by a manipulating servant, Fessenio, and a charlatan, Ruffo. The revelation of the twins' identity and the betrothals arranged for them with the son of Fulvia and Calandro and the daughter of another rich Roman family restore the Greeks to wealth and to each other, creating a new order in the Italian community, while the suppression of the truth about Fulvia keeps up the appearance of the old one. The total gain is appraised by the arch-trickster Fessenio, the character most nearly in control of the intrigue, who caps Lidio's jubilant, "We shall be better off here than we were in Modon!" with words that are as applicable to the principles of the new genre of *commedia* founded on and surpassing Attic New Comedy as they are to the happy conclusion of the drama: "Just so much better as Italy is worthier than Greece, as Rome is nobler than Modon and as two fortunes are more valuable than one. And we shall all triumph!"

16 "Annotationi," 166.

(V, xii).[17] Rounding off the play, the ringing humanistic boast echoes the first prologue, attributed until recently to Castiglione,[18] in which the superiority of new Italian comedy and its inheritance from Boccaccio and from Plautus are simultaneously proclaimed. The five acts that lie in between, a synthesis of characters and episodes displayed in prose that is at once modern and timelessly Boccaccian, held in dramatic tension by the contraction of time to a day and space to a street scene, confirm the claim.

The complication that Bibbiena practices in the disposition of his multiple *contaminatio* of raw materials creates a network of actions, a working model and probably the original inspiration of Ruscelli's formula for the ideal plot. Lidio's intrigue with Fulvia gives rise to Calandro's attempt at intrigue with Lidio; fleeing one labyrinth, Santilla is drawn into another by the charlatan's plan to dupe Fulvia. The confusion reaches such a pitch by the end of the fourth act that even Fessenio, who has previously taken a detached artistic pleasure in the ironic pattern of the intrigue, begins to believe that Lidio's feminine disguise has become a genuine metamorphosis. As Ruscelli recommended, the intrigue continues well into the fifth act, and Santilla's wail, "In what a labyrinth I find myself!" (V, ii)[19] is both a description of the plot and the vaunt of the playwright, shortly preceding the sudden revelation and concealment of the denouement.

The principle of complication implies not only some degree of causal interdependence of action but also multiplication of details and reflections of one pose or episode in another: a prostitute takes Lidio's place in the dark to fool Calandro about his mistress, Santilla takes Lidio's place with Fulvia to fool Calandro about his wife, and Fannio plans to take Santilla's place to fool Fulvia about her lover; the pivotal disguise in the comedy is that of Santilla as a boy, and Bibbiena multiplies it by four, decreeing transvestism for Lidio, Fulvia and Fannio as well; in addition to the crazy image of the affair between Fulvia and Lidio created by Calandro's coupling with the prostitute, there is another brief reflection of it in the quick tumble behind the door of the servants Samia and Lusco.

---

[17] Borsellino, *Commedie*, 1. All quotations are from this edition. "Staremo meglio che a Modon!" "Tanto meglio quanto Italia è piú degna della Grecia, quanto Roma è piú nobil che Modon e quanto vaglion piú due ricchezze che una. E tutti trionferemo."

[18] The prologue is shown to be Bibbiena's own composition by Giorgio Padoan in his edition of *Calandria* (Verona: Valdonega, 1970), 139–79.

[19] "In che laberinto mi trovo io!"

As an imitation of life, mirror of custom, and image of truth, *Calandria* represents the prevailing, but not unanimous sixteenth-century view of the proper subject of the genre. The reality Bibbiena brings onstage is not the Florence of the moment evoked by the language of Machiavelli or of Grazzini, not Annibal Caro's slice of Piazza Farnese or the contemporary Roman customs satirically surveyed by Aretino, still less the brutal postwar Veneto of the deracinated peasant Ruzante. The reality of *Calandria* is generalized, an updated Decameronian holiday world, tangible and plausible, a territory of common cultural ownership which was speedily accepted in the Cinquecento as the realm of life to be imitated by *commedia*. The coincidences permitted here by fortune are as unlikely and as exaggerated as the gullibility of Calandro, the tricks of Fessenio or the indiscretion of Fulvia, but they are nevertheless selections from real life, artistically heightened and related. Real old men can be stupid and lustful, dissatisfied wives really can run wild for love, real con men can make people believe almost anything, families can be separated in wartime, impecunious foreigners do cast about for means to financial security, and fortune really does play a disconcerting role in life; indeed, the dramatic force of the coincidences and of the extraordinary effects of love's tyranny depends on and requires the context of an ordinary, if generalized, reality. In its own time even the racy but literary prose of *Calandria* required and received warrant from objective extraliterary experience: although the dialogue is thick with stylized epigrams from Boccaccio, Ruscelli explains that the natural syntax has been twisted for the realistic purpose of imitating the way Greeks speak Italian.[20]

The units with which Bibbiena constructed his simulacrum of physically perceptible reality are not only generally prophetic of the materials of the genre for more than a century but also are specifically identical with the movable parts—commonplaces of theme, situation, character— of which *commedia* after *commedia* would be put together. Fortune, the force that moves and baffles the plots, now seconding the power of love, now allying itself with wit, now indiscriminately threatening all with its caprices, also figures throughout *Calandria* as a topos, beginning with Fessenio's opening words, "How true it is that for every design man makes, Fortune makes another" (I.i). "Women are fickle" (I.ii)[21] is another of the topoi which would be handed down from comedy to

[20] "Annotationi," 170.
[21] "Bene è vero che l'uomo mai un disegno non fa che la Fortuna un altro non ne faccia." "Le femmine sono mutabili."

comedy, here introduced as a preface to some joking about homosexuality. Patterns of verbal encounters are set in scenes like that between the *serva*, Samia, who returns breathless from running an errand and answers her mistress' anxious questions with gasps, irrelevancies and malapropisms (III.v). Such exchanges, like the give-and-take of *sententiae*, or the deceiving fragments of eavesdropped dialogues, are units of drama adapted from Boccaccio for the stage, or from Plautus to exploit Italian vocabulary and allusions. Synchronized with the crossfire of Tuscan proverbs, they emerged in *Calandria* as sections of a new vernacular structure which could be reassembled into other compositions in the genre, like the scenery for most productions of comedy.

The same holds true for the commonplaces of situation and nonverbal action first organized in *Calandria*: the repeated substitutions of lovers in the dark; the slippings in and out of that useful portion of the set, the *camera terrena*; the optical illusions created deliberately by costume changes and accidentally by family resemblances. So too the relationships which would be the human staple of the *commedia* are already well-developed in *Calandria*. There is a considerable range of *servo(a)-padrone(a)* combinations, calculated contrasts between the mistress' fiery passion and the servant's earthly lust, and between the association of sex and madness in Fulvia's sympathetically-presented love with that of sex and food in Calandro's ridiculed cravings. Had it been written forty years later as a compendium of generic structures, *Calandria* could not be more representative than it is of the *commedia* in its first half-century.

By attaching so much value to the principle of *contaminatio* even in the early Cinquecento when they were trying to free the ideal modern genre from its Latin swaddling clothes, Italian dramatists acted on that impulse to mix things which beat beneath most movements in Renaissance art. Although Annibal Caro could claim as late as 1543 that the law of comedy had not yet been entirely established,[22] the fact that the "innovation" he defended was rather a matter of quantity than of quality—a triple plot instead of a double one—shows that fundamental principles were no longer at issue. In the decades that followed, curiosity to know how much the structure of *commedia* would bear led to combining not only individual sources but the newly defined genres themselves. The results would be diverse hybrids of matter and of tone, displays of thematic chiaroscuro and variations on structural units in the superstructure of *intreccio* plot, with its prescribed denouement. It is an axiom

[22] *Gli Straccioni*, Prologue, Borsellino, *Commedie*, 2.

of criticism that Cinquecento *commedia* began in unity and ended in pieces, having produced a pathetic-sentimental strain which nourished the music drama and baroque tragicomedy of the Seicento, and a miscellany of comic turns and techniques which would be maintained by the *commedia dell'arte*. The second half of the Cinquecento, coinciding with the phase of Italian comedy closest to Shakespeare's time, witnessed developments in the genre which prepared for the ultimate disintegration. A modern preference for the pioneers of the genre sometimes obscures the fact that these developments also produced sophisticated theatrical instruments and demonstrated potentialities of comedy previously unrealized in Renaissance drama.

The impulse to mix was encouraged by interest in form no less than by appetite for varied content. An intense critical activity following the publication of Robortello's translation and explication of the *Poetics* in 1548 fostered attempts to extrapolate what Aristotle must have thought about comedy from what he said about tragedy. Although writers of *commedia* had long before learned from Plautus and Terence to accomplish recognition and reversal in their plots, Aristotle's praise of Sophocles' use of these means of resolution led to competition of comedy with tragedy and to such claims as Guido Decani made for Flaminio Maleguzzi's *La Theodora, commedia* in 1568: that the peripety employed in it is "the same as that in Oedipus Tyrant, so much celebrated by Aristotle; although that moves from happiness to woe, whereas this is exactly the opposite."[23]

Imitating *Oedipus* in comedy also meant transposing sombre dramatic irony into a happy key: unavoidable fate was replaced by unhoped-for providence. As a consequence, the peripety, primarily functional as a mechanism heretofore, became in itself a content-structure full of meaning for the times. An important goal of the Counter-Reformation campaign against fortune-telling and belief in fate, or in predestination, was the re-affirmation of the doctrine, defined by Aquinas and the church fathers before him, of the sovereignty of divine providence, limiting fortune's power and guaranteeing man's free will. The idea of a peripety which is not merely another turn of fortune's wheel but the unexpected result and revelation of a plan for human happiness made by a power greater than that of luck was perfectly formed to serve a Catholic re-

[23] Written before 1564 (Venetia: Domenico Farri, 1572), Dedication (1568), "l'istessa con quella d'Edipode Tiranno, tanto celebrata da Aristotele; se ben quella è di felicità in infelicità; ove questa è tutt' all'opposito."

indoctrination program. It was a case of dramatic criticism effortlessly seconding theological orthodoxy and responding to the Counter-Reformation appeal for an engaged art.

The abstract quality of much late Renaissance drama, often blamed on an Inquisitional censorship which made representation of social reality dangerous and satire nearly impossible, may be discerned even in external details. One need think only of the ideonyms that Borghini fastens on the leading *innamorati* in *L'Amante furioso* (1583): Filarete and Aretafila. What can be described as escapism, however, can also be attributed to receptivity on the part of playwrights to critical theory and to the spirit of the Counter-Reformation. The tendency toward abstraction moved in the same direction as the universalizing trend in drama which was furthered by Horace's principle of decorum and by Aristotle's preference of ideal fiction over real history as a subject for tragedy. At the same time, general moral and cultural currents were influenced by hope of a return to a universal church, away from the particularities of schism and heresy and from the moral empiricism associated with earlier Renaissance writers such as the banned Machiavelli. In comedy, one of the results was an intermittent symbolism that looked back to the allegory of medieval drama, but without sacrifice of the structural refinements developed by Renaissance humanistic experiments in the genre. The abstractness of late *commedie* originated in a meeting of near-classicism with neo-medievalism, of the form of New Comedy enriched by supercharged Aristotelian peripety with allegorical and didactic possibilities as strong, if not as direct, as those of Quattrocento *rappresentazioni* and *farse morali*.

Like other charter principles of regular comedy, its ideal definition as imitation of life, mirror of custom and image of truth remained in force but suffered an expansion. The delight in reproducing the appearance of concrete reality that had attended the début of vernacular comedy gave way in Tridentine times to an impatience with merely sensible objects of imitation and a manneristic scrutiny of the ironies and inadequacies of appearance. The challenge to make a theatrical image of a truth above custom and not susceptible of being reflected by a mirror was taken up in the line of sentimental comedies springing from the first efforts of Piccolomini and the other members of the Sienese Accademia degli Intronati of the 1530's, in which the invisible inner reality of the heart was brought onstage in pathetic situations and emotional scenes, often dominated by articulate women with strong feelings.

Extension of the idea of dramatically imitable reality was directed not only inward to the hidden motions of the heart but outward to the invisible workings of an eternal world in which the day's span of a comedy was a brief but possibly significant, even emblematic, moment. The concept of providence, central to the tradition of romance, inherent in New Comedy and indispensable to Christian doctrine, was one such reality toward which the generic structures of the *commedia* gravitated. The *intreccio* plot itself, so carefully perfected by practice of *contaminatio* and complication, could be used not only as a dramatic mechanism for rational organization of a selected reality but as the vehicle for a complex of ideas or as a metaphor for the twisted, fortune-ridden temporal appearance of human life, which is in reality an orderly design eternally present to the eye of providence.

Representation of such truths had to be achieved without loss of verisimilitude; the effect of wonder demanded from *commedia* by the neo-Aristotelians depended no less than before on strict plausibility. Although Castelvetro's insistence on pleasure and credibility and on limiting fictional time and place and actual length of performance[24] suggests an audience as weak of intellect and imagination as of bladder, the spectators of the comedies with an expanded field of reality were, in fact, being invited to perform the dual mental action of observing the pleasing fiction and perceiving the truth for which it was a sign.

One of the least-examined results of experiments with genre in this very active period—private drama now flourished in universities and petty courts, in the country as well as in the centers of Venice, Ferrara, Florence, Rome and Naples, and the professional troupes traveled everywhere—was the mutation of the *grave* comedy. The adjective that D'Ambra had used to distinguish Terence's tone from his own more playful Florentine note became a means of relating the best modern comedy to a tradition that included both D'Ambra and Terence, while simultaneously opposing it to the ill-constructed improvisations of the poorer sort of *commedia dell'arte* zanies. Girolamo Razzi was proud to record that his *commedia La Cecca* had been considered by some to be "too grave and severe, and, as you might say, too little *alla Zannesca*"[25] (*La Balia*, 1560, Prologue). *Commedia grave*, as the term was used by

---

[24] Lodovico Castelvetro, *Poetica d'Aristotele vulgarizzata, et sposta* (Basilea: Pietro de Sedabonis, 1576), quoted in H. B. Charlton, *Castelvetro's Theory of Poetry*, (Manchester University Press, 1913), pp. 84–85, n. 2.

[25] (Fiorenza: Giunti, 1564), "troppo grave e severo, e per dir cosi poco alla Zannesca."

Cristoforo Castelletti and Sforza Oddi for their own works and by Pompeo Barbarito to describe Della Porta's *L'Olimpia*, could refer, on one side, to firm interlocking structure and variety of substance fused by *contaminatio*, as forecast by *Calandria*, and on the other, to a seriousness that made comedy resemble its sister, tragedy, as Tasso put it in a sonnet praising Pino.[26] The admired *gravità* could include actions and characters fit for tragedy, the effects of "wonder, sorrow and pity"[27] of which Castelletti boasted (*Torti amorosi*, Prologue), or the symbolism of dramatic structure indicated by Luigi Pasqualigo's claim that the love plot of his *Il Fedele* makes manifest "the ordeals and deprivations suffered by him who, guided to safe harbor by the heavens' goodness, no longer fears fortune's evil power, because all things here below having been so disposed by the Great Maker that they are forever in continual motion, there is no one who is not more or less moved by the constant flow back and forth. . . ."[28] (1576, Prologue). Fortune's subordination to providence, briefly acknowledged in comedy by Ariosto (prose *Suppositi*, V, viii) and elaborated by Aretino as the Counter-Reformation began (*La Talanta*, V, i), had become a commonplace of structure by 1589, when Calderari called the peripety of *La Schiava* an "example to all that no man is ever so harried by adverse Fortune that in a moment, in a second, God may not make him happy and contented"[29] (V.ix.).

When Della Porta announced in a prologue that a new, wonder-arousing and well-balanced plot was the soul of comedy and that in his work peripety would be born of peripety and recognition of recognition, causing the ghosts of Menander, Epicharmus and Plautus to rejoice in

[26] Castelletti, *I Torti amorosi*, 1581, Prologue (Venetia: Heredi di Marchiò Sessa, 1591), and *Le Stravaganze d'amore*, 1584 (Venetia: Pietro Bertano, 1613), I.v; Oddi, *Prigione d'amore*, written 1570?, Prologue (Fiorenza: Filippo Giunti, 1592); Della Porta, *L'Olimpia*, Dedication (Napoli: Horazio Salviani, 1589); Torquato Tasso, *Le Rime*, ed. A. Solerti, 4 (Bologna: Romangnoli-dall'Acqua, 1902), 190. See Louise George Clubb, "Italian Comedy and The Comedy of Errors," *Comparative Literature*, 19, no. 3 (Summer 1967), 240–51, for other examples of *commedia grave*.

[27] "Meraviglia, dolore e compassione."

[28] (Venetia: Bolognino Zaltieri, 1576), "gli affanni e le miserie passate a chi in sicuro porto condotto per benignità de i cieli più non teme la malignità della fortuna, perche essendo cosi disposto le cose di qua giù dal Sommo fattore, che stanno sempre in continue moto, non è persona, che molto o poco non sia agitata da questo continuo flusso, e reflusso. . . ."

[29] (Vicenza: Agostino dalla Noce, 1589), "essempio a ciascuno: CHE non è giamai l'huom cosi perturbato dalla avversa Fortuna, che in un punto, in un'attimo Dio non lo renda felice, e contento."

being surpassed by the moderns, he was attesting the longevity of the first principles of *commedia* as well as boasting of progress. The comedy with which one version of this prologue appeared was *Gli Duoi fratelli rivali*, a well-developed specimen of late Cinquecento *commedia grave*, written ten or more years before its publication in 1601.[30] Its New Comedy ancestors and recent Italian antecedents are declared at every turn: by the verisimilitude, the Salerno street setting, the time span limited to a Tuesday and a Wednesday, the two *innamorati* with a clever servant apiece, the parasite, the braggart captain, the *contaminatio* of borrowings from *Mercator*, *Andria* and other Plautine and Terentian sources, with a primary plot from the Bandello tale which Shakespeare also used in *Much Ado About Nothing* (*Novelle* I, 22).

The choice of a romantic and nearly tragic novella, with its echo of Ariosto's courtly tale of Ariodante and Ginevra (*Orlando Furioso* V), and Della Porta's inclusion of scrambled facts from Salernitan history and from his own family records, however, illustrate the more comprehensive use of the principle of *contaminatio* in late *commedia*. The result is an *intreccio* of contrasting genres, a theatrical story of the rivalry of the nephews of the Spanish viceroy of Salerno for the love of Carizia Della Porta, one of two daughters of an impoverished nobleman. With the help of a clever servant, a venal glutton, a bawdy maidservant and a gullible braggart, the disappointed aspirant tricks his more fortunate brother into accusing Carizia of wantonness. Her apparent death elicits the truth, her return pacifies the new rivalry ignited by the viceroy's order that one brother marry her sister, and a double wedding averts the last threat of tragedy.

Details of characterization in *Fratelli rivali* reveal the reciprocity between *commedia grave* and the *commedia dell'arte* that co-existed with dramatists' attacks on the actors' often shapeless *zannate*. Della Porta's *miles gloriosus*, Martebellonio, for example, produces comic cadenzas which would be suitable for any braggart captain and may have been borrowed by actors for use in other comedies. Many of them, in fact, resemble the tirades for the mask of Capitano Spavento published by Francesco Andreini on his retirement from the stage in 1607.[31] The heroic passion and peril that are juxtaposed with broad foolery in *Fratelli rivali* likewise seem intended to exploit the range of the *comici*'s professional

[30] (Venetia: Gio. Batt. Ciotti, 1601).
[31] *Le Bravure del Capitano Spavento divise in molti ragionamenti in forma di dialogo* (Venetia: Giacomo Antonio Somasco, 1607).

skill, and they explain something of Della Porta's popularity with the actors. These darker elements also demonstrate the lengths to which *contaminatio* could be carried in comedy. Units developed when the genre was being defined and differentiated from others are loaded in this late play with non-comic weights. The groupings of *servo* and *padrone*, young lovers and old opponents, *innamorata* and *balia*, and their encounters in the street and at windows belong to the familiar bourgeois reality. But the major characters have been promoted to a social rank as high as that demanded for tragedy by Italian theorists. The long-established generic relation of nurse-to-girl decrees in *Fratelli rivali* the confidence that Madonna Angiola enjoys and the part she plays in the courtship; but Della Porta makes her Carizia's aunt, thereby establishing Angiola as a *duenna* instead of a *balia* and emphasizing the family's place in an aristocratic ambience equal to that inhabited by the analogous characters of Bandello and Ariosto. With the character of the viceroy Della Porta goes not only beyond earlier *commedia* but also beyond Bandello by adding to the novela plot from the tradition of comedy the figure of a guardian, but turning him from a foolish or menacing blocker of youth's desire into a potentially tragic ruler with an almost Shakespearean mission as restorer of order and arbiter of peace.

In disposing and entwining the multiple threads of this fabric, Della Porta fulfills the promise of his prologue and upholds his predecessors' principle of complication. His means are the generic topoi and movable parts of *commedia* but, like many writers of late *commedia grave*, he employs them both for achieving greater complexity of pattern and for representing feelings, moral example or some other incorporeal object. Many of the units observed in *Calandria* appear in *Pratelli rivali*: the originally Plautine scenes of questions and irrelevant answers (*Fratelli rivali*, II.ix.) and of eavesdropping (II.iv.), the topos of woman's frailty (II.ii.), the exchange of proverbs (III.i.), the substitution of partners at a rendez-vous in a dark *camera terrena* (II.xi.), the deflating comparison of love and food obsessions (I.iii.), among others. But the old structural units have become means to new ends. The hoary misogynistic saw leads into a scene in which Carizia's grace and virtue shine out so wonderfully as to convert even her detractor, an example of the spiritual embellishment of the *innamorata* that was undertaken in many *commedie gravi*[32]

---

[32] See Louise George Clubb, "Woman as Wonder: A Generic Figure in Italian and Shakespearean Comedy," forthcoming in Dale B. J. Randall, ed., *The Renaissance Background of English Literature* (Durham: Duke University Press, 1976).

and that is continued in *Fratelli rivali* by further vicissitudes of the plot, including false accusation, apparent death, resurrection and triumph. The exchange of contradictory proverbs is used to sum up the pros and cons of the deceit perpetrated by the brother who is associated with shifty Machiavellian ideas about fortune and efficiency, condemned by the explicit moral of the play. The deception in the dark is played for laughs but also for pathos and for echoes of the theme of false appearance and of the unreliability of human means of cognition, which resonates somewhat spasmodically throughout the comedy.

Revelation, rather than concealment, is the natural end of such *commedia grave*. In *Fratelli rivali* the venerable device of discovery of kinship is not needed as a literal passage to the idea revealed: the distance between what appears to be and what is, played on with every deceit and misunderstanding, at every turn of the intrigue, itself becomes the final revelation. Death, violence and disorder, the represented "facts," are proved at last to be unreal or transitory, dissolved by the real and the permanent: love, virtue and the supernatural power in whose plan of order chaos is merely a phase. The ways of the heart and the ways of providence are given as much theatrical substance as the limitations of the genre allow.

Late Cinquecento preoccupation with hybrid genre and with perfect peripety facilitated imitation of the invisible realities. Spectators long accustomed to appraise comedy according to generic conventions of content and of form could be brought not only to see that all ends well but to observe the ending as a peripety, to eye the design as connoisseurs and to recognize it as the image of a truth not confined by the fiction. Signs posted at turnings in the labyrinth of *Fratelli rivali*—"Give thanks to God. . . . He alone has decreed in Heaven that events so difficult and impossible to resolve be brought to so happy an end" (V.iii.)—are officially sanctioned by the concluding words of the civil and domestic authority, the viceroy, who casts himself as spectator of the events that are real to him and, thus, economically instructs the spectators offstage in how to see the play:

> In truth, as spectator, I greatly wondered at the cruel battle between two otherwise valorous and worthy noblemen; but now that I see so much beauty in Carizia—and likewise in her sister—I excuse and do not blame them, and I judge that God in his vastness governs these matters with secret and sure laws of the fates, and that long ago He had ordained these grave disorders that so worthy a pair of sisters might be matched with so

worthy a pair of brothers, for it seems that by His will they were born to be joined together.[33] (V.iv.)

Early and late, Cinquecento comedy was full of life. If its vitality is no longer self-evident, the *commedia* remains immeasurably valuable for the study of genre, being principled, fertile of structures and evolutionary. Ultimately it was a genre inhibited by its principles. The commitments to a nominally specific setting in present time and urban place and to a verisimilitude which obviated the use of some means which would have been useful for imitating intangible objects decreed that other genres or sub-genres would pre-empt the goal. The Italian genre that most programmatically did so was the pastoral tragi-comedy, the history of which is properly a chapter in the larger history of the comedy. Even Guarini's *Pastor fido*, which defined the new genre in 1590 and was proffered as an even blend of tragedy and comedy, owes more to the *commedia* on which experiments with Sophoclean form and content were tried than it does to tragedy directly.[34] As for the preliminary pastoral plays, from Beccari's *Il Sacrificio* of 1555 onward, in them the example of *commedia* is still more obvious, in the units of character and of grouping, of verbal encounter and of plot device, as in the *intreccio* structure which was the choice of almost all pastoral dramatists but Tasso. Escaping from the residual realism of *commedia grave* into the new third genre, comic types and actions moved farther toward the abstract, shedding specificity to become theatrical shapes of feeling or of idea, while the plots in which they figured became images of providential transformation of sorrow into joy or, as Thomas McFarland calls Shakespeare's pastoral comedies, "structures of hope."[35] Neither the wish to mix genres in a manner acceptable to neo-Aristotelian theory nor the desire to invent theatrical

[33] "Rendete grazie a Dio. . . . Egli solo ha ordinato nel cielo che i fatti cosi difficili et impossibili ad accommodarsi siano ridotti a cosi lieto fine." "Veramente mi son assai meravigliato, essendo spettatore d'un crudel abbattimento di due per altro valorosi e degni cavalieri; ma or che veggio tanta bellezza in Carizia—e cosi ancor stimo la sorella,—gli escuso e non gl'incolpo, e giudico che l'immenso Iddio governi queste cose con secreta e certa legge de' fati, e che molto prima abbi ordinato che succedano questi gravi disordini, accioché cosi degna coppia di sorelle si accoppiono con si degno paro di fratelli, che par l'abbi fatti nascere per congiungerli insieme."

[34] See Louise George Clubb, "The Making of the Pastoral Play: Some Italian Experiments between 1573 and 1590," J. A. Molinaro, ed., *Petrarch to Pirandello* (Toronto: Toronto University Press, 1973), 45–72.

[35] *Shakespeare's Pastoral Comedy* (Chapel Hill: University of North Carolina Press, 1972), p. 38.

means of imitating invisible realities of emotion and of universal order could be fully satisfied by the *commedia grave*, but when the hybrid genre was finally established in the form of the pastoral play, and theorists warred over its aesthetic propriety, there spoke decades of experimentation with comic principles: *et in Arcadia comoedia gravis.*

Comedy in the English Mystery Cycles:
Three Comic Scenes in the Chester *Shepherds' Play*

Lorraine Kochanske Stock
University of Houston

i

One of the most significant revolutions in the critical attitudes expressed about medieval vernacular drama has concerned the comedy which pervades the English Mystery Play Cycles. Earlier critics staunchly maintained that the craft cycles of religious drama were exactly that, and any comic or secular additions were infringements upon and deterrents from that basic religious purpose. Hardin Craig, probably the most adamant proponent of this position, stated that "The mystery plays after they fell into secular hands were not of course by any means faithful to their simple religious beginnings. They were full of aberrations. . . ."[1] Though not nearly as sanctimonious as Craig, Eleanor Prosser echoed Craig's basic complaint about comedy while establishing her own criteria for judging comedy in the cycle plays: "If the comedy breaks the mood, negates the theme, and destroys audience participation, sympathy, or necessary emotional response . . . is it not 'bad drama'?"[2] A more recent approach to the comic drama heralds the critical swing of the pendulum away from this attitude. As a result, more objectivity has been employed in an attempt to integrate the comic elements thematically into the basic structure of the particular pageants and the cycles which they compose. As his own interpretations of the comic sequences were seminal in the growth of this new trend, perhaps V. A. Kolve is their most appropriate and articulate spokesman:

> The one thing all these [comic scenes] have in common is their formal seriousness: however funny, bumptious, coarse, or improvisatory these

---

[1] Hardin Craig, *English Religious Drama of the Middle Ages* (Oxford: The Clarendon Press, 1966), p. 158.

[2] Eleanor Prosser, *Drama and Religion in the English Mystery Plays* (Stanford: Stanford University Press, 1961), p. 82.

comic actions may seem, they have their roots in serious earth; they are intimately and intricately involved in their play's deepest meanings.[3]

The critical controversy over these two diametrically opposed views of comedy in the English plays has eluded final settlement, moreover, because of the very problematic questions of definition, classification, and temporal perspective necessary to any generic considerations of such "comedy." For example, one must distinguish between its two very different medieval definitions: in its broadest sense Comedy refers to a literary piece having a fortuitous ending, as exemplified by Dante's *Divine Comedy*; in its narrower and more conventionally modern application, it refers to the inclusion of frankly humorous, even rowdy episodes which are often at variance with, or fancifully embroidered upon actual scriptural sources. We must also recognize that medieval generic comedy often includes and even relies upon the incidental humor for its effect. Beyond this initial reservation about definition, a further problem becomes apparent in the absence of critical unanimity with respect to what actually constitutes intentional incidental humor in the plays. Both this disagreement and the confusion resulting from the often-incorrect contemporary assumption that what strikes modern audiences as funny also necessarily elicited laughter from medieval audiences preclude even a superficial, much less any theoretical classification of such comedy. Furthermore, the many different manifestations of incidental comedy in the myriad guises of slapstick, farce, parody, comic anachronism, and grotesque or cruel humor compound the difficulties of serious discussion of the genre. And when, in the hope of deducing a consistent, all-inclusive theory of this comedy in medieval drama, critics attempt to apply any or all of these distinctions or criteria to the four very diversely-styled and unique major Mystery Cycles, the resulting permutations of these problems render the situation a hopelessly muddled one at best. Arnold Williams' recent, well-intended *tour de force* on comedy in the Cycle plays[4] demonstrates this dilemma. In attempting a comprehensive treatment of comedy in so brief a study, Williams succeeded at least in illustrating the complexities of such a mottled genre as medieval comedy, if not in actually resolving the assorted difficulties.

The shepherds' play has been the type of pageant most often treated as a representative example of the comic in medieval drama. If the Wakefield

[3] V. A. Kolve, *The Play Called Corpus Christi* (Stanford: Stanford University Press, 1966), p. 173.

[4] Arnold Williams, "The Comic in the Cycles," in *Medieval Drama*, ed. Neville Denny (London: Edward Arnold, 1973), pp. 109–24.

Second Shepherds' Play, being the most widely anthologized of all the English Mystery plays, has gained the greatest public exposure, it has also garnered, not undeservedly, the lion's share of critical evaluation and explication for its sophisticated employment of a comically parodic subplot. For these reasons, it is worthwhile to explore the shepherds' play as a yardstick by which to measure and perhaps evaluate Comedy in the drama cycles. By the same token, however, the critical attention lavished upon *Secunda Pastorum* at the expense of other examples of this sub-genre demands, in fairness, that another shepherds' pageant be appointed comic paradigm for consideration of comedy in the drama. Because we have been treated recently to a good new edition of the *Chester Cycle*,[5] and because the Chester version of the shepherds' play contains three controversially comic scenes, this study shall narrow its focus to the *Chester Shepherds' Play*, the type's most misunderstood particular specimen, in our exploration of comedy.

Unfortunately, *The Chester Shepherds' Play* has endured the slings and arrows of outraged critics whose literary criticism consisted mostly of condescending and uncomplimentary comparison of it with its counterpart in the Wakefield Cycle, which traditionally has been proclaimed the superior play. The shame has been that, as in the case of other critically ignored medieval plays,[6] tradition has contributed to the state of the play's critical record more than actual critical investigation. One of the earliest commentators on the Nativity pageants, for example, Samuel B. Hemingway, possibly initiated the tradition: "... the [Chester] *Shepherds' Play*, although as a whole a shapeless mass, contains much effective detail, which was used later by a real dramatist in the Towneley *Prima Pastorum*."[7] This early judgment on the play was accepted and echoed as recently as 1964 by Margery Morgan who said: "The Chester *Adoration of the Shepherds* is artistically inferior to the two Wakefield plays on the same subject: its characters are less convincing, its humor is less subtle, its action and the development of mood are less skillfully managed...."[8] I shall proceed now,

[5] *The Chester Mystery Cycle*, ed. R. M. Lumiansky and David Mills (London: EETS s.s. 3, 1974). All references to plays in the Chester Cycle will be from this edition of the text.

[6] See my discussion of *Mankind*, a play which endured a similar fate. Lorraine Kochanske Stock, "The Thematic and Structural Unity of *Mankind*," *Studies in Philology*, 72 (1975), 386–407.

[7] Samuel B. Hemingway, *English Nativity Plays* (1909; rpt. New York: Russell and Russell, 1964), p. xxvii.

[8] Margery M. Morgan, " 'High Fraud': Paradox and Double-Plot In The English Shepherds' Plays," *Speculum*, 39 (1964), 682.

by closely examining the three comic scenes of the *Chester Shepherds' Play*, to debunk some of these traditional critical assumptions and judgments and to reveal the serious thematic relevance of what has always been dismissed as gratuitous low comedy in the pageant. Hopefully, from this exploration of comedy in a particular play will emerge some bases for extrapolation about generic comedy in the English mystery cycles. I shall begin with the first major scene of the pageant, consisting of an expository introduction of the protagonists/shepherds and the controversial feast scene.

ii

The opening scene of the *Chester Shepherds' Play* is crucial because, as in any well-made play, it lays the foundation for the action which follows it. It begins with a long soliloquy delivered by Hankyn, the Primus Pastor, the content of which is a rather vainglorious exposition of the veterinary skills he practices on his ailing sheep, including a comically tedious, lengthy catalogue of both the diseases suffered and the medications applied to the sick sheep. Hankyn boasts that:

> From comlye Conwaye unto Clyde
> under tyldes them to hyde,
> A better shepperd on no syde
> noe yearthlye man maye have. (Play VII, ll. 5–9)

If the shepherd's life is fulfilling for the chance it presents him to play physician, it is also a lonely one for Hankyn, and he subsequently invites the company of his friend, the Secundus Pastor, by calling rather loudly to him as though he is deaf:

> Howe, Harvye, howe!
> Drive thy sheepe to the lowe.
> Thow maye not here excepte I blowe,
> As ever have I heale. (Play VII, ll. 45–49)

They decide that a feast is in order and extend the invitation to a third shepherd whom the first shepherd advises they call loudly also because he too is hard of hearing:

> Crye thow must lowd, by this daye;
> Tudd is deafe and may not well here us. (ll. 59–60)

Tudd, who finally hears them as he is washing out a pan he used to mix sheep medication—an act for which he comically fears his wife will give him a painful "clowte"—joins them after boasting about his own veterinary skills, "noe better [doctor]—that I well knowe— / in land is nowhere lafte" (ll. 83–84), and after meekly admitting "that eych man must bowe to his wife; / and commonly for feare of a clowte" (ll. 87–88). Tudd joins Hankyn and Harvey and they all settle down to a gargantuan feast, the consumption of which is verbally punctuated with the naming of all the various (and sometimes comically gross-sounding) foods, among which are included: green cheese that will grease well their cheeks, sour milk, a sheep's head, and "a puddinge with a pricke on the ende." As one of the shepherds perhaps ironically puts it, it is a "noble supper" indeed.

This expository scene has proved controversial to critics of the play. The "veterinary" section has been interpreted fairly consistently as an analogy to Christ's ministry as the Good Shepherd and as a reference to the common-place *topos* of Christ as healing physician of Matthew 9:12, especially since the shepherds will undergo a transmogrification at the play's end from shepherds and healers of sheep to pastors and healers of men, by virtue of their conversion and calling to a life of preaching.[9]

The "feast" section has prompted even more critical disagreement between those who deny the comic value of it[10] and those who acknowledge its comic intent but differ as to its explanation.[11] Actually, the feast can be considered successful on a variety of comic levels, not the least of which is as a lower class parody of the typically medieval catalogue of delicious comestibles that Chaucer had his own fun with in the description of the Franklin in the "Prologue" to the *Canterbury Tales*. Whereas the epicurean Franklin, whose

[9] See for example, V. A. Kolve, *The Play Called Corpus Christi*, pp. 152–55; Margery Morgan, "High Fraud," p. 682; Rosemary Woolf, *The English Mystery Plays* (Berkeley: University of California Press, 1972), p. 186. Miss Woolf equates the sheep dying of the rot with mankind before the Incarnation.

[10] Han-Jürgen Diller, "The Composition of the Chester Adoration of the Shep-herds," *Anglia*, 89 (1971), 190.

[11] Interpretations of the feast have ranged from the sublime to the ridiculous. See Leah Sinanoglou, "The Christ Child As Sacrifice," *Speculum*, 48 (1973), 491–509. Sinanoglou discusses the spiritually restorative properties of the foods. See also V. A. Kolve, pp. 160–65, who relates the feast to the end of the Advent fast, and whose theory is respected by Rosemary Woolf, p. 186; Margery Morgan who thinks the feast evokes the feast of the Mass: "High Fraud" pp. 683–84; John Gardner, *The Construction of the Wakefield Cycle* (Cardondale: Southern Illinois University Press, 1974), p. 81, thinks the play parodies both the Christmas feasts of aristocrats and the feast of the Eucharist; Arnold Williams, "The Comic in the Cycles," p. 113, who thinks the meal is a remnant of pagan ritual and folk festivals; Maurice Hussey, *The Chester Mystery Plays* (London: Heinemann, 1971), p. xviii, who thinks that the feast is "proof that the plays were written before the Black Death removed many items from the menu."

house "snewed . . . mete and drynke," presided over a bord boasting such elegant edibles as "fat partrich," "breem," "luce," and "other deyntees," the fare which the Chester Shepherds, on the other hand, pull from their literal bags of tricks is considerably humbler; indeed, more often than not, only marginally esculent! In defense of what might possibly be dubbed the "gratuitous" humor of the gluttons' litany recited by the three shepherds, we should consider the universality of the comedy associated with food and overeating. The humorous appeal of some of Shakespeare's most durable comic characters—Sir Toby Belch and Jack Falstaff come most immediately to mind—derives from their rather lavish eating habits. Indeed, we know that Falstaff would have sold his soul to the devil on Good Friday for a cup of Madeira and a cold capon's leg (*Henry IV, Part I*, I.ii.). The shepherds' feast scene is just as funny and just as thematically salient as Falstaff's gustatory penchants, and it does not require a tremendous leap of the imagination to see the shepherds' feast as a generic ancestor of the Shakespearean comic gourmandisings.

We can extend beyond the level of incidental comedy, moreover, if we consider the feast scene along with the expository/veterinary scene which precedes it in the play. Surely, in the long catalogues of diseases and remedies, we are meant to recognize a microcosmic suggestion of the post-lapsarian state of spiritual disease inherited by all of mankind from Adam's disgrace, which can only be healed by the Incarnation of Christ, who will act as both Good Shepherd and physician, and ultimately by the restorative properties of the Redemption. We must recognize, too, that the shepherds occupy morally ambivalent positions at the start of the play. The images of both healer[12] and patient—by virtue of the fact that they are pointedly shown to be deaf—inform their characterizations in this scene. And if their roles as shepherds identify them with Christ the Shepherd (an association which the playwright capitalized upon in their conversion to Christ, the New Adam, in the Adoration scene), the comic foibles they exhibit also mark them as sons of the Old Adam and inheritors of the post-lapsarian human condition. In this context their gluttonous feast suggests Adam's sin of gluttony in eating the forbidden fruit; their pride—or if pride seems too strong a term for their boasting of being the best shepherds, let us say their vainglory—reflects the motivation of Adam's sin in Eden; their henpecked submission to their wives suggests Adam's failure to overrule *his* wife's fateful whim about eating the fruit, the action which precipitated the Fall.

[12] The pattern of shepherds (men) curing sheep as a reversal of Christ, Lamb of God, curing men is relevant here.

Thus, the shepherds' assorted foibles suggest, in a comically parodic but thematically meaningful way, the proclivities to the very sins which were responsible for Adam's Fall and which necessitated the healing agency of Christ's Incarnation. As such, these comic peccadilloes can best be seen as the real symptoms of the disease of men, not sheep, which constitutes the main theme of the first scene of the Chester *Shepherds' Play*. And the comic feast which ends the scene provides the thematic bridge to the equally controversial wrestling scene, about which we shall speak next.

iii

The wrestling scene of the Chester *Shepherds' Play* has been viewed with so much scorn and disfavor that in some editions it has actually been excised from the rest of the play.[13] Few critics have tried to see anything in it beyond rough, purposeless, slapstick humor designed to obviate possible boredom among the bumpkins presumed to be the play's audience,[14] though the exception to this rule is V. A. Kolve, who interprets the scene as a reflection of the theme of *Deposuit Potentes* deriving from a verse of the Magnificat, a reading which Rosemary Woolf has endorsed.[15]

The scene itself is brief and full of both action and significance. After their own gluttony has been surfeited, the three shepherds decide to offer the "bytlockes" of their meal to their absent servant boy, Trowle, who defiantly refuses their offer of the leftovers and remains in solitude on his "hill," guarding their sheep. Inexplicably, it would seem, the three shepherd/masters frantically, almost maniacally, try to cajole Trowle into eating their food. Trowle continues to refuse, though his reasons make his refusal both comic and understandable: he says, "the dyrte is soe deepe" on the food, and complains that at their house, from which the food has been obtained, "the grubbes thereon do creepe" (ll. 214–16). Finally, in exasperation, the third shepherd challenges Trowle to "wrastle . . . here on this wold." Trowle is quick to accept the challenge and agrees to take on all three masters in the match, throughout which the three shepherds continue to tempt Trowle with blandishments of food, false

---

[13] See I. and O. Bolton King, *The Chester Miracle Plays Done Into Modern English and Arranged for Acting* (London: Society For Promoting Christian Knowledge, 1930); Maurice Hussey, *The Chester Mystery Plays, op. cit.* Neither version includes the wrestling scene.

[14] Arnold Williams, "The Comic In The Cycles," p. 113, thinks it is another vestige of folk and pagan ritual; M. Morgan, "High Fraud," pp. 684–85, says the scene "effects the overthrow of decency and good order."

[15] V. A. Kolve, pp. 155–58; Rosemary Woolf, p. 187.

deference, and power, all the while attempting to prove their mastery over him. Not very surprisingly, Trowle resists all their wheedlings and threats and easily manages to throw successively all three of his masters in the wrestling match, to the acknowledged "shame" of the three masters. Trowle absconds with the choicest leftovers and his dejected masters are left to grumble, "that wee bine thus cast of a knave" (l. 289).

V. A. Kolve's interpretation of the wrestling scene is the most persuasive and least superficial proffered to date. While Kolve invites us when we read the scene to think of the Christ Child, in the human expression of the Hypostatic Union, overthrowing the mighty earthly rulers, he very gingerly backs away from pursuing the idea to its logical conclusion when he warns:

> I am not suggesting that we read the shepherds' wrestling match as an allegory for, or a figure of, the overthrow of Herod—or a better parallel—for the Harrowing of Hell. Trowle is not Christ, not by a long way, nor a figure of Him; the shepherds are neither Herod, nor Jewry about to lose its Messiah, nor Satan.[16]

A closer reexamination of the wrestling scene, however, reveals that not only can Trowle and the shepherds be read as allegorical or typological figures, but even more interestingly, the entire scene can be viewed as a comic parody of Christ's three Temptations by Satan, with the three shepherds setting the comic snares representative of Satan's three Temptations of Christ, and Trowle enacting Christ's triple overcoming of temptation by overthrowing (literally and physically) his masters. The playwright successfully orchestrated such a complex use of the comic double-plot by echoing the language of the shepherds' temptings in the later play of Christ's Temptation and by providing, as a final, formal demonstrative proof of his design, a "Doctor" at the end of the *Temptation* Pageant, whose duty it is to make clear the correspondences.

Notwithstanding Kolve, a close look at the ambiguous language used to introduce the character Trowle, replete with *double entendre*, leads to an inevitable association of him with Christ.[17] Trowle's introduction into the play is announced when, after the three have gorged themselves

---

[16] V. A. Kolve, p. 158; R. Woolf has also shied away from admitting such a possibility.

[17] The very fact that a fourth character is added to the usual number of three shepherds (an obvious parallel of the three magi) should tip us off to the importance of the odd character. Consider Mak, who is the extra character in the Wakefield *Secunda Pastorum*.

sufficiently, the first shepherd suggests: "Fellowes, nowe our bellyes be full, / thinke wee on him that keepes our flockes" (ll. 149–50), an ambiguous statement which, to an audience unaware that another character, much less another shepherd, is yet to occupy the stage, might imply *the* shepherd who watches over *all* flocks, Christ, the Good Shepherd. In light of the many examples of Christological anachronism throughout the earlier scene, one of which was the presumably rhetorical invitation uttered during the shepherds' feast a few lines prior to this, "Come eate with us, God of heavon hye" (l. 139), this first reference to Trowle sounds suspiciously like a Christological allusion. The false assumption is of course undercut when in the next line the shepherd suggests that they call after Trowle, not Christ, whom the audience mistakenly might have believed to be the referent. Other statements the shepherds make in Trowle's characterization carry similar ambiguity, especially since they are resonant with the fulfillment of the typological relationship, the depiction of Christ by Satan in the *Temptation* Pageant. The third shepherd says of Trowle, "such a lad nowhere in land is" (l. 158), which resembles Satan's admiration of Christ, "Sythen the world first begane / knew I never such a man" (Play XII, ll. 25–26). When the first shepherd calls to Trowle with his horn he does so loudly enough "that hee and all heaven shall here" (ll. 162), which suggests that Trowle is associated with the object of Satan's temptation game, of whom Satan says, "Hit seemes that heaven all should be his" (XII, l. 15).

Trowle betrays his likeness with Christ in what he says of himself, moreover, for while rhetorically addressing his sheep, he utters an ambiguous compliment which (because he prefaces it with the vague referent, "we") may refer either to the sheep or to himself: "Noe better may bee / of beast that blood and bonne have" (VII, ll. 171–72). Satan's description of Christ as "Blotles eke of blood and bonne" echoes the line and increases the probability that Trowle is being characterized as a figure of Christ. Trowle's defiant refusal to descend from his "hill" (in the Temptation Pageant Christ is also occupying a "hill") further strengthens the association:

> For kinge ne duke, by this daye,
> ryse I will not—but take my rest here.
> Now wyll I sitt here adowne
> and pippe at this pott like a pope.
> Would God that I were downe
> harmeles, as I hastelye hope,

At me all men lerne mon
this Golgotha grimly to grope.[18] (ll. 186–93)

Trowle's simile comparing himself to the Pope, Christ's representative on earth, and the mention of Golgotha, the scene of Christ's passion, are obvious enough allusions. The expressed desire to be "downe harmeles" may refer either to the agony on the cross or, more probably, to the leap from the pinnacle of the temple which Satan attempts to persuade Christ to make in the *Temptation Play*. At any rate, there is certainly enough implied and direct comparison between Trowle and Christ in his initial depiction to suggest that we pay closer attention to Trowle and his behavior than critics have done.

Trowle proves himself worthy of the comparison in his reaction to the temptations urged upon him by the shepherds. We have already commented upon the manic attempts of the shepherds to force Trowle to eat their food, which is an obvious parallel to Satan's desire to tempt Christ into breaking his desert fast "with speach of bread him to betraye" (XII, l. 54). Satan's second temptation involves his promise to Christ, "I shall shape honour for thee," if Christ consents to come down from the Pinnacle of the Temple "by sleight" (l. 114), an act which will prove His "maistrye." This second temptation has its comic and parodic equivalent in the first shepherd's promise of honor to Trowle, who had previously called himself a "poore page":

Trowle, better thow never knewe.
Eate of this, meate for a Knight. (ll. 238–39)

Though the shepherd flatters Trowle with the honor of implied knighthood if he eats their grubby food, Trowle's response, as was Christ's, is to rebuke the false honor. The first shepherd's angry reply to the rejected honor further implies the second Temptation because he threatens Trowle by saying, "One this grownd thow shall have a fall" (l. 251)— ironically, the very action that would have most pleased Satan. Satan's third temptation of Christ takes place on a "hill" where Satan promises Christ that He may be "lord . . . of all this realme and royaltie" if only Christ will "kneele down and honour" Satan (XII, ll. 134–36). We recognize the comic parallel of the third temptation when the second shepherd asks for the same honor, ironically without the power promised in Satan's trick:

[18] Lines 192–93 are found in M. S. Harley 2124.

> Boye, lest I breake thy bones,
> kneele downe and axe me a boone.
> Lest I destroy thee here on these stones,
> sease, lest I shend thee to soone. (ll. 258–61).

As Trowle is too smart to cavil to such an empty threat, he throws the temptor to the ground even as he did his other two temptors. And just as the shepherds, after their unsuccessful attempts to prove their mastery over Trowle, must suffer the ignominious and embarrassing physical overthrow of their plans by a boy who "shames and shendes" shepherds (l. 268), so too must Satan face defeat by admitting:

> Alas, for shame I am shent.
> With hell-houndes when I am hent
> I must be ragged and all torent
> and dryven to the fyre. (ll. 153–56)

And if Satan rues his foiled "gamon" (XII, l. 4) with Christ because he must return to the pains of hell-fire, the shepherds are served, at the end of their "game" (VII, l. 246) with Trowle, the comic figure of Christ, a rather similar fate in his curse upon them: "To the devyll I you betake, / as traytors attaynt of your tache!" (ll. 284–85). Similarly, while Trowle's reward for overcoming his three temptors is to "catch" the choicest morsels of food, Christ will do his own "catching" by absconding with the souls Satan has so jealously guarded, when He harrows Hell. Thus the structure, content, imagery and action of the wrestling scene comically parody the well-known New Testament event of Christ's Temptation by Satan, to which subject each one of the four mystery cycles devoted a pageant. It remains to ponder *why* such a comic double-plot was constructed by the Chester playwright. For that explanation, thankfully, he provides us with the "Doctor" at the end of the Temptation Pageant, who reveals the exegesis of what we have just witnessed. The Doctor instructs the audience about the typological relationship which can be inferred from this second set of temptations. If Adam, our forefather, was overcome by succumbing to temptations of the vices—gluttony, vainglory, and "covetous of highnes"—Christ rectified Adam's three mistakes by withstanding successfully the three traps Satan set for him in his temptation game.

> That Adam was tempted in gluttonye
> I may well prove appertly,

> when of that fruite falsly
> the devyll made him to eate.
>
> And tempted hee was in vayneglorye
> when hee height him great maistrie,
> and have godhead unworthelye
> through eatinge of that meat.
>
> Alsoe hee was tempted in avarice
> when he height him to be wise,
> knowe good and evill at his devise
> more then he was worthye. (XII, ll. 177–88)

The Doctor proceeds to explain that Christ was tempted to gluttony when Satan urged Him to turn the stones into bread; in vainglory when he told Him "down to goe / the pinnacle of the temple froe / an unskillful gate"; and in covetousness when he offered Christ riches and power in return for honoring Satan (XII, ll. 193–208). The typological opposition of the Old Adam and New Adam is summarized succinctly in the Doctor's final comment: "But Adam fell through his trespas, / and Jhesu withstoode him through his grace" (ll. 214–15).

Though this Doctoral exposition insures the conveyance of its meaning, even without it the structural and thematic significance of the wrestling match becomes clear in light of the action of the *Temptation* Play which, because it followed it in all the cycles, would have been an anticipated part of the meaning of the entire cycle for the audience. If the three shepherds betray, through the exhibition of their foibles in the first scene, an inherited proclivity toward the weaknesses of their ancestor the Old Adam, what action could be more appropriate to a Christmas play than that Trowle, the potential figure of the New Adam, comically resist their attempts to implicate him in the same three vices which precipitated Adam's Fall, and which Christ would later resist at his own symbolic reversal of the Fall in Satan's Temptation? We shall return to this crucial scene later. Meanwhile, we shall investigate the comic turning point of the play, the shepherds' parodic singing of the "Gloria in excelsis Deo," a scene which has also met with critical derision.

iv

While recovering from the wrestling match, the shepherds discern the bright light of the star of Bethlehem and are treated to the angel's song which proclaims the Incarnation, after which they seemingly mock the

Latin words of the song and make a comic mish-mash of the message. The scene has been violently denounced by some of the critics, while the remainder have either lamely attempted to justify it or have accepted it for the wrong reasons. Eleanor Prosser pointed to the scene, which she considered "a travesty of the announcement of Salvation," as the primary example of how comedy, inappropriately placed, made for bad drama.[19] Rosemary Woolf considered it a "stupid misunderstanding."[20] Arnold Williams sees it as another situation drawing from festival spirits, while F. M. Salter enjoyed it for its "breath-taking colossal impudence" and justified it on the grounds that in the Middle Ages God was considered to have a sense of humor.[21]

The angelic parody, like the other comic scenes of the play, assumes important thematic relevance when we view it in context of the entire play. We have already established that the shepherds, especially in the first scene, have been implicitly designated the representative invalids suffering from the post-lapsarian spiritual malaise inherited from Adam. The Chester playwright needed a physical infirmity which emblematically could suggest this spiritual disease endemic in all post-Adamic humanity to be represented by these shepherds. Because the impending cure of spiritually ailing mankind (the Incarnation) would be announced by an angel to these representatives *in song*, the playwright's typological sensitivity would make him select an aural difficulty for the disease. Indeed, the playwright's conscious depiction of the shepherd's deafness in the first scene, if only in terms of typological "rightness," was nothing short of inspired. Acknowledgement of the deafness suffered by the shepherds to a great extent accounts for the comic difficulties they have with the message they do not *quite* hear from the angel, and also renders unnecessary the difficulties critics have encountered in the scene. Never mind that the message is delivered to these rustics in Latin, though this undeniably contributes to their comic misunderstanding. What critics have either ignored or failed to notice is that their deafness would surely prevent the shepherds from deciding conclusively what the exact words of the message were, much less from deciphering their meaning!

If we examine the scene closely we notice that the first shepherd's immediate reaction to the song is to question whether his companions had been able to *hear* anything: "Fellowes in feare, / may yee not

[19] Prosser, pp. 81–82.
[20] Woolf, p. 188.
[21] Arnold Williams, pp. 113–14; F. M. Salter, pp. 103–104.

here / this mutinge on highe?" (ll. 358–60). What follows of course is the shepherds' concerted efforts to piece together what they all must have had difficulty hearing. Initially, they cannot decide whether they heard "glore" or "glere," "grorus glorus" with a "glee," etc. Though their hearing impairment causes their uncertainty about the *content* of the message, it does not diminish, nevertheless, its tremendous effect upon them. The first shepherd says:

> Naye, on a 'glor' and on a 'gloy' and a 'gly'
> gurd Gabryell when hee so gloryd.
> When hee sang I might not be sorye;
> through my brest-boone bletinge hee bored. (ll. 400–04)

In their desire to comprehend the message, the shepherds seize upon what is familiar to them in search of some clue. The one above thinks of his sheep's bleating; Trowle thinks he recognizes in "terra" the word "tarre," one of the medications they used to cure the rot in their flocks. Now, however, by virtue of being the privileged recipients of celestial tidings, an experience which begins to heal them of their own postlapsarian infirmity, the shepherds are transformed from mere veterinarians into potential healers of men, the roles they will assume at the play's end, when they become hermits and anchorites. Trowle confirms this suggestion of their cure from spiritual deafness to the "Word" when he says, "Hee sange alsoe of a 'Deo' / me thought that heled my harte" (ll. 430–31).

The foibles and petty sins of the shepherds—the gluttony displayed in their comic feast, the preoccupation with things of this world, the backhanded generosity implied by the wormy leftovers they proffer to Trowle, which was tantamount to greed, and the personal antipathy which ultimately erupted into the wrestling match—all are transformed by the angel's song into harmony, generosity and "bona voluntas." In the medical metaphor so prominent throughout the pageant, they have been healed, as Trowle admits, by the mystifying contact with "Deo," and we may assume that though Trowle refers to his "herte" being healed, the deafness which emblematically implied their spiritual insensibility was also healed. The second shepherd concurs with Trowle: "never in this world soe well I was. / Singe wee nowe, I rede us, shryll / a mery songe us to solace" (ll. 441–44).

But perhaps in emulation of the splendid celestial song they have just heard with newly healed ears, Trowle quickly assumes leadership of their quartet: "All men now singes after mee, / for musicke of mee learne yee maye (ll. 445-46). In keeping with the adroitness—moral and otherwise—exhibited by Trowle earlier in the wrestling scene, we may presume that the song they sing will be anything but "shrill." Also at his insistence, the shepherds pursue the star to Bethlehem, where they are inspired by their adoration of the Christ Child to reform, become hermits and anchorites, and forego the healing of sheep for the pastoring of men. Thus, the third major comic scene, the shepherds' supposed mocking parody of angelic song, proceeds neatly to the obligatory adoration scene found in the other cycles' counterparts of the *Shepherds' Play*, but thematically enriched in the Chester version by the moral transformation of the shepherds from herders and doctors of sheep to pastors and spiritual healers of men.

v

We have demonstrated, hopefully, that the comic scenes—the feast, the wrestling match, and the angelic parody—are more thematically integral to the purportedly "serious" religious drama cycle that contains them than has previously been admitted. To draw generic conclusions and extrapolations from the study of a single play may seem presumptuous. We dare do so because the shepherds' play occupies a very special, pivotal place in the medieval drama cycle. And if Redemptive Comedy is built into the overall structure of the Mystery Play genre—as its movement from the tragedy of the Fall to the joyfully triumphant denouement of Christ's Redemption suggests it is—then the fulcrum of the balance between tragedy and the ultimate comedy in the cycle is the shepherds' play, making it the most appropriate play for the generic exploration of comedy.

The Chester playwright understood the central importance of the shepherds' play in the cycle and exploited its pivotal nature wherever and however possible. Because it is typologically the transitional play between the Old and New Testament pageants, between material devoted to the Old Adam and the New Adam, and at the heart of the cycle's depiction of its "Divine Comedy," the Chester playwright staged within his shepherds' play the comic recapitulation of Adam's temptation, which at the same time emerges as a joyful adumbration of the temptation Christ will successfully undergo in order to cancel the effect of Adam's failure. This scene is the wrestling match, the one that, as often as not, was deleted from the play because critics failed to realize its importance within the comic/Divinely Comedic structure of the drama cycle depicting Salvation history.

The careful characterization of and emphasis upon the centrally important character Trowle, moreover, was warranted by virtue of his midcenter position between the Old and New Adam. As a shepherd and member of the race of mankind he partakes of Adam's sin-spotted heritage. Yet after his successful thwarting of his masters' traps, and after his witnessing of the mystery of the Incarnation, he is inspired to reform and resolves to become an anchorite and to preach the mystery he has just seen. Thus, Trowle becomes the first beneficiary of Christ's Redemption, and, as such, heir of the New Adam.

If, as earlier critics did, we consider the purpose of the dramatic enactment of Salvation history to be didactic and intended for the spiritual edification of its audience, then the *Chester Shepherds' Play* is ideally executed for such an effect. The shepherds who follow Trowle's example by reforming and adopting a religious life are the closest to being civilians and extra-Biblical characters in the entire cycle, especially since they are specifically localized in Chester, England. Because of this, they serve as proxies for the audience, who can participate in the comic humor of the cycle by laughing at their antics, and at the same time vicariously participate in the Divine Comedy implied by the cycle's sweep of Salvation history by imitating their example and becoming followers of the New Adam. If comedy—even the seemingly gratuitous but thematically crucial, low comedy of the three scenes explicated in this study—is capable of such an effect, then we must (contrary to received opinion) entertain the possibility that the comedy is the *foundation* for the dramatic structure rather than a gay frieze applied to the already existing dramatic edifice.

Redemptive Laughter: Comedy in the Italian Romances

Peter V. Marinelli
University of Toronto

i

Stories about the contemporary reception of literary works are often a case of "se non è vero è ben trovato," but perhaps a contrast will serve to make a point. Recall the vignettes of the solicitude of the imperial family for their poet—the reading of the Sixth Book of the *Aeneid* by Virgil himself to the empress Livia and her stricken reaction to the moving tribute to Marcellus; or the desire of Augustus to preserve the poem at all costs from the destruction to which its author had consigned it. Think then of the famous sarcasm of Cardinal Ippolito d'Este upon being presented with the *Orlando Furioso*: "Messer Ludovico, dove mai avete trovato tutte queste———(rude word)." And remember too, while we are in this vein, the irritated comment attributed to Lord Burleigh when about to deny Spenser his fifty pounds for the *Faerie Queene*: "All that for a song?" Comparatively speaking, the romancers have had no easy day of it, however diligently they sought to glorify the dynasties of their patrons in emulation of Virgil. Something about this literature of knights and damsels in glimmering forests and enchanted seascapes suggests, at first glance, something less hard won, less tragically satisfying than the gravity and grandeur of true epic, whether we are dealing with the martial severity of the *Iliad*, the stoic moral elevation of the *Aeneid*, the dark ferocity and residual mystery of the Germanic epic, or the religious-patriotic fervor of the *Chanson de Roland*. And, truth to tell, it is hard to set Achilles or Hector or Aeneas (or Adam, to include Milton) beside Orlando or Ruggiero or Arthegall and resist a smile. Purely as images commanding immediate emotional responses, they are a world apart. But what finally tips the scale in favor of epic and sends the romance flying light-witted into the air is the fact that it often confuses Thalia with Calliope and abandons itself to laughter. Spenser, of course, has enough obvious high seriousness to counterbalance his comedy, but the case with the Italian romances is different. The lamentable truth is that comedy is sovereign there, and there is not an *o altitudo* in the lot. To the generality of literary critics and readers then, comedy in the Italian romances usually means a rootless, unanchored hilarity supposedly proper to an ebullient and volatile people. Stalwart and serious North, adorable but ingenuous South: the dichotomy exercises a perennial fascination.

Little wonder then that the chivalric narrative has, rather like some slightly raffish social upstart, hyphenated its name and re-emerged as the more toney epic-romance. To what end, a reader well may ask. Under that torn umbrella all manner of peculiar, fundamentally unlike things are made to shelter. There we shall find, at the two extremes, the *Morgante Maggiore* of Pulci and the *Gerusalemme Liberata* of Tasso—the freakish Carolingian extravagance of a witty brain cohabiting oddly with a solemn, Aristotelianly structured epic on the Crusades. And there too we find, in middle position, the *Orlando Innamorato* of Boiardo and the *Orlando Furioso* of Ariosto, two poems (*pace* C. S. Lewis) as unlike as could be imagined, given that they share the same personnel, events and general outlines. Clearly, this lumping together of highly individualized poems will not do (and we have not even included the *Faerie Queene*, with its own set of problems). More and more the generic embrace seems a critical default in the face of irreducible complexity. Hoops burst, buckles fall apart: what these poems (some of them) have in common (sometimes) is a Carolingian background; passages of inordinately overwhelming loves alternating with others of uncontrollable martial fury; episodic construction interrupted at strategic intervals by skillfully recounted novelle; division into cantos; and one or two things more. It is scarcely enough to establish a genre, one would think, but since the romantic epic and the epic-romance are patently here to stay, it would be well to mark out their boundaries more precisely and point out that they contain provinces with different mores and manners.

This essay is concerned with three poems—the *Morgante Maggiore* and the two *Orlandos*—in which the comic impulse provides their reason for being. In the following pages, I shall attempt to differentiate and distinguish among these works by differentiating the comedy of which each is the vehicle. In the course of that confrontation, I hope to assert the unique and essential character of each poem and, as well, the increment of meaning and moral and intellectual complexity visible in the process. In that movement we may see the chivalric romance gradually but ever more firmly disentangling itself from its unseemly plebeian connections and reflecting the humanistic values and interests of the courts of Florence and Ferrara. We shall find, if I am not mistaken, that in moving from Pulci to Boiardo to Ariosto, we move really on three separate planes. In the first, we have a poem divided uncertainly between parody and burlesque in its first part and almost total seriousness of treatment in its second: "comic" romance and "serious" epic are distinctly walled off from each other. In the second poem, we have an only slightly more formally successful work informed by satire of Pandemian love in Orlando and Angelica, set against a comedy of a higher human love in two mythical prototypes of the d'Estes, Bradamante and Ruggiero: an epic theme of dynastic love, colored by medieval romantic tradition, has begun to interpenetrate the comic romance. And in Ariosto, we move to a poem which builds on this foundation imperfectly but fascinatingly erected by Boiardo; the result is a comedy in which an overall Neoplatonic view of life and love mingles with the very tissues of the Carolingian romance to become, finally, vision and form. The process is cumulative. There are elements of burlesque and parody in Pulci that are in Boiardo and Ariosto as well; but the comedy of animal and human love on two planes of an implied Neoplatonic ladder is something that Boiardo shares only with Ariosto, who refines and develops it unimaginably; while the unique comedy and mastery of form that distinguishes Ariosto as he contemplates his poem from an ironic godlike perspective is his and his alone. In this triple movement, we recapitulate the process by which laughter moves on three levels: aristocratic parody of Italian proletarian hilarity—occasional, fragmentary, intermittent; satire of the popular romance's obsession with the world of eyeless passions, alternating overwhelming lusts and insensate rages against a background of the Saracen invasions of France; and finally in Ariosto, a vision of the meshing of conflicting human motives and desires in this sublunary arena, a scrutiny of the theater of the world and the driving excesses of its passions viewed *sub specie aeternitatis*. With the *Furioso* we are overtly in the presence of a Christian Lucianist, scanning the complexity of human desire with wonder and laughter; and of a Christian Democritus as well, who watches the spectacle of the unwearying hunt of mortals for earthly satisfaction in terms of a cosmic hilarity. What was before, in Pulci and often in Boiardo, merely the superior smile of the aristocrat patronizing the romantic playthings of the people becomes, in Ariosto, the reflective laughter of a mind detached from acquisitive passion even as it anatomizes it in its own literary creation. The distanced objective comedy of the *Furioso* is entirely proper to an Horatian poet who inscribed over the lintel of his doorway "Parva sed apta mihi," and in whose contemporary biographies the theme of restricted desires and circumscribed ambitions sounds a dominant note.

These are strange claims for a work in which no less a critic than C. S. Lewis saw nothing more than the diversion of an idle hour and the relief of a convalescent desirous of not being mentally taxed. But it is not often mentioned in literary criticism, either Italian or English, when speaking of Boiardo and Ariosto, that they were both Latinists of note, Lucianists both, both prominent members of courts solidly Neoplatonic in their philosophic, literary and artistic orientation; that Boiardo was the cousin of Pico della Mirandola and no doubt had some acquaintance with the concept of the two Venuses; that Ariosto was only one of a stable of Neoplatonizing poets and painters, including Mantegna and Perugino, cultivated and patronized by Isabella d'Este and that every one of his works is modelled upon the work of some ancient writer— Plautus and Terence in the comedies, Horace in the *Satires* and Latin lyrics, and Virgil in the epic. In such a society, laughter was no limitation on the intellect; it was the revelation of the intellect at work.

The ability to speak truth laughingly is embodied in two phrases common in the writings of Renaissance Neoplatonists—*serio ludere* and *ridendo dicere verum*. It was the aesthetic creed of Erasmus and Thomas More, who were Lucianists and anatomizers of human folly both. And it is not surprising (quite the opposite) to find that the chief poem of the Italian Renaissance, a hearty Carolingian romance employed by its author for the serious purpose of praising a contemporary dynasty and emulating Virgil, should be cast in a comic mode. In speaking of the comedy of the *Furioso* then, we shall have to bear in mind not only the gleeful indecorousness of an Orlando who skewers brigands on a spear like frogs or later runs hilariously amok among shepherds, but also the vision of earthly mutability conferred by special grace upon Astolfo from the perspective of the Sphere of the Moon. And we should especially bear in mind that the end of this comedy is the marriage of the dynastic forbears of the d'Estes, who after long testing and tribulation are united in a Paris from which the Saracens are finally expelled. In these endearing personages of comic romance, a renovated society is about to be transplanted to a future Ferrara. Their vicissitudes have served as a model of human love with all its imperfections striving for fulfillment. Their contemporary descendants are meant to laugh sympathetically and knowledgeably, and in laughing to note and to learn.

ii

Historical circumstances alone would have ensured that comedy should be the vehicle for the great poets of Florence and Ferrara. For the poems of Ariosto and Pulci and Boiardo represent a third stage in the development of Carolingian and Arthurian materials in Italy from roughly the twelfth to the sixteenth centuries. Not native to Italy, they were imported from France in late Middle Ages, diffused by storytellers among the populations of the Veneto and Tuscany, and only then, in the fifteenth century, readopted into an aristocratic atmosphere at the courts of the Medici and the d'Estes. It is inevitable therefore that aristocratic and learned authors who adopt the Matters of France and Britain will always stand at a satiric distance from them, because they come colored by the hyperboles and rich misapprehensions of the laboring classes who adopted it as their own. The mind boggles at what a horny-handed bourgeois would make of the egregious conventions of the degenerating courtly code (no fool, he would probably recognize much of it as satirical and not be far off the mark). In fact there is a living survival of this demotic rehandling of aristocratic materials in the puppet traditions of modern Sicily. Still, in Palermo, gilded and silvered knights clank about in towering rhetorical rages, thwacking and walloping Saracens whose limbs and heads fly from their trunks with phantasmagorical dispatch— and the help of some clever mechanical contrivances. It is a joy to have seen, if only because one luxuriates in playing Thesus and Hippolyta to Bottom and his cohorts. Our relish in this is absolutely unshadowed by thought. Melancholy sets in only when we reflect that critics see no difference between this nonsense or the prose romances of Andrea da Barberino and the poetry of Ariosto—give or take a dollop of Irony and a dose or two of Crocean Pure Art.

It becomes readily apparent in Northern Italy of the late fifteenth century that the aristocrats have designs upon the plebeian romances and mean to redeem them from their indecorous contaminations. But in the initial stages they manifest a curious ambivalence toward them. Clearly they are amused by their extravagance and stand at a readily discernible satiric distance from them; on the other hand, it is difficult to ascertain the satire in cases where the poems go on and on and reflect the aristocrats' own very evident delight in the mimicry of popular motifs and adventures. Popular literature always seems to present this difficulty; to take two examples from our own day, is it really possible to satirize Mickey Spillane or James Bond? And if it is, at what length? In a paragraph? a chapter? Certainly not an entire book. In any case, the process of reclaiming the romance was initiated tentatively and not wholly successfully by Luigi Pulci. There may be more than fable in the story that he undertook the *Morgante* at the request of Lucrezia de' Medici, Lorenzo's pious mother, who first suggested that he attempt to redeem the characterization of the aged Emperor Charles from the tasteless buffoonery into which it had fallen: a weeping booby of an incredible ancientness, constantly befooled by his errant paladins and childishly helpless in the face of the Saracen invaders. But the *Morgante* draws its weakness as well as its strength from the same source—its derivation from and essential proximity to the very kind of literature it originally sought to elevate. In the nineteenth century it was revealed that the first twenty-three cantos were a reworking, never very far from the source, of an earlier popular poem called the *Orlando*; while the last five cantos (a later addition by Pulci, accounting for the *Maggiore* of the title) were based upon a poem called *La Spagna*. In its two parts, therefore, Pulci's poem bears the stamp of a divided sensibility, one amorous and chivalrous, retailing the conquests in love and battle of paladins like Astolfo and Rinaldo, and the other martial and heroic, describing with dignity and fervor the lofty action at Roncesvalles, an action in which a soldierly, faithful Orlando is at the center of attention. There is no attempt at integration of the erotic and the irascible impulses, no attempt to reconcile heroic strength and romantic meandering.

Pulci's treatment of his sources is interesting: it involves the addition of a line of droll, deflating commentary here, a stanza of humorous farcing out there. Throughout his poem we are aware of the unmistakable presence of a witty manipulator and commentator, but it is obvious also that he follows in the lead of his sources and goes where they direct. Obviously he has not brought the whole poem under his control and established a unifying presence in its divergent parts. The material remains fundamentally unchanged and his work is one of *rifacimento*, a canto-by-canto touching up rather than a total dissolution and recasting of materials under the pressure of an indubitable creative intellect. But that is to ask for an Ariosto.

Whatever Pulci's inability to stretch his hand decisively over these elusive materials, there is never a question of a lack of intelligence here—it flashes out constantly in bizarre turns of language and descriptions of untoward events; on a more considerable level, it manifests itself in the high-water mark of Pulci's art, the original creation of two of his major figures, Margutte and Astarotte, respectively a Vice-figure bulging with sinful vivacity, and a comic Devil whose humor constantly shades off into an affecting melancholy. Into the mouths of these outsized, grotesque and flagrant creatures, especially the latter, Pulci puts all kinds of extraneous materials, scraps from the intellectual banquets of the Medici circle. The Matter of France is utilized as the poet sees fit, and Pulci infuses into it— more correctly, he forces it to accommodate—his own intellectual interests and those of his society. Hence those astonishing interpolations and digressions—philosophical, theological, geographical—dealing with God's foreknowledge, the problem of free will, damnation, the impermanence of religions, the possibility of human life beyond the Pillars of Hercules, the circularity of the earth, etc. Interesting in themselves, none of these is truly incorporated into the work or related one to the other. They inhere only in the speaker to whom they are assigned and their resonance is confined to the moment at which they occur. They strike us with the force of their enormous comic incongruity, and there is no question that they have enraptured readers, from the Medici courtiers to Byron and beyond, with their wonderful liveliness. But there is no question in Pulci of comedy attaining a form and a central perspective.

Pulci's diffuse comic effects radiate from no unifying center. Boiardo gains over his predecessor by focussing his laughter on love, specifically, on romantic love, and on the absurdities and follies it creates in those who succumb to its madness. The impress of a more learned mind than Pulci's makes itself apparent in the very opening of his poem, perhaps in its very title. *Orlando Innamorato* is meant to carry the force of an amazing newsflash: here is the most unimaginable of all happenings, the chaste paladin totally enslaved to a passion for a pagan enchantress Angelica within moments of first seeing her. The devastation is universal; any number of his compeers are similarly stricken by the sight of her beauty, nor is the aged Charlemagne himself exempted. It is not difficult to see what Boiardo is about: in enveloping Orlando himself in the meshes of Cupid, he has taken the love-motif of the popular romance to its logical conclusion; but he has also framed that love in a particular category that defines and limits it for the judicious reader. Orlando's love, delineated in the first canto, has all the hallmarks of what Dante and Cavalcante, to say nothing of Robert Burton, would recognize as heroic love. It is sensually motivated, begins in sight of the beloved's physical beauties, reveals itself as sudden passion to which the will and then the reason succumb, and grows increasingly obsessive in its refusal to acknowledge any but visceral longings. Ficino would have termed it the effects of Venus Pandemos; Pico, "amor ferinus" or "amor bestiale." Certainly the paladin himself, ninny though he is, recognizes his condition for what it is. He phrases his dilemma in the words of Ovid's Medea and alludes significantly to the bridle of Temperance, which he feels himself rather horsily to have slipped (I, 1, st. 30–31).

All this, of course, is matter equally for tragedy or comedy. Ariosto will make us fully aware of the darker reverberations of Orlando's downfall, but that is because he is hard-minded about attributing consequences to any action set afoot by his characters. The case is different with Boiardo: within moments of the poem's opening, he presents us with a situation—Orlando crazy with love—that remains fundamentally static. For sixty-eight cantos more, he will preserve the paladin in that ludicrous posture as an irrational lover; it requires Ariosto to push him over the edge into real madness. Boiardo's is a poem in which the forward movement is accomplished by the constant introduction of novelty and surprise, one of the chief ones being that though Orlando is represented as being a sensualist in love, he is also an inept sentimentalizing booby (perhaps the two things are really one) who, even on those occasions when the prize of Angelica's "flower" is presented to him, lets the occasion slip and the prize depart. On one of the few occasions when allegory is introduced into the poem, Penitence appears in a storm and whips Orlando for failing to take Occasion by the forelock. We do Boiardo an injustice if we fail to remark the fine irony. Love, he says over and over again, makes a man virtuous and valorous, and never did Orlando accomplish so many marvellous feats as when he was in love: an ambush for the reader, when he finds himself pursuing the hero into one delicious stupidity after another, with no sign of functioning intellect visible on the part of Orlando, who is all brawn, no brains.

The essentially outrageous nature of events and personages in Boiardo is a witness to the poet's good sense and aristocratic taste: he has deliberately pushed things to an extreme which juveniles might enjoy for its phantasmagorical excesses, while he aims his irony over their heads at the more judicious members of his courtly audience. The technique is unmistakable: everything in the poem is gargantuanized and made excessive—illimitable armies, hyperbolical heroes with stupendous armor and chargers, their inordinate and overwhelming appetites for territory, women, horses, lances, swords and marvelous shields. Flames and fires from the internal conflagrations of love and hate burn on every page and the words "soperchio" or "excessive" and "roina" and "rumore" appear on nearly every page, while every battle is designated as greater and more terrific than the last. In Boiardo's comedy, love-passions monstrous in their instantaneous ability to overwhelm the intellect lead constantly to equally hyperbolical rages. He raises the traditional popular inflammability of characters to a transcendent level; desire and wrath become the governing emotions of the poem as it oscillates constantly between enormous battles and scenes of romantic pursuit, for arms and love are the only two things in Boiardo's poetic world. The author is fully conscious of this, and his transitions reveal that he looks upon it with a certain complacency: "I haven't shown you a lovely sword-fight for a long time now," he will announce, after he has delayed for a time in magic gardens of romance; or conversely, "My head is beating with the noise of this battle; let's discourse of love for a while."

The emphasis on monstrosity is an aspect of Boiardo's art that links it to Pulci and to the popularizing romancers before him. But unlike Pulci and the others, Boiardo gives his readers a fixed, conscious standard by which to measure these disorderly, extravagant passions. The concept of the "dismisurato"—the "unmeasured" in the sense of the unregulated and intemperate (cf. the Latin *mensura*)—permeates his vocabulary and is almost a tic in his rhymes. "Dismisura" is the negative aspect of an implied standard of moderation, reason and restraint. Over and over again it is given visible embodiment in Boiardo's deliriously restless personnel and their unrestrained appetites and actions. In nothing do his characters exist more than in their excesses, and the world they inhabit is a world of appetite alone. All is "soperchio" and "fuor di misura." In their extremities of desire and rage, they are stripped to their essential governing passions and become single-minded personifications of appetitive motion. The technique is close to allegory, though it lacks the particularized, schematic organization that the latter demands. But there are moments, when Orlando chews his nails in anger or jealously clashes his teeth together in furious rage at his rivals, when one tends to think in terms of capitalized Zelotypia and Furor. In this severely delimited world of regularly alternated choler and concupiscence, unrelieved except by some gracious novelle of gentler emotions, the interior landscape of the *Innamorato* reveals itself inevitably as the lower third of the Neoplatonic body, the seat of the irascible and concupiscible passions. For chivalric poetry gets its name not only from the mode of conveyance of its heroes, but from the inner black and white horses of Plato as well.

What we have been describing is Boiardo's aristocratic satire of certain tendencies in proletarian romance: the technique is that of comic inflation and exaggeration. It is forever delightful and remarkably fresh, but a certain repetitive element does make itself felt in the course of its cantos. It is no surprise therefore that the opening of Book II announces a change of perspective, a shift into weightier epic materials to counterbalance the laughable oddities of Orlando. In this wholly unexpected development lies one of the most momentous developments in the development of romantic epic, for it involves nothing less than the interweaving of an essentially epic theme of dynastic love with the ironic satire of the madly enamored Orlando. Proletarian comedy and courtly epic attempt to effect a union. The attempt is not wholly successful, but it is a rich and promising beginning.

Aware that the audience has wearied a bit of Orlando and of his carnal but inept love, Boiardo turns to another hero, the young Ruggiero, whom he proffers as a counterpoise in an epic setting. We must narrow our attention on this figure for a moment, for though he bears the considerable burden of having to function as the ancestor of the d'Estes, his appearance on the literary scene is altogether abrupt and mysterious. We know of a Latin poem by one of the Ferrarese courtiers that made mention of this hero and his marriage to Bradamante, the heiress of the house of Clairmont, but all we possess of it is a fragment, and indeed that is all that may ever have existed. The poem provides only the slenderest of clues, but it reveals a desire to link the Empire of Charlemagne with the dynasty of Ferrara. We have no way of knowing what was available to Boiardo; most likely he wrought from his own imagination an African childhood and youth for his young hero before he followed the invader Agramante to France; and it seems clear that his intention was to pursue the theme of the courtship of the two mythical lovers to its end in their dynastic marriage.

By whose suggestion the comic Carolingian romance that Boiardo already had in hand was made so surprisingly to accommodate the love story of the d'Este ancestors is likewise enveloped in mystery. The fact remains nevertheless that the appearance of Ruggiero and Bradamante is a momentous one: for the first time since Virgil, a ruling dynasty is praised through the heroic careers of prototypes who embody the ideals and aspirations of the race. There is a difference, however, and it is the difference between the epic and the romance. Where Virgil concentrated on Aeneas and left Lavinia in shadow, medieval romance tradition dictated that Bradamante be given at least an equal share of attention, and that the history of their preparation include an education in love. The *Roman d'Eneas* is a landmark in that development; and perhaps it should be recalled also that in fifteenth century Italy, the humanist Maphaeus Vegius had provided a thirteenth book for the *Aeneid*, in which the marriage of Aeneas and Lavinia was celebrated. It was a precedent that no imitation, especially in the form of the epic-romance, could afford to ignore.

The introduction of Ruggiero into the poem at the beginning of Book II is alive with promise; it heralds a more sophisticated comedy of love than that of the beef-witted Orlando. Boiardo is increasingly and constantly aware of the theme of the two loves as the poem progresses and some of his most superb passages occur in the Proems of Book II where he hymns a Venus of concord and fruitfulness: the ones at II, iv, st. 1–3 and II, xii, st. 1–3 are especially fine. Unfortunately, the poem only fitfully begins to incorporate this material, so that the encounter between Bradamante and her destined consort must wait till the fifth canto of Book III, only four cantos before the poem was so sadly broken off by Boiardo's death. Nevertheless, the moment is well worth waiting for: it counterbalances the first encounter of Orlando and Angelica in the most remarkable way and reveals that with a greater sense of structure and a sharpening of the oppositions implicit in the two pairs of lovers, Boiardo might have made something truly fine of this material: but structure was not one of Boiardo's concerns. The lovers meet by chance on the battlefield, withdraw apart to exchange challenges, and when Bradamante doffs her helmet, revealing herself as a beautiful young woman, Ruggiero suffers the same visual bewitchment as Orlando. But there is a significant difference: though attracted by each other immediately, the lovers-to-be exchange not vows of love, but genealogies: marriage is, humorously enough, in the air from the start. The course of this love is pitched against a background of dynastic fatality from the first, and their love is viewed as part of an historical process over which providence ineluctably presides. This idyll of cognitive love is brusquely interrupted by an inconvenient intruder, and the couple parts, never to be reunited in the few remaining cantos of the *Innamorato*. But this incipient comedy of love on a human scale, poised against the animalistic fervor of Orlando for Angelica, is among the most successful things in Boiardo. It is one of the first threads in the torn web of the poem that Ariosto picks out to manipulate immediately in his own poem. However tardily, then, however fragmentarily, the comic romance had begun to accommodate an epic Virgilian theme. In so doing, it had revealed it could serve to frame a subject of enormous interest to Neoplatonizing courts, the variety of loves—animal, human and divine—available to mortal men.

All of the unfinished threads of the *Innamorato* are woven, sooner or later, into the complicated tapestry of the *Furioso*, and Boiardo is the most important immediate source of Ariosto's poem. But this is clearly the place to assert that the true background for the *Furioso* is to be sought in the love-writings of Ficino and Pico, in the *Asolani* of Bembo, with its three dialogues on the triple nature of love, and in Book IV of Castiglione's *Cortegiano*, a book dedicated to Alfonso Ariosto, the poet's cousin, in which Pietro Bembo, Ariosto's intimate friend and his closest literary advisor, is the chief speaker on the subject of the Neoplatonic hierarchies of love. Another fruitful path might be followed in the discourses of the relative merits of the active or civil and contemplative lives, from Landino onward. And it would not be altogether unrewarding to think, in this context, of the room in the Louvre where seven paintings that Isabella d'Este commissioned for her Studiolo are still hanging all together. The titles of several of them are interesting and require no comment: Mantegna's "Minerva Triumphing over Venus," Perugino's "The Conflict of Love and Chastity," Costa's "Allegory of the Virtues (The Triumph of Virtue)," and his "Allegory of the Vices (Man a Slave of the Vices)," and Correggio's "The Dream of Antiope (Venus and a Satyr)," lately more correctly identified as a representation of animal love, and a counterpart to a Correggio canvas now in the London National Gallery, "Cupid Educated by Mercury and Venus," a representation of the higher love.

The misreading of Ariosto derives almost wholly, I believe, from the failure to appreciate his mode of handling his source in Boiardo. Let us consider for a moment what Ariosto had before him in the poem whose interrupted action and arrested personnel he chose to set in motion again. The *Innamorato* provided him with most of his matter, either fully developed or still in embryo: of ribald, robustious comedy concerning passionate love, more than enough; of human love about to encounter obstacles to its fulfillment in marriage, only a faint but fruitful beginning; but of transcendent spiritual love, nothing at all. The passionate variety embodied in the Orlando-Angelica story, and the rational variety embodied in the Ruggiero-Bradamante story, Ariosto develops from Boiardo's beginnings; the portrayal of the highest love is his own most amazing contribution and testifies to the stunning element of surprise he hoped to elicit from knowledgeable readers familiar with his predecessor's romance.

Where in the madly ardent and intemperately passionate world of the *Innamorato* had the standard of Reason appeared? If it was perceptible at all, it was by implication in the ironic gestures of its creator, in his stance as a courtly man of sense addressing other men of sense over the heads, as it were, of his puppet creatures. But Ariosto brings Reason into the poem by incarnating her in the figure of Logistilla. Her Platonic connections under her Italianate Romance name are unimpeachable: "to logistikon," the reasoning faculty. Shortly after the poem opens, Ariosto engages our attention in a full-dress allegory that usually embarrasses critics: Ariosto's wings of iridescent fantasy appear to be clogged by an unexpected pedantry. The Logistilla allegory is there for a purpose, however, and it has resonances beyond itself, if we will only think for a moment. In a poem in which the hero goes mad and loses his reason, the presence of Reason herself should not be so lightly dismissed. The Logistilla episode is an allegory of the tripartite human body, divided between Reason and Passion. On an island—the human body as island is well-known from Neoplatonic allegories of Homer and from Phineas Fletcher's *The Purple Island* as well—Logistilla occupies the northern vastnesses into which she has been driven by her two rebellious and usurping sisters, Morgana and Alcina. These two are enchantresses deriving from Boiardo, where they are said to be sisters, and where they are associated with indolent lust and avarice, respectively. But Ariosto himself single-handedly invents Logistilla, thus capping Boiardo's representations of passion with the element always missing in him, rationality. He creates, in other words, a hierarchy of reason over will and passion: a heroine whose name is learnedly and wittily formed from a Greek word signifying Reason is made the topmost, beleaguered member of a sisterly trinity whose lower representatives have names deriving from degenerate vulgar romance, and are associated with sensual indulgence and treasure and power. The island is clearly the fallen human body, two-thirds passion, one-third reason chased into a narrow place in the head and always at bay. The three sisters embody the three potentialities of the human body, its three loves, its three possible lives—feral and passionate, human and active, divine and contemplative. Nor is it difficult to see in them a cunning romantic transformation of the three goddesses in the Choice of Paris—Venus, Juno and Athena. In this episode, Ruggiero is in pride of place as the father of the d'Estes and as the hero therefore who has to make a Choice of Life. It is he who is brought face to face with Alcina, Morgana and Logistilla on their allegorical island; it is he who has to learn to negotiate the distance between them. But even as he makes his painful way between Vice and Virtue, between Unreason and Reason, history is tellingly interleaved with that of two other warriors: with that of Astolfo, whose journey we shall deal with in a moment; and with that of Orlando, who is even now preparing to desert Paris and embark on a wilful journey to insanity. In his maniacal quest for sensual satisfaction, the two sisters achieve the final figurative overthrow of Logistilla's shrunken kingdom. Orlando's madness at this point is fifteen cantos away, Ruggiero's moral struggles continue to the very end of the poem: clearly, the Logistilla-Alcina allegory reverberates beyond the half-dozen or so cantos in which it appears. In it, Ariosto asserts his artistic independence and in a Neoplatonic programme hierarchizes, schematizes and in general orders the dishevelled, unruly elements of Boiardo's romance.

In this building of a classical humanist edifice on a grounding of apparently frivolous romance materials, we can see a major characteristic of Ariosto's comic art in the *Furioso*, an essential way of proceeding in his literary creation. I have given one example, but there are literally hundreds to suggest that he transforms and redeems whatever he touches, though we shall have to know his source as thoroughly and completely as he did in order to perceive the metamorphosis. This surely is to play seriously and laughingly to tell the truth.

Another example will reinforce the point. Till Ariosto, the Carolingian romance had kept its feet on the ground; if nothing else, it is of the earth, earthy. Love, wrath and avarice are its ruling passions and all its concerns are worldly concerns. What a wonder then to see how enormously Ariosto has expanded its horizons as he strives to bridge the distance between the comic and the serious, the chivalric and the epic. The universe of the Carolingian poem is now only the middle ground between the heavens and the underworld; the loves enacted on its bosom have either an upward aspiration or a downward inclination. The fires and smoke of hell open under our feet, and our eyes catch a distant glimpse of the jewelled walls of the Heavenly Jerusalem.

How powerful the irony therefore that dictates that Astolfo should be the paladin who achieves this height on his winged horse; and achieve it, not by his own volition or merit, but by special grace and election, as St. John, his host, and the type of Contemplation, tells him so clearly. Of all the multitudinous personnel of Carolingian romance, Astolfo is, if we consider his origins, least likely to qualify for this exalted position. He is there by the sovereign will of the poet, who even in this detail reveals how determined he is to redeem and purify the buffoonery of his sourcs. In every previous incarnation in the popular poems as well as in Boiardo, Astolfo has been renowned for two things and two things only: endearing hot-headedness linked to a wonderful sense of self-preservation, and a really remarkable penchant for falling from his horse. His is the chivalric version of the comedian's pratfall. Yet, by an unimaginable leap, except to a Neoplatonist, Ariosto makes him the man who, once turned into a vegetative tree for his lust with Alcina, is redeemed and brought to Logistilla, who teaches him to temperately bridle the hippogriff and soar to the heavens. In her role of Minerva Frenatrix or Athena Hippodamia, she teaches the same lesson to Ruggiero, who learns the lesson less well, and whose course of virtue is longer and more painful: the man who seeks kingdom and rule in the civil active life is lower on the scale than the one who gives himself up to the life of the mind entirely. In effect, then, this is Ariosto's private and most uncynical joke with the tradition he inherited: the man who could least control his horse now gains the heavens by bridling his horse under the direction of Reason. The winged horse as a symbol for the soul in its upward or downward flight would have given no trouble to Ariosto's contemporaries; let alone to Donatello, whose Neoplatonic "Bust of a Young Man" in the Bargello wears a medallion round his neck with exactly such a charger on it, or to Annibale Carracci, whose painting "The Choice of Hercules," now in the Naples Pinacoteca, shows a winged horse spreading wings for heaven in the part of the painting given over to the life of virtue. Here again, therefore, as Astolfo, in the Sphere of the Moon contemplates the littleness of the earth and the absurdity of the acquisitive hunts with which it is overrun, we realize that a popular motif has undergone a learned, witty transmutation. "Earth conquered gives the stars." "Felix qui potuit cognoscere causas. . . ." The philosophic calm and merry detachment of a converted Astolfo are in the tradition of Boethian and Macrobian philosophy and Lucianistic literature: what an exaltation for a creature with his earlier pedigree!

Only Ariosto, too, could have reminded us of the medieval tradition of the Apostles as millers separating the grain of the prophets from the chaff when he tells us, with his usual crafty innocence, that the hospitable saints who greet Astolfo remember as well to give his hippogriff good store of forage. With what other thing does one feed the soul than with the grain of the spirit? This, of course, is not Dante's heaven, though even Dante might have spared a smile for the rendering of the most serious things in terms of an unoffending and marvellous laughter. In the country of Dante, only a fool would have attempted to storm the heaven of heavens in poetry and strain the interior eye for a vision of the circles of the Trinity. Ariosto was not a fool; for him, the Sphere of the Moon was exaltation enough, and he was content to keep within the decorum of the comic poem, for which he is often abused by those who have never even conceived of such a thing.

The hippogriff is associated with two riders, Astolfo and Ruggiero. The latter's flights are less highly directed; they suggest the volatility and unmanageability of the spirits of youth, and a taking wing for the false heavens of pleasure. Where the obedient hippogriff bears Astolfo to the Circle of the Moon, it rebelliously takes matters into its own wings and wafts Ruggiero into the arms of Alcina. Clearly, "horsiness" in this chivalric poem has less to do with merely equine interest than with the team in Plato's *Phaedrus*. But even Boiardo has this learned laughter as an underlay to his most suggestive bawdiness, as when Angelica is tempting Rinaldo: "Don't be afraid to come into my arms, for I can carry you through the air. You'll see an infinite space of earth pass beneath your feet in an instant. I can fulfill your highest desire, if you have ever had a desire to fly. Come, mount me, gallant baron; perhaps you'll find me no worse than your Bayard" (II, ix, st. 17). Perhaps the reader will also recall an uprising recently of female airline personnel, concerned with suppressing an advertisement showing a stewardess under a slogan reading "Fly me." The impulses leading to Renaissance allegory are often universal and eternal.

Significantly, Orlando and the hippogriff are strangers: his horse, unlike that of Ruggiero and Astolfo, is allowed no wings. He represents the brute passionate existence—"insania" as Ficino saw it—that finds its correlative in the life of the stable. Angelica, too, for all that it outrages readers who expect a modern psychological consistency in her portrayal, is constantly associated with horses. She functions only as a symbol of attraction, more important for what befalls her than for what she does, which is little more than to evade her suitors. We are put on our guard about horses and Angelica very early in the *Furioso*, when Sacripante's horse hilariously collapses on him when he is frustrated in his attempt to rape Angelica; we are warned by the triumphant appearance of Bayard in more than a horse's guise at the climactic moment of Canto I, a canto aswirl with fleshly hunts of various kinds. We should be even more alerted when Angelica in Canto VIII becomes the prey of an old hermit whose "jade" is insufficient to match his longings; in Canto XI we should have our eyes opened completely when Angelica finds it necessary to hide from pursuers and spends a night (completely unnoticed, says the poet slyly) in a stable among mares; in Canto X we should spy a connection when Ruggiero spies her, dismounts in frenzy from his hippogriff, and can scarcely restrain himself from climbing onto a different mount. Surely, however, nothing will prepare us for that last terrific appearance of Angelica when, coming unexpectedly across a now thoroughly bestialized and swinish Orlando, she attempts to evade his instinctive and unrecognizing chase, disappears by turning her magic ring, and falls unceremoniously from her palfrey: a poor beast that Orlando confuses with Angelica herself, into whose saddle he leaps with brute ferocity, and which he rides mercilessly to death, finally tying it to his leg and dragging it on the ground after him till its flesh is worn and rubbed away. Never was the burden of the flesh so gruesomely depicted. Levity, forsooth.

Orlando's madness is the lowest point to which any hero falls in the whole of the *Furioso*; Astolfo's visit to heaven marks the highest point any hero attains. They represent, respectively, the two poles of the human potential, an inferno of animal passion and a paradise of angelic transcendence. For Ruggiero, as dynast, warrior and husband, the path is longer and more complex, and interest centers on him increasingly as the poem approaches its conclusion. We can trace the general pattern his voyage describes.

Ruggiero's course, though it is directed to a destiny of active rule, almost exactly parallels Astolfo's, for the active man's life requires a contemplative element. Significantly, it shares a likeness with Orlando's only in its initial stages, when all three warriors begin their journey, and diverges notably from it thereafter. All three heroes begin at the same moral point: Astolfo is trapped inside a tree to indicate a loss of humanity in his lust for Alcina; Ruggiero is similarly enthralled for the moment to a Circean Alcina; and Orlando is locked in a spasm of torment for the departed Angelica. Orlando's course is irremediably downward, till Astolfo, whose course is set in a completely opposite direction, effects the comic redemption of his wits. Ruggiero's course fluctuates between the two poles, as befits a creature whose life in the world is conceived as the mean between outright hedonism and complete transcendence.

Generally speaking, Ruggiero's problems are sensual at the beginning, increasingly worldly in the middle, spiritual at the end. In his repeated moral entanglements, there is a move from lust to wrath and avarice to pride, overtly pointed by the poet in the proems to the cantos concerned. His responsibility grows greater as the possibility of error grows more serious in its consequences. The question here treated fictionally is the question more drily treated in the treatises on the civil life: the making of the dynast, the dynast as moral and intellectual being. Ariosto submits this forefather of the d'Estes to one calamity after another: he gives an earnest account of his eventual triumph in his choice of Logistilla over Alcina, but it requires the length of the entire poem to bring him its fruition. After the sensual episodes with Alcina and Angelica, in the first third of the poem, lust presents no very significant obstacle to his career; his promise to Bradamante to be baptized marks the end of a stage. The pull of a false honor to his pagan lord Agramante begins the next set of tribulations, capped when he encounters a forceful opponent to his marriage in the person of Bradamante's mother, Beatrice. She is cast in the mold of Virgil's Queen Amata, and she is similarly unwilling to give her daughter to a landless stranger: the theme of women and avarice is many times repeated in the poem. Ruggiero is driven to envy, wrath and desperation, especially when he learns that his rival is Leo, the son of the Emperor of Greece, whose Bulgarian subjects are in rebellion against him. In a swift dash to the East, he sets himself at their head, and through chance as well as a desperate valor achieves a triumph and a kingdom. Worldly satisfaction and self-conceit conspire to throw him from the top of Fortune's wheel, and he soon finds himself in the dungeons of the enemy he thought vanquished. Rescued—even in the mere narration we can see the whimsical alternation of Fortune, whose lunatic power is asserted in the proem to Canto XLV—he falls into despair and thoughts of suicide, till once again the fortunate intervention of a generous dis-position in his one-time rival causes the poem to end happily in an exchange of courtesies and reciprocal self-sacrifice. Marriage is the crown of Ruggiero's success and the feasting and final victory with which the poem closes marks the zigzag, providentially fortunate end of the true comic hero.

I have presented a mere outline of the dynast's career; there are other complexities that would require too long a discussion. But even from an outline we may be willing to admit that the world did not have to wait for Spenser's Britomart and Arthegall for portraits of dynasts-to-be who are moral beings and mirrors of the values of their race. As a classicist choosing to glorify his patrons, Ariosto had the example of Virgil before him, and Virgil was of course a Mantuan. Need we recall that Isabella d'Este Gonzaga was the Marchesa of Mantua? And need we recall that the voyage of Aeneas was commonly read in the Neoplatonic commentary of Landino and others as an illustration of the relative merits of the contemplative and active lives? From the "L'arme, gli amori" of its opening phrase to the indignant flight of Rodomonte's spirit at its very end, the *Furioso* courts comparison with the *Aeneid*. And never more than in this, that for the emphasis of the pagan poem on the workings of "fata," Ariosto everywhere asserts an elevated, omniscient, omnipresent, all-directing and inescapable Divine Providence.

Providence is benign, it moves towards laughter in order and reconciliation. As poet and maker of his own poetic universe, Ariosto Neoplatonically associates his own artistry with the all-seeing, timeless wisdom and rational order of the macrocosm. From that perspective, he scrutinizes the wilful short-sightedness of all his creatures as, driven by irrational puffs of momentary passion, they launch courses of action whose ends Providence alone will shape, rough-hew them how they will. In the erring, perverse entanglement of will with striving will, Providence finds means to achieve its own distant and inescapable ends; just as the poet serenely manipulates the tangled narrative threads of his own romance to an harmonious and ordered conclusion. Repeatedly, he represents himself as both weaver and musician, and in his certain knowledge of the immense reverberations to any action his characters may unthinkingly set afoot, he preserves a never-failing irony. Ariosto's constant theme is the imperfection of human understanding, the limits of human vision, the fallacy of trust in the ceaseless movement of the visible world. The choice of a romance form of interlacing narrative movements, abruptly suspended at crucial moments to leave the reader in a posture of baffled ignorance of its outcome, perfectly mirrors his choice of theme:

various actions are separately propelled into motion and ramify unimaginably, enormous consequences grow from their apparently slight beginnings, and all maintain a separate life and direction till they unexpectedly merge, revealing a most unaccidental design. The reader's view initially is that of a segmented, episodic, meaningless world; he operates horizontally, in time and space, short-sighted and bewildered, where the poet works vertically, allowing the poem leisure to unfold and reveal its controlling idea. Only the poet has the whole web in his view at one and the same moment.

In the persons of Ferrau and Sacripante, Agramante ,Mandricardo, Gradasso, Orlando and a host of others, the poem launches one arc of maddening desire after another—whether for a kingdom or a woman, or a set of fabulous armor—whose trajectory is gradually but certainly intersected by another, then deflected, then ruefully confounded in a baffling welter of wholly unexpected events. To take one example among dozens, what wonderful consequences follow from the mere act of Orlando's casting his sword away in his madness, what far-flung disruption in the camp of the quarreling invaders, who by this wholly fortuitous rivalry for a mere sword, become eventually—for God has a long hand, says Ariosto—the creators of their own destruction and expulsion from France. To know the *Furioso*, we must know the beginnings of its every action in Boiardo, and we must pursue its every twisting and turning wherever and however the poet inexorably drives it home to its extraordinary conclusion. The relentless, concealed logic of this process makes for humility in the reader. No less than the characters of the poem, he is trapped in a canto-by-canto progression, never sure till the very end of the interlacing action that it has a pattern and form. Then only does he realize that he is in the hands of a Great Mover of a poet, who regularly refers all order to a Great Mover of the universe.

From the opening canto of the poem, characters regularly put themselves, like Ferrau and Sacripante, "in arbitrio di Fortuna," and Fortune plays her usual freakish tricks upon them whether we are dealing with the lustful chase for a woman by two horsemen wittily depicted as galloping wildly on one horse, or as in the case of Agramante, with a king who attacks another's realm, only to lose his own in the process. Lust and avarice constantly procure their own ambush, and we are frequently reminded in Ariosto of the Renaissance depictions of the goddess Nemesis, with the attributes of Temperance, indicative of an innate world-order inescapably circumscribing those who cannot put bounds to their own desires. Orlando, as St. John tells Astolfo in the Circle of the Moon, has suffered precisely this fate: in his excess lay his punishment, the blinding of his inner eye by "voler divino."

Against this chaos of passion subject to the power of Fortune, Ariosto immediately pits the power of human love directed by Providence: it is Bradamante against Angelica from the very first canto. We learn first of the intervention of Providence in the poem when it begins to curb and direct the course of the future progenitress of the d'Estes. In an episode directly modelled on that of Aeneas in the Sybil's cave, Merlin tells her that it is by the will of God ("voler divino") and the disposition of heaven that she is to be set on her course of love; all her future journey is a learning to adjust her own contumacy and pride in the realm of time to the eternal pattern foreseen for her by Providence in eternity. The very same language is used by St. John when Astolfo attains the Sphere of the Moon on his hippogriff: he has ascended to that height by "voler divino," the Saint tells him, and he is not to attribute his coming there to his own intelligence or courage. Constantly, then, the poem interweaves the themes of human wilfullness ("voglia") and "voler divino," and from the clash between the two much of the divine laughter of the *Furioso* grows. Why, the wonder becomes, has the poet gained a renown for being coldly elegant, worldly, cynical, heartless and faithless, when he was in fact being only Neoplatonically wise?

He was especially wise about himself, both as poet and man. The poem gives us, in the self-dramatization of its author as a persona in the poem, two separate aspects, which we may designate as the Orlando-figure on one hand, the Astolfo-figure on the other. They alternate mercurially, thus furnishing yet another example of that mutability overwatched by stable fixity that is probably the poem's chief image. In the opening canto, Ariosto represents himself as a lover who, like his paladin, is the victim of a rooted concupiscence which frequently deprives him of his wits. In the third canto, however, the canto in which her providential destiny is revealed to his heroine, he is the priest of Apollo and the celebrator of a higher love. The former is the man who finds excuses later for Orlando's excesses, for like him he carries the same disease in his very bones. The latter is equally clearly the poet whose intuitive and unlimited comprehension of all his poem's concatenated complexities, past, present and to come finally resolves them into a divine unity. The self-dramatization involves an act of cognition. In the Sphere of the Moon, with all the waste and rubbish of human desire present to his view in the form of lovers' vows and toppled kingdoms and the praises and flatteries of princes, the freakish Orlando-aspect is made, in effect, to accuse itself of avarice in the writing of a poem dedicated to the praise of a chief sublunary vanity, dynasties and the glorifying of patrons. In the end, nothing escaped Ariosto's passionate, piercing intelligence, especially not himself.

This then is the poem that ends, to all intents and purposes, the aristocrat's determination to win back the Matter of France. In the light of the *Furioso*, all future attempts to write a Carolingian poem are superfluous. The *Morgante Maggiore* and the *Innomorato* are, by comparison, provincial poems of particular societies; the *Furioso* is a world poem. In its large embrace, the poem had caught every manner, plebeian or exalted, to which the Matter had been subjected in the course of centuries, and in the unified vision and philosophic perspective of its poet, it had encompassed and assimilated every diversity. All the heroes had been gathered up and returned home from their far-flung adventures, every incomplete action brought to its rounded and sometimes highly unexpected fulfillment. In its art, learning and sheer beauty, the humanist educational programme of Ferrara in the fifteenth century found its finest harvest. And this was the poem presented to Ariosto's patron, the Cardinal Ippolito, a man of so temperate and regulated a nature that he had his brother's eyes put out in a jealous rage on hearing them praised by his own mistress. We know of Ariosto's dissatisfaction with his unlovely master from the *Satires*, poems in which he gave a shape and a meaning to his indignant resentment of a courtier's existence. But "Messer Ludovico, wherever did you find all this————" must have been the cream of the jest. Messer Ludovico had earned his right to his comic outrage.

NOTE

In these pages I have presented the skeleton of an argument developed at greater length and in a different form in a book now finally nearing completion, *The Dynastic Romance: Studies in the Chivalric Poetry of Boiardo and Ariosto*. The problem of providing sufficient documentation in so restricted a space presents insuperable difficulties. I have determined to take the bold course of presenting none at all, and of deferring the notes to another occasion. My hope is that this essay is as self-contained and self-explanatory as possible.

INDEX